U·X·L Encyclopedia of U.S. History

U·X·L Encyclopedia of U.S. History

VOLUME 1: A–B

Sonia Benson, Daniel E. Brannen Jr., and Rebecca Valentine
Lawrence W. Baker and Sarah Hermsen, Project Editors

U·X·L
A part of Gale, Cengage Learning

GALE
CENGAGE Learning™

Detroit • New York • San Francisco • New Haven, Conn • Waterville, Maine • London

GALE
CENGAGE Learning™

U•X•L Encyclopedia of U.S. History

Sonia Benson, Daniel E. Brannen Jr.,
and Rebecca Valentine

Project Editors: Lawrence W. Baker
and Sarah Hermsen

Editorial: Julie Carnagie

Rights Acquisition and Management:
Margaret Chamberlain-Gaston,
Kelly A. Quin, and Jhanay Williams

Composition: Evi Seoud

Manufacturing: Rita Wimberley

Imaging: Lezlie Light

Product Design: Jennifer Wahi

Cover Design: Rokusek Design

© 2009 Gale, Cengage Learning

For product information and technology assistance, contact us at
Gale Customer Support, 1-800-877-4253.
For permission to use material from this text or product,
submit all requests online at www.cengage.com/permissions.
Further permissions questions can be emailed to
permissionrequest@cengage.com.

While every effort has been made to ensure the reliability of the information presented
in this publication, Gale, a part of Cengage Learning, does not guarantee the accuracy of the
data contained herein. Gale accepts no payment for listing; and inclusion in the publication
of any organization, agency, institution, publication, service, or individual does not imply
endorsement of the editors or publisher. Errors brought to the attention of the publisher
and verified to the satisfaction of the publisher will be corrected in future editions.

LIBRARY OF CONGRESS CATALOGING-IN-PUBLICATION DATA

Benson, Sonia.
    UXL encyclopedia of U.S. history / Sonia Benson, Daniel E. Brannen Jr., and Rebecca
Valentine ; Lawrence W. Baker and Sarah Hermsen, project editors.
        p. cm. --
    Includes bibliographical references and index.
    ISBN 978-1-4144-3043-0 (set) -- ISBN 978-1-4144-3044-7 (vol. 1) --
ISBN 978-1-4144-3045-4 (vol. 2) -- ISBN 978-1-4144-3046-1 (vol. 3) --
ISBN 978-1-4144-3047-8 (vol. 4) -- ISBN 978-1-4144-3048-5 (vol. 5) --
ISBN 978-1-4144-3049-2 (vol. 6) -- ISBN 978-1-4144-3050-8 (vol. 7) --
ISBN 978-1-4144-3051-5 (vol. 8)
    1. United States -- History -- Encyclopedias, Juvenile. I. Brannen, Daniel E., 1968- II.
Valentine, Rebecca. III. Title. IV. Title: UXL encyclopedia of US history. V. Title:
Encyclopedia of U.S. history.

E174.B46 2008
973.03--dc22   2008022347

Gale
27500 Drake Rd.
Farmington Hills, MI 48331-3535

ISBN-13: 978-1-4144-3043-0 (set)   ISBN-10: 1-4144-3043-4 (set)
ISBN-13: 978-1-4144-3044-7 (vol. 1)   ISBN-10: 1-4144-3044-2 (vol. 1)
ISBN-13: 978-1-4144-3045-4 (vol. 2)   ISBN-10: 1-4144-3045-4 (vol. 2)
ISBN-13: 978-1-4144-3046-1 (vol. 3)   ISBN-10: 1-4144-3046-9 (vol. 3)
ISBN-13: 978-1-4144-3047-8 (vol. 4)   ISBN-10: 1-4144-3047-7 (vol. 4)
ISBN-13: 978-1-4144-3048-5 (vol. 5)   ISBN-10: 1-4144-3048-5 (vol. 5)
ISBN-13: 978-1-4144-3049-2 (vol. 6)   ISBN-10: 1-4144-3049-3 (vol. 6)
ISBN-13: 978-1-4144-3050-8 (vol. 7)   ISBN-10: 1-4144-3050-7 (vol. 7)
ISBN-13: 978-1-4144-3051-5 (vol. 8)   ISBN-10: 1-4144-3051-5 (vol. 8)

This title is also available as an e-book.
ISBN-13: 978-1-4144-3274-8, ISBN-10: 1-4144-3274-7
Contact your Gale, a part of Cengage Learning, sales representative for ordering
information.

Printed in the United States of America
1 2 3 4 5 6 7 12 11 10 09 08

Contents

VOLUME 4: H–J

VOLUME 5: K–M

Reader's Guide

U•X•L Encyclopedia of U.S. History introduces students to the history of the United States from pre-Colonial America to present day. This 8-volume set explores the timeline of America: its founders, key historical figures, wars, events, political environment, economy, and culture. Entries were selected with guidance from the National Council for the Social Studies (NCSS) Curriculum Standards for Social Studies— Middle School, which were adopted in 2002. The NCSS standards' eras are: Three Worlds Meet (Discovery of the New World, beginnings to 1620); Colonization and Settlement (1585–1763); Revolution and the New Nation (1754–1820s); Expansion and Reform (1801–61); Civil War and Reconstruction (1850–77); the Development of the Industrial United States (1870–1900); the Emergence of Modern America (1890–1930); the Great Depression and World War II (1929–45); Postwar United States (1945 to the early 1970s); and Contemporary United States (1968 to the present).

U•X•L Encyclopedia of U.S. History features nearly 700 entries— arranged alphabetically across the set—with more than 400 images and maps to help better illustrate the text. Each entry contains bolded terms that indicate cross-references to other entries within this set. In addition, several sidebar boxes offer additional insight into the people, places, and events that have occurred in American history. All eight volumes contain a general bibliography and a comprehensive cumulative subject index that provides easy access to subjects discussed throughout *U•X•L Encyclopedia of U.S. History.*

Acknowledgments

Much appreciation goes to authors Sonia Benson, Daniel E. Brannen Jr., and Rebecca Valentine. Dan Brannen is grateful to project editor Larry Baker, who makes his challenging role seem easy, thus easing the writer's task. Warm regards to Phil, film lover and fellow Coppola fan. Kisses to Kaya, Malina, and Liam, for punctuating long working spells with riveting Italian soccer matches over homebaked pizze and calzoni. To Jen, who shouldered countless tasks to make possible this book and our life in the Desert Ocean: ti amo molto e sempre! Rebecca Valentine thanks Max, Tuck, Tavia, and Bella, who managed without her more than they would have liked.

Additional thanks go to copyeditors Carol Brennan, Anne Davidson, Jessica Hornik Evans, Christa Gainor, Erika-Marie S. Geiss, Ellen Henderson, and Leslie Joseph; proofers Leslie Joseph and Amy Marcaccio Keyzer; the indexers from Factiva, a Dow Jones Company; and typesetter Datapage Technologies International, Inc.

Recognition is also given to the following advisors, whose comments and suggestions helped shape *U•X•L Encyclopedia of U.S. History:*

- Carol Deviney, Librarian/Teacher, Murphy Middle School/Plano ISD, Murphy, Texas
- Maria Kardick, Librarian, Eighth Grade Center, Spring-Ford School District, Royersford, Pennsylvania
- Nina Levine, Library Media Specialist, Blue Mountain Middle School, Cortlandt Manor, New York
- Jacqueline A. Plourde, Retired Director, Learning Resource Center, Madison Junior High School, Naperville, Illinois

Comments and Suggestions

We welcome your comments on *U•X•L Encyclopedia of U.S. History* and suggestions for other topics to consider. Please write: Editors, *U•X•L Encyclopedia of U.S. History,* U•X•L, 27500 Drake Rd., Farmington Hills, Michigan 48331-3535; call toll free: (800) 877-4253; fax to (248) 699-8097; or send e-mail via http://www.gale.cengage.com.

U•X•L Encyclopedia of U.S. History

A

Ralph Abernathy

Ralph David Abernathy and **Martin Luther King Jr.** (1929–1968) founded the **Southern Christian Leadership Conference** (SCLC) in 1957 to promote civil rights for black Americans. Abernathy has sometimes been called the "other side" of King, his longtime friend and associate. Abernathy found it easy to relate to the poor while King, at least in the early years, appealed more to the middle class. Together, the two men were a powerful team, attracting thousands of followers to the struggle for civil rights.

Early life

Ralph Abernathy was born on March 11, 1926. His father, William Abernathy, was a Baptist deacon and farmer. Abernathy aspired to be a preacher, but when he graduated from high school he was drafted into the U.S. Army to serve during the last months of **World War II** (1939–45). After the war, Abernathy enrolled at Alabama State College in Montgomery, **Alabama**. He was ordained a Baptist minister in 1948 and graduated with a bachelor's degree in mathematics in 1950. He earned a master's degree in sociology from Atlanta University the following year.

With King in Montgomery

In 1951, Abernathy became pastor of First Baptist Church in Montgomery. Three years later, King became pastor of another black church in Montgomery, Dexter Avenue Baptist. The two men became fast friends. Sharing a mutual interest in the struggle for civil rights,

Ralph Abernathy (above), along with Martin Luther King Jr., founded the Southern Christian Leadership Conference and inspired thousands of people to get involved in the civil rights movement. AP IMAGES

Abernathy and King discussed how to go about bringing an end to **segregation** (the separation of blacks and whites in public places) in an orderly, nonviolent manner. Despite having been a soldier, Abernathy, like King, was convinced that nonviolence was the only acceptable means of protest.

Bus boycott

In 1955, Montgomery became the site of a huge civil rights event when a well-respected African American woman, **Rosa Parks** (1913–2005), refused to give up her seat to a white passenger on a city bus. She was arrested and fined. Parks's arrest touched a nerve in the community. The local Women's Political Council called for all black people of Montgomery to protest by refusing to ride the buses.

King and Abernathy quickly formed the Montgomery Improvement Association and held meetings to spread the word about the **Montgomery bus boycott**. They instructed local ministers to explain from their pulpits how the boycott was to be conducted and arranged for taxis and carpools to take people to work. The boycott began on December 5, 1955. Despite threats and intimidation, it lasted for more than one year, but it was successful. The U.S. **Supreme Court** ruled that segregation on Montgomery buses was illegal.

The SCLC

In 1957, King and Abernathy arranged a meeting in Atlanta, **Georgia**, with other Southern ministers. They formed the Southern Christian Leadership Conference, an organization of churches and civic groups that would lead nonviolent protests across the South in pursuit of desegregation (ending the separation of blacks and whites in public places). King was elected president of the SCLC; Abernathy was its secretary-treasurer. While Abernathy was at the SCLC meeting, his home and the First Baptist Church were bombed, as were other homes and churches in

Montgomery. Although his wife and children escaped unharmed, the warning was clear.

In 1960, King moved to Atlanta to devote more time to the SCLC, and the following year Abernathy joined him there, becoming pastor of West Hunter Street Baptist Church. During the next few years, the two ministers led nonviolent marches, sit-ins, and rallies in the major cities of the South. (See **Sit-in Movement**.) They were arrested a number of times and threatened often, but they attracted support across the nation. Little by little, they made progress against the segregation and discrimination faced by African Americans in the South. In 1965, Abernathy became the vice president of the SCLC.

Poor People's Campaign

By the mid-1960s, the **civil rights movement** had changed many laws and policies, but many African Americans were still disadvantaged and poor. To draw attention to poverty, King organized a Poor People's Campaign in 1968. He intended to march on **Washington, D.C.**, but he was assassinated on April 4, 1968, before he could carry out his plan. It was left to Abernathy to complete the task.

Soon after King's death, Abernathy, the new president of the SCLC, led a march to Washington to demonstrate for economic and civil rights. He and his followers set up a campsite called Resurrection City near the **Lincoln Memorial**, to which poor and homeless people came from across the country. The results of their efforts were disappointing, largely because Congress was preoccupied with the problems of the **Vietnam War** (1954–75).

Last years

As president of the SCLC, Abernathy led several protests against segregation in the South. He was often compared to King and was generally perceived as lacking the charisma and poise of his friend. He resigned from the SCLC in 1977 to run for Congress, but he failed to gain the seat. Undaunted, he formed an organization called the Foundation for Economic Enterprises Development (FEED) to teach job skills to African Americans.

Abernathy published his autobiography, *And the Walls Came Tumbling Down*, in 1989. Because the book revealed that King had been carrying on extramarital affairs, critics accused Abernathy of betraying his long-deceased friend. He died the following year.

Abolition Movement

Abolition is the goal of abolishing, or completely eliminating, **slavery**. There were two significant eras of abolition in the United States. The early movement took place between 1770 and 1830 and focused on eliminating the African slave trade. Abolitionists of this early era assumed that prohibiting the importation of slaves from other countries would eventually result in eliminating slavery altogether. Thus, when the United States prohibited the foreign slave trade in 1808, many early abolitionists lost interest in the abolitionist cause. A second phase of the abolition movement—the "new abolitionism"—began in the 1830s and continued until the American **Civil War** ended in 1865. New abolition-

Members of the Pennsylvania Abolition Society, with well-known abolitionist William Lloyd Garrison seated bottom right. Garrison and the society used speeches, pamphlets, and newspapers to call for the immediate abolition of slavery.

ists opposed gradual methods. They wanted immediate, unconditional emancipation (freeing of slaves). Other antislavery forces developed in this era that sought restrictions on slavery and were more agreeable to gradual emancipation through political negotiation.

Early abolitionism

The first group to speak out against slavery in the United States was the **Quakers**, a Christian group founded in England on the belief that each individual is able to communicate with God and understand right and wrong through his or her own "inner light," or conscience. Beginning in the 1750s, Quakers in England took a strong moral stand against slavery. They helped to abolish the slave system in the British Empire by 1833. Quakers took early leadership in American antislavery activities beginning in the mid-eighteenth century. They were largely responsible for the first American abolition society, called the Society for the Relief of Free Negroes Unlawfully Held in Bondage, which was founded in 1775.

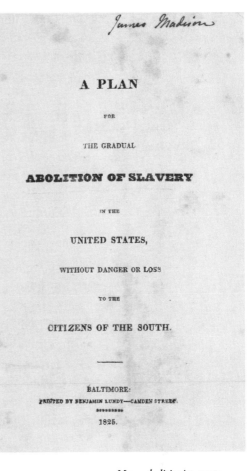

Many abolitionists wrote papers or distributed pamphlets suggesting ways to end slavery. This pamphlet from former U.S. president James Madison proposes the gradual abolition of slavery without endangering the economic and social stability of the South. © CORBIS

The **American Revolution** (1775–83) gave the United States even more reasons to oppose the injustices of slavery. Slavery not only violated the law of God, it contradicted the rights of human beings spelled out in the **Declaration of Independence**. Opposition to slavery was widespread in the new nation. By the 1780s, abolitionist societies had formed in most states, including the upper South. In the decades after the Revolution, many northern states abolished slavery. In **New Jersey** and **New York**, legislation demanding immediate emancipation failed. There, abolition groups passed laws freeing slaves when they reached a certain birthday.

In 1808, the U.S. Congress prohibited foreign slave trade, although people could still buy and sell slaves within the United States. The abolitionists' hopes that this act would result in the end of slavery proved to be unfounded. The South resisted pressure to emancipate slaves. Most

Americans assumed that the U.S. **Constitution** left the issue of slavery to state governments and that the U.S. Congress could abolish slavery only in new territories. Many people in the North and South accepted slavery as a necessary evil.

American Colonization Society

In the early nineteenth century, a plan for ending slavery arose that appealed to slaveholders and abolitionists alike: freeing African slaves and then sending them to live somewhere outside of the United States. Most reasons for relocation were based on racism. Many whites—Southerners and Northerners alike—were uncomfortable with the idea of having freed slaves living and working in their communities. If former slaves could be relocated outside the United States, slaveholders might be less reluctant to free them, and nonslaveholding whites might be less anxious about competition for work. Some Northern reformers approved of relocation on the grounds that it would be kinder to the freed slaves, since they believed American society would never treat black people fairly or accept them as equals.

The **American Colonization Society** (ACS) was founded in 1816 as the major relocation, or colonization, organization for freed slaves. It acquired land in Liberia, Africa, for its proposed colony of freed slaves and rapidly won the approval of church and government leaders in the North and South. But the efforts of the ACS were slow; it sent only a few thousand blacks to Liberia before 1830. Enthusiasm for the movement faded as doubts grew about its practicality. A large group of black and white abolitionists united in their opposition to sending freed slaves to Africa.

Garrison and the American Anti-Slavery Society

By 1830, abolitionists who rejected the idea of relocating former slaves had set a new goal: the immediate, unconditional end of slavery. Characterizing their strategy for achieving this end as "moral suasion," or persuasion by appealing to people's conscience, the new abolitionists employed agents to work throughout the country as missionaries in the antislavery cause. These missionaries converted as many people as they could to abolitionism and organized their converts into local antislavery societies. The new abolition movement spread rapidly. In 1832, eleven persons formed the New England Anti-Slavery Society; by 1837,

Massachusetts had 145 societies, New York had 274, and **Ohio** had 213. In December 1833, sixty-three men (only three of them black) formed the American Anti-Slavery Society (AASS). By 1838, the AASS claimed 1,350 affiliated societies, with membership approaching a quarter million participants.

The best-known of the new abolitionists was William Lloyd Garrison (1805–1879). Garrison had formed strong alliances with black abolitionists such as James E. Forten (1766–1842), a wealthy black Philadelphian, in the anticolonization campaign. Garrison launched a Boston-based abolitionist newspaper, the *Liberator,* in 1831; the great majority of its readers were black. Garrison's book *Thoughts on African Colonization* (1832) persuaded many young reformers to change loyalties and follow Garrison's course, calling for the immediate abolition of slavery and rejecting all compromises or half measures.

Garrison and the AASS used tactics of moral suasion and not politics in their war against slavery. Through speeches, pamphlets, newspapers, and individual contact, they spread the word to the nation that slavery was a sin. They hoped that clergymen and other opinion leaders would be persuaded and exert pressure on slaveholders. Their movement gained the greatest following in the Northeast. A growing middle class deemed slavery at odds with its religious beliefs and the free-labor system. Churches, though, generally remained aloof from the movement, and community leaders were generally hostile to the ardent reformers. Abolitionists were denounced as troublemakers who wanted to interfere with local authorities.

Political abolitionism

When the churches failed to respond to their message, some abolitionist leaders began to press for change through political legislation. These abolitionists tended to be less uncompromising than Garrison and his followers. They wanted to focus on restricting slavery and were not willing to engage in some of the other reforms Garrison had taken up, such as women's rights. In 1840, when Garrison appointed a woman to a committee, a conflict arose among leaders of the AASS over the role of women within the organization. A second abolitionist group, the American and Foreign Anti-Slavery Society, split from the AASS. Members of this new group favored a political strategy to end slavery. They supported the new Liberty Party in 1840 and 1844. By 1846, support for that party had faded, and most political abolitionists gave their votes to the new antislavery **Free Soil Party** in 1848.

The Free Soil Party grew dramatically in the 1850s, due mainly to the outrage of Northerners over the Fugitive Slave Act of 1850, which required people in nonslaveholding states to return runaway slaves to their owners in slaveholding states. (See **Fugitive Slave Laws**.) At this time, there was also a huge public response to the abolitionist novel *Uncle Tom's Cabin* (1852), written by Harriet Beecher Stowe (1811–1896). When chaos and violence broke out in the new territory of **Kansas** between those who wanted slavery and those who opposed it, antislavery sentiments in the North soared. Unlike Garrison and the AASS, the political abolitionists compromised on their goals, generally accepting slavery in the states in which it already existed and even in some new territories. Garrison, by contrast, had counseled abolitionists to stick to the moral high ground by firmly denouncing the injustice of all slavery and racism.

Black abolitionism

Black abolitionists tended to favor political action, but they complained repeatedly that white abolitionist organizations put blacks primarily in supporting roles. After 1840, black abolitionists met more frequently within their own organizations, held their own conventions, and supported their own newspapers, such as Samuel E. Cornish (c. 1795–c. 1858) and John Brown Russwurm's (1799–1851) *Freedom's Journal* and abolitionist and orator **Frederick Douglass**'s (c. 1817–1895) *North Star.*

Douglass had been closely allied with Garrison and the AASS, but by the 1840s he turned more frequently to separate "Negro Conventions" as the best institution through which to organize against slavery and racial prejudice. Like Douglass, other black abolitionists garnered significant support. Among the more popular speakers were former slaves William Craft (c. 1824–1900), Ellen Craft (c. 1826–c. 1897, **Sojourner Truth** (c. 1797–1883), and William Wells Brown (c. 1815–1884). Each was skilled at depicting the horrors of slavery, and they all sold personal narratives and gathered funds to support the movement.

The appeal of violence

By 1850, many black leaders ceased talking about "moral suasion" and began to talk about violent rebellion. If whites did not concede to blacks the right to self-defense, some leaders asked, and if blacks never showed their willingness to fight, then how could Southern slavery and Northern injustice ever end? Even white abolitionists began to contemplate warfare. Those who followed Garrison believed proslavery leaders dominated the political system. At one public meeting in 1854, Garrison denounced the Fugitive Slave Act and burned the Constitution. White abolitionist John Brown (1800–1859) was so convinced that violence was the only way to achieve abolition that he planned an all-out war against slavery in the South. In 1859, he led a raid on a federal arsenal in the city of Harpers Ferry, in what is now West Virginia, intending to steal weapons to give to slaves. (See **Harper's Ferry Raid**.) The raid was a dismal failure, but it drew the divided nation's attention to the urgency of the problem.

The end of slavery

In 1854, political abolitionists formed the **Republican Party**, which was dedicated to stopping the spread of slavery into the western territories. In 1856, this party carried eleven northern states in the presidential election, and numerous Republicans were elected to the U.S. Congress and state offices. As a candidate for the U.S. Senate and later as a presidential candidate, **Abraham Lincoln** (1809–1865) never came out against slavery in existing states, but he did insist that slavery be prohibited in the new western lands, a point that many Southerners interpreted as a clear antislavery stance. When he was elected president, seven southern states seceded, or withdrew, from the United States. Four more seceded when Lincoln began to gather his army for war in 1861.

The onset of the American Civil War (1861–65) unified the antislavery factions. White and black abolitionists joined Douglass and Garrison in lobbying for immediate emancipation and the enlistment of free blacks in the Union (Northern) army. Other abolitionists focused on organizing aid for the thousands of former slaves who, as soon as war broke out, had fled to the Northern states. Sponsored by church groups and freedman's aid societies, reformers moved to **Washington, D.C.**; New Orleans, **Louisiana**; and Port Royal, **South Carolina**, to be near the former slaves and to provide material aid and basic schooling. These efforts continued and expanded after the war.

Midway through the war, Lincoln took two giant steps toward freedom for African Americans. In January 1863, Lincoln issued the **Emancipation Proclamation**, freeing all slaves in the United States. He also announced the formation of black military units. All abolitionists hailed the passage in January 1865 of the **Thirteenth Amendment** to the Constitution, prohibiting slavery in the United States, as completing the legal process of abolition.

Abstract Expressionism

Abstract Expressionism, a visual arts movement that emerged in the late 1930s and 1940s, challenged accepted standards of what was art. Embracing improvisation (simultaneous creation and production), individuality, and energy, it was the first art movement with origins in America. Abstract art moved beyond representing reality as everyone experienced it daily. Rather than depicting people, landscapes, familiar objects, or elements from nature, the Abstract Expressionists used color, shapes, lines, and space to evoke another part of reality.

European artists in the 1920s—the Surrealists, Expressionists, and Cubists—had painted canvases in which objects and people were still recognizable but far from realistic. When **World War II** broke out in Europe in the late 1930s, many influential artists fled to the United States. Their experiments and explorations had a great influence on American painters. New York City, rather than Paris, became the center of artistic activity. Rejecting the goal of representing the world around them, instead the so-called New York School of painters wanted to convey spontaneous emotions and the subconscious mind (the part of thinking that is not in our awareness).

Many Abstract Expressionist paintings were done on very large canvases. Jackson Pollock (1912–1956) dripped and flung paint onto canvases to allow movement and color to express the subconscious mind. In his paintings, Mark Rothko (1903–1970) achieved great emotional effects by layering and stacking rectangular fields of color, with the colors bleeding into each other at the edges.

Abstract Expressionism was a radical break from traditional art, and at first it was difficult for many to accept. In the political climate of the

Cold War in the 1950s, however, Abstract Expressionism became a symbol of American freedom and the quest for the new. Whereas the Soviet Union strictly controlled artistic expression, in the United States Abstract Expressionists were free to experiment as they wished—in keeping with the American ideals of democracy, freedom of expression, and innovation.

Acquired Immune Deficiency Syndrome
See **AIDS**

John Adams

John Adams was the first vice president of the United States (from 1789 to 1797) and the second president of the United States (from 1797 to 1801). During the **American Revolution** (1775–83), he served as one of the leading politicians in the first and second Continental Congresses. (See **Continental Congress, First** and **Continental Congress, Second**.) He was well regarded by his fellow politicians as a man of strong intellect.

John Adams, the second president of the United States and one of the leading politicians in the first and second Continental Congresses.
THE LIBRARY OF CONGRESS

Early life

Adams was born in Braintree (later called Quincy), **Massachusetts**, on October 30, 1735. His father, also named John Adams, was a farmer and leather goods maker who also served as a church deacon, town selectman, and lieutenant in the local militia. The elder Adams and his wife, Suzanne Boyleston, also had two other sons, Peter and Elihu.

Adams spent much of his youth outdoors in rural Braintree and planned to be a farmer when he grew up. Adams was educated by two private tutors and attended a public school called Dame School. In 1751, Adams's parents sent him to Harvard College to study to be a clergyman.

John Adams helped negotiate peace with Great Britain and signed the Treaty of Paris, which ended the American Revolution in 1783.
© CORBIS

Among the twenty-eight initial students in his class, Adams eventually ranked in the top three.

After graduating from Harvard in 1755, the nineteen-year-old Adams moved to Worcester, Massachusetts, thirty miles west of Boston. There he started to teach grammar school. He lived in the house of James Putnam, a Harvard graduate and lawyer. Adams studied law under Putnam and in 1758 returned to his parents' home in Boston to practice law.

In 1764 Adams married Abigail Smith, the daughter of a clergyman. She too was intelligent, and their marriage was marked by loyalty and friendship. Together they had five children: Abby, John Quincy, Susanna, Charles, and Thomas. Susanna died when she was just one.

Law and activism

In the 1760s, Adams continued to study law and slowly built his law practice. He also became in-volved in revolutionary politics. When the **French and Indian War** ended in 1763, victori-ous Great Britain had amassed great debts. To pay them, the British Parliament enacted a series of tax laws that became known in America as the Intolerable Acts. Many Americans began to feel it was unfair for Parliament, in which America had no elected represen-tatives, to tax Americans.

After Parliament enacted the **Sugar Act** of 1764 and the **Stamp Act** of 1765, John Adams's cousin, statesman Samuel Adams (1722–1803), organized protests in Boston. John Adams attended meetings and emerged as an effective spokesman against Britain's imperial policies. In August 1765, he published the first in a series of four essays in the *Boston Gazette* newspaper. The essays, later published in Britain, described how colonists had emigrated to America to establish civil governments based on liberty and freedom.

In his law practice, Adams worked on a variety of cases, including divorce, wills, rape, and trespass. Adams defended John Hancock (1737–1793), who would be the first signer of the **Declaration of**

Independence, against smuggling charges brought by British customs officials. In 1770, Adams defended Captain Thomas Preston, the British officer in charge at the **Boston Massacre** of March 5, 1770. That event happened when British soldiers fired upon a crowd of colonists, killing five of them. Adams received much criticism for defending Preston. Adams, however, believed every man deserved a fair trial, and Adams won the case.

American Revolution politics and diplomacy

In 1774, the First Continental Congress met in Philadelphia to seek solutions to America's problems with Great Britain. Adams was chosen to attend as a representative from Massachusetts. Not yet in favor of independence, Adams recommended a system of equal parliaments in America and Britain with common allegiance to the crown.

In April 1775, the Revolutionary War began with the **Battle of Lexington and Concord**. Adams served that May in the Second Continental Congress, where he supported future president **George Washington** (1732–1799; served 1789–97) to lead the Continental Army. By then, Adams believed independence was necessary. In February 1776, he gave Congress a pamphlet called "Thoughts on Government," in which he proposed a system of governments for the colonies. Later that year, Adams seconded the motion in Congress that led to the adoption of the Declaration of Independence on July 4, 1776.

Adams served America during the war as a commissioner in France, seeking foreign aid for the American cause. Returning to Boston in 1779, Adams attended the state convention that prepared the Massachusetts state constitution, which Adams drafted. Along with **Benjamin Franklin** (1706–1790) and John Jay (1745–1829), Adams served as commissioner to negotiate peace with Great Britain and eventually signed the **Treaty of Paris** to end the war in 1783. From 1785 to 1788, Adams served as America's first minister to Great Britain, missing the action as America drafted a **Constitution** to form a new plan of government.

In the federal government

Adams returned to America in 1788 and was chosen to be the nation's first vice president. He served under President Washington throughout both of Washington's two terms, from 1789 to 1797. Writing to his wife, Abigail, Adams called the office of vice president insignificant.

Washington's decision to retire after two terms gave Adams a chance to seek the presidency. Adams was a member of the **Federalist Party**, which generally favored a strong federal government. Adams's chief opponent for the presidency was the leader of the **Democratic-Republican Party**, **Thomas Jefferson**. The Democratic-Republican Party, whose members also became known as Jeffersonian Republicans, generally favored a smaller role for the federal government but strong state governments.

Adams defeated Jefferson and took office as president in Philadelphia, **Pennsylvania**, on March 4, 1797. Jefferson became vice president because he received the second most electoral votes; this system eventually was changed by the **Twelfth Amendment** to the Constitution in 1804.

One of Adams's first decisions as president was one he eventually called one of his greatest mistakes: keeping Washington's cabinet instead of creating his own. The cabinet is the group of people who lead the major departments in the executive branch of government. In 1797, those positions included the attorney general, the secretary of state, the secretary of the treasury, and the secretary of war. Keeping Washington's cabinet was an error because they were very loyal to former attorney general **Alexander Hamilton** (1755–1804), the leader of the Federalist Party, with whom Adams had many problems throughout his presidency.

Foreign affairs

When Adams became president, America was being drawn into a naval war between Great Britain and France. The two European countries had been fighting since 1793 over issues related to commerce and imperial power. Amidst that conflict, Great Britain began capturing American merchant vessels and forcing the ships' sailors into naval service for Great Britain.

America tried to end its problems with Great Britain by signing a treaty in 1795. France considered this to be a violation of France's own treaties with America. So France began to capture American merchant vessels carrying goods to Great Britain and to force American sailors into service for France.

Adams wanted to avoid war as much as possible. Many members of the Federalist Party, however, wanted America to align with Great Britain and fight France. Hamilton was among that group, and his desire for war with France contributed to his problems with Adams. Democratic-Republicans, including Vice President Jefferson, tended to favor France and to prefer that America stay out of the conflict if possible.

Early in March 1797, Adams proposed to send a Democratic-Republican, future president **James Madison** (1751–1836; served 1809–17), to negotiate the problems with France. Opposed to Madison, Adams's cabinet threatened to resign, so Adams dropped the idea. He instead sent a bipartisan commission to Paris, France, in July 1797. The commission consisted of **South Carolina** governor Charles Pinckney (1757–1824), **Virginia** politician John Marshall (1755–1835), and former U.S. representative Elbridge Gerry (1744–1814) of Massachusetts.

Anonymous French agents told the commission that negotiations could not begin without a monetary bribe from the Americans to help France in its war with Great Britain. The scandal led to a louder cry for war with France. Adams allowed American merchant vessels to arm themselves. Congress passed laws breaking all treaties with France and authorizing the seizure of French ships that endangered U.S. commerce. It also created the Department of the **Navy** in April 1798 and added the U.S. **Marine Corps** in July.

Domestic affairs

The conflict with France led to the passage of the **Alien and Sedition Acts** in 1798. These were four laws that increased the time for foreigners to become U.S. citizens, empowered the president to deport foreigners under certain conditions, and made it a crime to publish "false, scandalous, and malicious" things about the government. One newspaper at the time wrote, "It is Patriotism to write in favor of our government—it is sedition to write against it."

Adams did not actively enforce the Alien Acts. His administration, however, used the Sedition Act to file criminal charges against many newspapers editors who favored the Democratic-Republican Party. Hamilton did not think Adams was doing enough to enforce these laws, which added to the problems between the two men.

The federal budget nearly doubled during Adams's administration. To raise money, Congress passed a tax law called the Window Tax in July

1798. When three Pennsylvanians were jailed in early 1799 for refusing to pay the tax, John Fries (1764–1825) led a rebellion to force federal marshals to release the prisoners. Adams ordered the rebellion to cease and sent federal troops to crush it. Fries and his supporters were sentenced to death for treason, but Adams pardoned them for their crimes. This increased his unpopularity with the Federalists.

A number of government offices were formed during the Adams administration, including the U.S. Public Health Service in 1798 and the Library of Congress in 1800. The **Mississippi** and **Indiana** territories were created in 1798 and 1800. Also in 1800, Adams became the first president to reside in the White House after the federal government relocated to **Washington, D.C.**

Peace with France and the campaign of 1800

Adams arranged his final diplomatic mission to France in February 1799. He sent Ambassador to the Netherlands William Murray (1760–1803), Chief Justice Oliver Ellsworth (1745–1807), and **North Carolina** governor William Davie (1756–1920) to negotiate for peace. In October 1800, they signed the Treaty of Mortefontaine, finally reaching peace with France.

News of the peace failed to reach America in time to help Adams win the presidential election of 1800. Division in the Federalist Party allowed Jefferson, the Democratic-Republican candidate, to emerge the victor. The Democratic-Republican Party also won control of Congress in the election.

In the wake of defeat, the Federalist-controlled Congress passed a judiciary act before the end of the term. It empowered Adams in his last months in office to appoint new judges—aligned with the Federalist Party—to federal courts.

Retirement

At the age of 65 in March 1801, John Adams returned to his home and farm in Quincy, Massachusetts, where he spent the rest of his life. He wrote often to family and friends, and from 1802 to 1806 he worked on his autobiography. His wife, Abigail, died in 1818, which was a profound loss to Adams. In 1824, Adams had the paternal honor of seeing his son, **John Quincy Adams** (1767–1848; served 1825–29), elected as the sixth president of the United States.

Around 1811, Adams resumed his friendship with Thomas Jefferson. The two spent the remainder of their lives corresponding about politics, philosophy, theology, and personal matters. By historic coincidence, they both died on July 4, 1826, fifty years after the adoption of the Declaration of Independence.

John Quincy Adams

John Quincy Adams was more effective in his term as secretary of state than he was during his one term in the White House. His efforts as president were frustrated by opponents and by his inability to compromise. An intelligent and committed politician, he went on to a distinguished eighteen-year career in the U.S. House of Representatives.

Growing up in the Revolutionary War years

Adams was born on July 11, 1767, into a highly distinguished New England family in Braintree, **Massachusetts**. His father, **John Adams** (1735–1826; served 1797–1801), would become the second president of the United States. As a young boy, Adams was intrigued with all that was happening in the years leading up to the **American Revolution** (1775–83), the war for independence from Great Britain. Adams was an exceptionally intelligent young man. He attended private schools in Europe, graduated from Harvard College, and then studied law.

While still in school, Adams served as secretary to his father in Paris, France, during negotiations in 1783 to end the American Revolution. In 1794, President **George Washington** (1732–1799; served 1789–97) appointed him minister to the Netherlands. After his father became president in 1796, Adams served as minister to Prussia, in present-day Germany.

A change in political course

In 1803, Adams was elected to the U.S. Senate. His father was one of the founders of **Federalism**—a school of political thought that supported a strong national government and an industrial (business and manufacturing) economy. Adams's supporters in Massachusetts fully expected him to support **Federalist Party** policies, but as he watched the new nation

John Quincy Adams had a prominent eighteen-year career in the U.S. House of Representatives after serving as the sixth president of the United States. THE LIBRARY OF CONGRESS

take shape, his sympathies turned toward the **Democratic-Republican Party**, which favored states' rights over federal power and an agrarian (farming) economy. Adams frequently voted in favor of the policies of the Democratic-Republican president, **Thomas Jefferson** (1743–1826; served 1801–9), including the **Louisiana Purchase** in 1803, which nearly doubled the size of the United States. Having infuriated many of the people who elected him, he joined the Democratic-Republican Party (which was also known as the Jeffersonian Republican Party) at the end of his term in the Senate.

Secretary of state

Adams served in important overseas missions under President **James Madison** (1751–1836; served 1809–17) and was appointed secretary of state under President **James Monroe** (1758–1831; served 1817–25) from 1817 to 1825. In this position, he used his keen diplomatic skills to build and strengthen the United States. In the aftermath of the **War of 1812** (1812–15), a conflict over trade between Great Britain and the United States, he hammered out an arms-reduction agreement with Great Britain. He also negotiated with Great Britain to establish the boundary between British Canada and the United States. In 1819, Adams convinced Spain to cede **Florida** to the United States.

In 1823, President Monroe presented the **Monroe Doctrine** to Congress, which declared that the United States would not tolerate European interference in, or colonization of, the independent countries in the Western Hemisphere. Adams was a principal author of the Monroe Doctrine, which has served as the foundation of U.S. foreign policy since that time.

President

Adams joined the race for the presidency in 1824, running against four other Democratic-Republican nominees, one of whom was the popular military general **Andrew Jackson** (1767–1845). Although a majority of the popular vote went to Jackson, the race was close, and it fell to the House of Representatives to choose the new president. The House chose Adams as the sixth U.S. president. Many felt that Jackson was robbed of the presidency.

Adams moved into the White House full of ideas. He planned to expand the country's roads and canals, build a national university, improve bankruptcy laws, create a standard system of weights and measures for American business, and much more. Once in office, though, he discovered that every move he made was fiercely opposed by Jackson's supporters in Congress. The Jacksonians were not his only problem. Adams refused to play the customary political game in Washington, D.C., neglecting to reward his supporters with the political appointments they expected. His instincts were honorable, but his lack of charm and unwillingness to compromise prevented him from gaining a popular following. He lost the election of 1828 to Jackson.

Post-presidential years

In 1830, the former president was elected to the U.S. House of Representatives. Adams served with distinction from 1831 until his death in 1848, earning the nickname "Old Man Eloquent" for his speeches. His crowning achievement was his opposition to the "gag rules" that prevented antislavery petitions from being read on the floor of the House. Adams argued that the rules violated the **First Amendment** of the U.S. **Constitution**, which protects the freedom of speech and the right to petition the government. The House discarded the "gag rules" in 1844. While never officially declaring himself to be in favor of abolishing **slavery**, Adams became an outspoken champion of the antislavery movement in Congress.

In 1848, Adams suffered a stroke on the House floor. He was carried to the Speaker's room, where he died two days later.

Jane Addams

Jane Addams was the first woman to be awarded the Nobel Peace Prize. She dedicated her life to caring for others and co-founded one of the first settlement houses in the United States.

Born on September 6, 1860, Laura Jane Addams was the eighth child of Sarah and John Addams. The Cedarville, **Illinois**, family prospered, thanks to the good business sense of Addams's father, who owned a mill and eventually a bank. Addams lost her mother to illness before her third birthday, and her eldest sister, Mary, took over the responsibility of raising the children. Addams formed an especially close relationship with her father, who instilled in her a strong sense of morality and responsibility in helping others.

After graduating at the top of her class in 1881 from Rockford Female Seminary, Addams enrolled in medical school, but she did not stay there long. Her father died suddenly of a burst appendix, and around that time Addams's own health took a turn for the worse. She spent years in and out of the hospital and took six months of bed rest to recover from spinal surgery. Afterward, Addams traveled around Europe for nearly two years. She took another two years to write and decide what she wanted to do with her life.

Jane Addams founded Hull House, which became a key component of the immigration experience in Chicago and was one of the most famous settlement houses in American history. THE LIBRARY OF CONGRESS

Finds inspiration in England

During another trip to Europe, this time in 1888, twenty-seven-year-old Addams and her close friend Ellen Gates Starr (1859–1940) visited a settlement house (community center) in London. Toynbee Hall was Great Britain's first university settlement. There, college students could work together to help improve the lives of the city's poverty-stricken population. Addams and Starr were so impressed with the settlement project that they returned to America determined to develop their own settlement house. (See **Settlement House Movement**.)

The following year, the two women leased a large, rundown building in the heart of Chicago's immigrant slum (a district marked by intense poverty and filth). Starr and Addams moved into the building with the goal of restoring it and providing neighborhood families with a place to go where they could improve themselves while forging a sense of community with one another. They named the building Hull House (real estate tycoon Charles Hull

[1820–1889] had once lived in the building). Although Hull House was not the first settlement house in America, it would become the most famous.

The birth of Hull House

The settlement became a key component of the immigration experience in Chicago. Historians estimate that in 1890, 68 to 80 percent of Chicago's population was foreign-born. Immigrants who sailed to America's shores and headed for Chicago went directly to Hull House, where they knew they could find trustworthy people to help them locate jobs, homes, and food. That year Hull House was servicing two thousand people each week.

Once Hull House proved itself a worthy cause, Addams and Starr had little problem securing monetary donations to help keep it running. Free medical care was provided, as was relief for the unemployed. Addams made sure Hull House clients received education not only in academics but also in skills necessary for daily life. She and her colleagues taught immigrants the English language and how to count money and perform simple math calculations. She taught them how to read and made sure they learned how to use the political system to their advantage.

Through the decades, Hull House continued to provide a safe gathering place for its neighborhood citizens. In 1961, the University of Illinois at Chicago decided it would build its campus on the site of Hull House. Although the neighborhood fought the decision, Hull House officially closed in 1963. Closing of the settlement house proved to be a major loss for Chicago's poor and displaced, as they now had one less place to which they could turn for help.

Addams goes national

Addams became involved with other organizations as her reputation grew. In 1905, she was appointed to the Chicago Board of Education and elected as chairperson of the School Management Committee. Three years later, she helped found the Chicago School of Civics and Philanthropy (charitable giving), and she became the first female president of the National Conference of Charities and Corrections in 1909. That same year, she helped establish the **National Association for the**

Advancement of Colored People (NAACP), an organization that promotes equality between the races and is still active in the twenty-first century. From 1911 to 1914, Addams was vice president of the National American Women's Suffrage Association, one of the key women's organizations of the era. All the while, she remained at the center of social reform in Chicago. Addams headed investigations involving city sanitation issues and even accepted a position as a garbage inspector.

Throughout, a feminist

Addams believed women should have voting rights, and she encouraged women to create their own opportunities for growth and development. She was also a pacifist (one who is against violence of any kind), and she traveled the country speaking on the importance of peace. She gave lectures against America's involvement in **World War I** (1914–18) and was made chairperson of the Women's Peace Party in 1915. Shortly after that, she was elected president of the Women's International League for Peace and Freedom, a position she held until 1929.

Addams's public disapproval of America's involvement in the war brought attacks upon her in the newspapers and political magazines. Addams did not let the controversy weaken her position; she chose instead to work with **Herbert Hoover** (1874–1964), who would soon be elected U.S. president, in a program that provided food supplies to the women and children of America's enemies in the war. For her tireless humanitarian efforts, Addams was awarded the Nobel Peace Prize in 1931.

In addition to her many social and political activities, Addams found time to write. She authored numerous magazine articles on social reform issues and published seven books on social reform and pacifism. Addams died of cancer on May 21, 1935.

Affirmative Action

Affirmative action refers to federal requirements for employers that are made to protect minorities and women from discrimination (being treated differently) and to increase minority representation in the workforce. Although few people would deny its beneficial effects in bringing opportunities to more minorities and women, affirmative action has been highly controversial since it came into being in the mid-1960s.

Established in two acts

Affirmative action began with the **Civil Rights Act of 1964**, particularly Title VII of the act, which made it illegal for employers to discriminate against anyone on the basis of race, color, religion, sex, or national origin and required them to provide equal employment opportunities for everyone. It soon became apparent that Title VII, simply by prohibiting present-day discrimination, could not make up for the continuing effects of past discrimination. Many people argued that members of minority groups, having been the victims of discrimination for many generations, had often been deprived of the education, experience, and connections of those who had never been the target of discrimination.

To address this disparity, in 1965 President **Lyndon B. Johnson** (1908–1973; served 1963–69) initiated affirmative action when he signed Executive Order 11246, which required federal contractors to "take affirmative action to ensure that applicants are employed, and that employees are treated … without regard to their race, color, religion, or national origin." The overall goal was to bring groups that had been discriminated against in the past into the workforce at a more rapid rate than natural. Employers were required to compare the percentage of minorities in their present labor force with the percentage of minorities in the general population. If the employers identified situations in which minorities were underrepresented in their company, they were to file written plans that included goals, timetables, and strategies to correct the situation.

Certain affirmative action hiring processes were not allowed. Ruling in *Griggs v. Duke Power Company* (1971), the **Supreme Court** allowed affirmative action recruiting practices that were designed to increase the pool of female and minority applicants but prohibited quotas—numerical goals for the hiring of women and minorities.

Growing restrictions

During the 1970s and 1980s, as jobs became more scarce in the United States, opposition to affirmative action increased. Opponents felt that when an individual belonging to a minority was hired under affirmative action, someone else, probably a white male, was disqualified. In 1977, the Supreme Court took up a case that addressed this kind of "reverse discrimination," or discrimination against someone from the majority. In *Regents of the University of California v. Bakke,* white applicants who had been rejected from the University of California-Davis Medical School argued that the school had discriminated against them to fill a minority quota. The Supreme Court struck down the university's racial-quota admissions system but upheld the basis of affirmative action, ruling that it was acceptable to take race into account as a positive factor in admissions as a way to create a diverse student body.

In 1994, the **Republican Party** became the majority party in the U.S. Congress and promised to curb or end affirmative action programs. At the same time, **California** governor Pete Wilson (1933–) began tearing down his state's affirmative action structure, beginning with admissions and hiring procedures at the University of California. Governors in other states soon announced their own renunciation of affirmative action programs.

In 1995, the U.S. Supreme Court heard the case *Adarand Constructors, Inc. v. Peña.* Adarand, a **Colorado** highway guardrail company owned by a white male, filed the lawsuit to challenge the constitutionality of a federal program designed to favor minority businesses when awarding contracts. The Court ruled that federal affirmative action programs must be tested, calling for "strict scrutiny" in determining whether discrimination existed before using a federal affirmative action program. The ruling greatly restricted affirmative action practices. In response, President **Bill Clinton** (1946–; served 1993–2001) called for major changes in the way affirmative action was carried out and prohibited quotas, reverse discrimination, and preferential treatment for unqualified individuals.

College admissions and an uncertain future

In the 1996 case *Hopwood v. University of Texas Law School,* the U.S. Court of Appeals overturned the 1978 *Regents of the University of California v. Bakke* decision, which had supported race as a determining factor in school admissions. In *Hopwood,* the Court asserted that diversity was not necessarily in the interest of the state. Texas public universities were required to change their admissions processes so that race would no longer be a factor. In 2003, however, the Supreme Court upheld the University of Michigan Law School's affirmative action admissions policy, acknowledging that the school could benefit from a diverse campus, thus ruling that race could be a factor in admissions as long as it is not an overriding factor.

Affirmative action programs survived into the twenty-first century, though greatly reduced from their original character. The subject remained highly controversial, with neither opponents nor supporters showing any sign of changing their position.

Afghanistan Conflict

The invasion of Afghanistan by U.S. forces in October 2001 began as a quick and effective strike, ousting a tyrannical government and sending terrorist forces into hiding. For a number of reasons, the Afghanistan War dragged on for years after the invasion, allowing the enemy a chance to regain some of its power.

Retaliation for a terrorist attack

Within hours of the **September 11, 2001, terrorist attacks** on the World Trade Center and Pentagon, the administration of President **George W. Bush** (1946–; served 2001–) determined that members of the **al-Qaeda** terrorist network were responsible for the attacks. Two airliners crashed into the Twin Towers of New York City's World Trade Center, a third airliner crashed into the Pentagon, and a fourth jet crashed into a Pennsylvania field before arriving at its intended target. Al-Qaeda was led by the Saudi Arabian multimillionaire Osama bin Laden (1957–) and others who had embraced a radical form of Islam while fighting in Afghanistan during that nation's ten-year war with the Soviet Union (1979–89). Al-Qaeda was headquartered in Afghanistan, where the ruling Islamic regime, the Taliban, had been providing it shelter. After September 11, the Bush administration demanded that the Taliban turn bin Laden and other al-Qaeda leaders over to the United States. The Taliban stalled for weeks, claiming no knowledge of bin Laden's whereabouts.

The Bush administration prepared for war. Since an invasion of Afghanistan could be viewed as an act of self-defense, the administration did not seek United Nations approval for a multinational force. Instead, Bush called on the help of Great Britain. Canada and Australia later also contributed troops to the allied force. This mission was named Operation Enduring Freedom (OEF).

These two Canadian soldiers are part of the NATO mission to fight insurgents and stabilize Afghanistan. SHAH MARAI/AFP/GETTY IMAGES

The invasion

On October 7, U.S. and British forces launched air strikes against Afghanistan. At the same time, the United States provided the Northern Alliance, a loose coalition of Afghan military groups that had long op-

*Northern Alliance fighters
patrol the fallen northern city
of Mazar-e Sharif,
Afghanistan.* OLEG NIKISHIN/
GETTY IMAGES

posed the Taliban, with funding and support for an offensive against the
Taliban on the ground. The strikes initially focused on the area in and
around the cities of Kabul, Jalalabad, and Qandahār. Within a few days,
most al-Qaeda training sites had been severely damaged, and the
Taliban's air defenses had been destroyed. The air strikes then targeted
the Taliban's communications systems.

By November 9, 2001, the northern city of Mazar-e Sharif had
fallen to the Northern Alliance; four days later, a combination of allied
air assaults and ground maneuvers by the Northern Alliance forced the
Taliban to surrender Kabul, the capital. On November 18, the Taliban
announced that it would no longer provide protection to bin Laden, but
the U.S. government was no longer inclined to believe the regime's
promises. A week later, opposition Afghan leaders met in Bonn,
Germany, with U.S. support to plan the post-Taliban government.

Some five hundred U.S. **Marines** landed in Afghanistan on
November 26, the first major entry of American troops. Within hours of
the marines establishing their base, U.S. planes launched air strikes
against a Taliban stronghold outside the southern city of Qandahār.

The Taliban surrendered Qandahār on December 7. But both bin
Laden and Taliban leader Mullah Muhammad Omar (c. 1959–) had escaped from the city. December 16 saw the fall of Tora Bora, a cave complex that had provided a fort for al-Qaeda and the Taliban. Six days later,

on December 22, a temporary Afghan government was established, with Hamid Karzai (1957–) sworn in as chairman. At that point, the Bush administration's invasion appeared to be complete and successful, but in many ways the war had just begun.

Afghan-Pakistani border region

Although the opening offensives of the war came to a close at the end of 2001, the Taliban and al-Qaeda forces had not given up. They had simply moved into the region that surrounds the border between Afghanistan and Pakistan. There they were able to reorganize more or less in the open. The Taliban arose from a large tribal group called the Pashtuns, who number about forty million and live in tribal units in eastern and southern Afghanistan and northwestern Pakistan. When Pashtuns in Pakistan learned of the U.S. invasion of Afghanistan, they joined with other anti-Western groups in the area to offer refuge to the fleeing Taliban and to al-Qaeda. Pakistan had long been an ally of the Taliban in Afghanistan, and the new war strengthened ties between the Taliban and certain Pakistani groups. The president of Pakistan, Pervez Musharraf (1943–), had vowed to help the United States in its war against terrorism, but the Pakistani government was apparently unable to stop the buildup of insurgents in the remote regions of northwestern Pakistan.

In the border regions in 2002, the Taliban began to build training camps and recruit new soldiers from both sides of the border. The new recruits soon began launching car bombs and suicide bombings against the U.S.-U.K.-Northern Alliance coalition. They managed to regain control, at least temporarily, of areas that had already been liberated by the coalition forces.

On March 2, 2002, the United States launched Operation Anaconda, the largest ground operation of the war. Involving some two thousand U.S., Afghan, and allied troops, its purpose was to eliminate any Taliban and al-Qaeda fighters remaining in the mountains of southeastern Afghanistan. An estimated one thousand to five thousand al-Qaeda and Taliban forces had gathered in the Shahikot mountains in early 2002, where they could use the high-altitude caves to fire upon approaching coalition soldiers from relative safety. When the Anaconda offensive came to a close on March 17, the mountain caves were cleared and there were many enemy casualties, but hundreds of al-Qaeda and Taliban soldiers escaped once more into the border areas of Pakistan.

To build a state, or not

Afghanistan had long been a very poor country. Many Afghan people hoped that, after ousting the Taliban, the United States would bring in enough money and resources to supply stability and build a new economy. Among the top Bush administration officials there was disagreement. To commit large amounts of troops and money to bring political and economic stability was seen as "state-building" or "nation-building," the attempt of a powerful country to build the political and economic institutions of a weak or failing nation, and most conservatives opposed such a plan, saying it overstepped the federal government's authority. The administration wavered on these issues, announcing major reconstruction efforts but not providing the number of soldiers or amounts of money that the Afghan advisers requested.

NATO steps in

In 2002, the United States began to talk with other countries, mainly European, who were willing to help stabilize Afghanistan. In this peacekeeping and reconstruction plan, called the International Security Assistance Force (ISAF), Germany was to train an Afghan police force, Japan would disarm the warlords and their armies, England would fight the drug business, Italy would help Afghanistan reform its court system, and the United States would train a large Afghan army. The United States, wanting to carry out its war on terrorists, committed an additional eight thousand troops to searching out al-Qaeda and Taliban insurgents. None of these efforts was very successful.

In November 2003 Zalmay Khalilzad (1951–), an Afghan American, was appointed to serve as U.S. ambassador to Afghanistan. Upon becoming ambassador, Khalilzad convinced the Bush administration to put more resources into the war in Afghanistan. He played a very strong role in his year and a half as ambassador, from November 2003 until June 2005. Khalilzad helped the new government draft a constitution, hold democratic elections (in which Karzai was elected president), and organize a parliament. But as things began to improve, President Bush urgently needed him for another post—in Iraq.

In March 2003, the Bush administration had launched an attack on the nation of Iraq. (See **Iraq Invasion**.) At first, the engagement went smoothly and did not require the efforts of the military personnel in Afghanistan. By 2005, though, the experienced military leadership in Afghanistan were being recruited in large numbers to help calm the insurgency (uprising) in Iraq.

At the end of 2005, the North Atlantic Treaty Organization (NATO; a mutual security and self-defense agreement formed in 1949 among European and North American nations to block the military threat of the Soviet Union) took command of the fight against insurgents in Afghanistan. NATO forces there were comprised of 31,000 to 37,000 soldiers from 37 countries; approximately one-third of them were from the United States. The NATO mission was to stabilize Afghanistan.

In 2006, Afghanistan experienced a major increase in deadly attacks by suicide bombers and individuals with homemade explosives. The trend continued into 2007. Insurgents poured into Afghanistan from the training camps in the Pakistan borderlands. While pursuing the insurgents, NATO and U.S. air strikes have killed a large number of Afghan civilians, resulting in widespread anti-American and anti-Western sentiment. Poverty in Afghanistan was widespread, and years of war had taken a heavy toll on the population.

The U.S. Department of Defense announced in early 2008 that the number of U.S. troops in Afghanistan was around twenty thousand, the highest number since the war began in October 2001. An additional three thousand troops were expected to be sent there by summer to combat the increasingly formidable Taliban forces.

AFL-CIO
See **American Federation of Labor–Congress of Industrial Organizations**

African Americans
See **Black Codes; Black Panther Party; Black Power Movement; Buffalo Soldiers; Civil Rights Movement; Great Migration; Jim Crow Laws; Lynching; National Association for the Advancement of Colored People; Race Riots of the 1960s; Segregation; Slavery**

AIDS

Acquired Immune Deficiency Syndrome (AIDS) is an infectious disease that suppresses the immune system and prevents its victims from successfully fighting off infections that would not be of major concern in healthy people. The disease is caused by the human immunodeficiency virus (HIV), which is part of a group of viruses known as retroviruses.

Although the disease did not have a name until 1982, the first known cases of AIDS occurred in 1981. In the spring of that year, both **California** and **New York** reported an increase in the number of cases of Pneumocystis carinii pneumonia (PCP), a life-threatening form of pneumonia. In June, the Centers for Disease Control (CDC) reported five cases of PCP in Los Angeles, all without identifiable causes. The report is referred to as the beginning of a general awareness of AIDS in America. Before the end of the year, the first case of AIDS was reported in the United Kingdom.

Because the first documented cases of AIDS involved young homosexual men, the disease was originally believed to be exclusive to that population. Intravenous drug users were also transmitting the disease. It soon became apparent that AIDS could be acquired through blood, as evidenced by the death of a twenty-month-old child who had received blood transfusions in 1982. With this discovery, scientists and medical experts knew the disease was caused by an infectious agent, but HIV was not identified as that cause until early 1985.

How it works

AIDS was not publicly mentioned until September 17, 1985, when U.S. president **Ronald Reagan** (1911–2004; served 1981–89) was asked about funding for the disease at a press conference. That same year, a thirteen-year-old boy from Indiana named Ryan White (1971–1990) was diagnosed with AIDS. White was a hemophiliac (someone who has blood that does not clot) and had been infected with HIV via contaminated blood. Although White posed no risk to other students, he was banned from attending school and became a national symbol for the AIDS movement. White died in 1990 at the age of eighteen.

The public was terrified of this new disease, and little was known about it. Two scientists, French immunologist Luc Montagnier (1932–) and American immunologist Robert Gallo (1937–) and their teams discovered HIV as the cause around the same time (1983 and 1984), although they worked independently. HIV leads to AIDS because it destroys a certain type of blood cell necessary to maintaining a healthy immune system. Although a person can live for years with HIV and not know it, HIV always leads to AIDS. And AIDS is a fatal disease.

Since the advent of AIDS, researchers have learned much more about how the disease is transmitted. HIV is spread by sexual contact with an infected person, by sharing needles or syringes with someone

Several groups often gather to raise AIDS awareness. One of the most significant gatherings happened in October 1996 in Washington, D.C., when thousands of people created the AIDS Memorial Quilt to honor those who had died from and were living with the disease. THE GALE GROUP

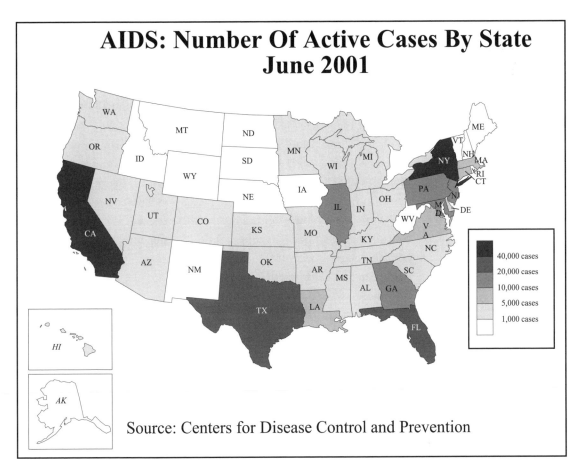

AIDS: Number Of Active Cases By State
June 2001

Source: Centers for Disease Control and Prevention

This map shows the number of active cases of AIDS in 2001. However, the number is continuing to increase and by 2007 North America had over 1.3 million people infected with AIDS and HIV. AP IMAGES

who is infected, and by receiving transfusions of infected blood. Babies born to women who are HIV-positive can become infected either before or during the birth process. HIV-positive mothers who breastfeed may transmit the disease to their babies. Sweat, tears, and saliva of infected people have never been shown to transmit the disease.

AIDS in the twenty-first century

No country is immune from AIDS. According to a United Nations publication, 33.2 million people lived with HIV in 2007, up from 29 million in 2001. Around 2.5 million of those living with HIV in 2007 were newly infected that year.

The most severely impacted region of the world in 2007 was sub-Saharan Africa, where 22.5 million people live with HIV. Sixty-one percent of these people are women. More than three-fourths of all AIDS-related deaths in 2007 occurred there. In North America, 1.3 million were infected, and approximately forty-six thousand adults and children were newly infected in 2007.

Medical treatment of HIV and AIDS has made many advancements since the 1980s. In 1986, a drug called azidothymidine (AZT) was shown to slow the attack of HIV. Since that time, other drugs have been found to be effective. Antiretrovirals interfere with the reproduction of HIV; protease inhibitors interfere with the enzymes HIV requires to take control of specific body cells; and nonnucleoside reverse transcriptase inhibitors interfere with HIV's ability to sort its genetic material into the viral code that leads to AIDS.

Although modern medicine helps delay the onset of AIDS in HIV-positive patients, there is no medicine that will prevent AIDS. The medicines available are expensive, and those who need them most can least afford them. AIDS remains one of the leading causes of death across the globe and is the leading cause of death in Africa.

Air Force

The U.S. Air Force (USAF) was once part of the **Army**; it was officially established as its own branch of the military on September 18, 1947, with the passage of the National Security Act. Under that act, the USAF's mission is to provide prompt and sustained offensive and defensive air operations in combat, to preserve the peace and security of the United States, and to fly and fight in air and space.

Before 1947, the Army and the **Navy** provided military aviation. The army's aviation section, the U.S. Signal Corps, was created in 1914. The USAF has fought in every war in U.S. history since **World War I** (1914–18). Like other branches of the military, the Air Force also participates in humanitarian efforts worldwide. One of the most famous was the Berlin Airlift of 1948–49.

According to *Air Force Magazine,* the 2006 USAF had a combined active duty and reserve field consisting of 302 flying squadrons.

Despite the fact that the USAF is the aviation branch of the military, most members never leave the ground; instead, they fill the hundreds of support positions necessary to maintain successful missions, working as mechanics, computer specialists, civil engineers, hospitality (restaurant) workers, lawyers, drug counselors, and others.

The most dangerous jobs in the Air Force are in the Pararescue, Combat Control, and Combat Weather divisions. These sections consist of enlisted members who go on special operations missions to rescue personnel, call in air strikes, and set up landing zones. The Air Force provides all training for almost every one of these enlisted jobs. After recruits go through basic training, they attend a technical training school for the particular positions they have chosen or been assigned.

Officer candidates train at the Air Force Academy in Colorado Springs, **Colorado**. The academy was established on April 1, 1954, and the first class entered in July 1955. Women were first accepted in 1976. Graduates can be commissioned by any of the branches of the military. The USAF Academy is one of the most selective colleges in the United States.

Al-Qaeda

Al-Qaeda (pronounced al KYE-dah; Arabic for "the base") is a worldwide terrorist network of organizations and individuals dedicated to *jihad* ("struggle" or "holy war") for the cause of Islam. Its goal is to rid Muslim countries of what it perceives is the corrupting influence of Western culture and to install fundamentalist Islamic regimes—governments that rule according to a literal interpretation of the Muslim sacred texts (the Koran and the Hadith) and enforce sharia (Islamic law). Al-Qaeda is only one of a number of closely linked Islamic terrorist and insurgency groups. The size of al-Qaeda is not known, but estimates run between several hundred to several thousand members. Some scholars believe, however, al-Qaeda is actually a small group that has received undue publicity for acts that have originated with other, connected terrorist groups. Al-Qaeda became notorious in the United States for its actions in the **September 11, 2001, terrorist attacks**, when members of the group hijacked four U.S. airplanes. Two of the aircraft destroyed the World Trade Center in New York City; a third crashed into the Pentagon near **Washington, D.C.**; and the fourth crashed in a field in **Pennsylvania**.

Osama bin Laden trained militant recruits from all over the world, creating the al-Qaeda organization.
AP IMAGES

Roots of al-Qaeda

In 1979, the Soviet Union invaded Afghanistan. Muslim leaders around the world called for a jihad, fearing the Soviets would establish a secular (nonreligious) government in the Muslim country. Thousands of Muslim men, primarily of Arab origin, volunteered to assist the Afghan resistance fighters against Soviet troops. With assistance from the United States, Saudi Arabia, and Pakistan, the Afghans and foreign fighters—or mujahideen (holy warriors), as they came to be known—defeated the Soviet Union in February 1989. The victory was celebrated as a triumph for God by the "Afghan Arabs," Muslims who had traveled to Afghanistan from Arab countries and joined the war in the name of Islam.

Osama bin Laden (1957–) was among the thousands of mujahideen who fought in Afghanistan. From a wealthy and prominent Saudi Arabian family, bin Laden brought financial support to the cause. After the war with the Soviet Union, bin Laden and his associates started to recruit soldiers and develop training camps. Bin Laden believed that defeating the Soviet Union was only the first step in a worldwide jihad campaign to support Muslims and promote Islamic governments. In Afghanistan, bin Laden's early supporters included members of the radical Egyptian group al-Jihad al-Islami, which was involved in the assassination of President Anwar el-Sadat (1918–1981) of Egypt in 1981. Bin Laden soon joined forces with the prominent al-Jihad leader Ayman al-Zawahiri (1951–), who favored terrorism and violence as the means by which to wage this international jihad.

Many "Afghan Arabs" returned home after the defeat of the Soviet Union ready to spark jihad in their own societies. Bin Laden returned to Saudi Arabia for a short period, but he was stripped of his Saudi citizenship in 1994 because of his extremist views. He set up his organization briefly in Sudan, but soon international pressure forced Sudan to crack down on him. Bin Laden moved to Afghanistan in 1996, where he was sheltered by the Taliban, the tyrannical ruling Islamist group.

In Afghanistan, bin Laden set up new training camps for militant recruits from all over the world, and his organization came to be known as al-Qaeda. Bin Laden was one of several primary leaders, including al-Zawahiri. Al-Qaeda represents itself as an Islamic group based on religious ideas, but its versions of the fundamental teachings of the Koran (the Muslim holy book) often differ greatly from mainstream interpretations. For example, bin Laden reinterpreted the concept of fatwa, a formal legal opinion. In Islam, believers are encouraged to seek answers to questions they have about Islam by submitting them to an Islamic cleric, or teacher. The teacher issues a fatwa in response to the question, clarifying the issue based on the writings of the Koran. Bin Laden issued his own "fatwas," which were neither responses to questions nor issued by Islamic clerics.

Declaration of jihad against the United States

During the U.S.-led **Persian Gulf War** (1991) against Iraq, the United States established military bases in Saudi Arabia. In bin Laden's view, this was an occupation of the holy land of Islam in Arabia, where the holy Islamic sites of Mecca and Medina are located. On August 23, 1996, bin Laden issued his first fatwa identifying the United States as an enemy and urging Muslims to kill American military personnel abroad. In 1998, he issued a second fatwa, this time in the name of the International Islamic Front for Jihad Against the Jews and Crusaders, urging all good Muslims to kill not only U.S. military personnel but also U.S. civilians.

Operations

Al-Qaeda's structure is based on secrecy. It is a worldwide network of organizations and cells (small groups of three to five people, who are secretly part of the organization but live undercover in society). Terrorist attacks are often planned, organized, and carried out by small groups called "sleeper cells," which remain dormant, or inactive, in foreign countries for long periods of time. Some of the September 11 hijackers, for example, lived in the United States for several years, using the time to plan the attack and learn the skills they needed (in this case, piloting commercial aircraft). To ensure secrecy, most members of terrorist cells do not know the identity of or the nature of the tasks carried out by other members of the organization or even their leaders. By maintaining

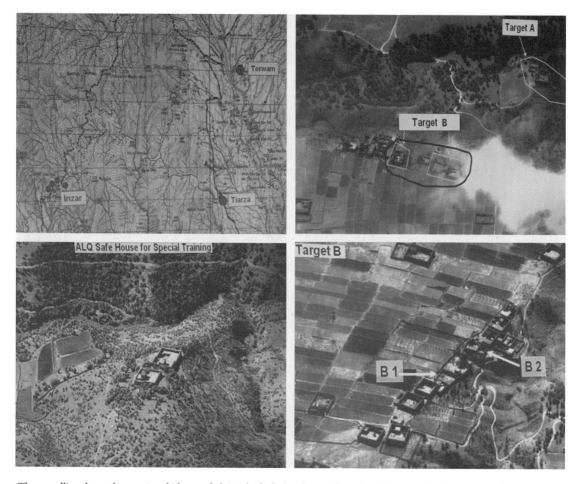

These satellite photos show various hideouts of al-Qaeda–linked militants along the Afghanistan border. Due to substantial funding from bin Laden himself, al-Qaeda is able to access the Internet, television, and other media while hiding in remote areas. AP IMAGES

secrecy in this way, al-Qaeda has been able to evade most counterterrorism efforts.

Al-Qaeda has a sophisticated structure. A primary factor has been bin Laden's access to money. He inherited about $250 to $300 million from his father. With a college education in business, bin Laden was able to set up a complex financial network. To collect money under the guise of religious purposes, he created a number of Muslim charities around the world, including in the United States. Although stationed in remote areas, al-Qaeda employed satellite communications (the use of artificial satellites stationed in space for communications using radio technology at microwave frequencies) for access to the Internet, television, radio, and other international media. Bin Laden and al-Zawahiri used the international media to voice their beliefs and goals and, most importantly, to gain worldwide attention. Some experts believe that they placed hidden messages in their media statements to communicate to al-Qaeda cells awaiting instructions.

History

The U.S. government began to identify bin Laden publicly as an international terrorist in the mid-1990s, when evidence connected him to attacks on U.S. military personnel and assets in Somalia (1992) and Saudi Arabia (1995–96). In addition, bin Laden was tied to several unsuccessful terrorist plots, including plans to assassinate Pope John Paul II (1920–2005) in 1994 and U.S. president **Bill Clinton** (1946–; served 1993–2001) in 1995.

Nineteen servicemen and women were killed in 2000 when the USS Cole *was bombed in Yemen by al-Qaeda suicide bombers.*
AP IMAGES

On August 20, 1998, in the wake of the al-Qaeda–led bombings of the U.S. embassies in Kenya and Tanzania that killed 224 people and injured thousands, President Clinton added al-Qaeda to the U.S. list of Foreign Terrorist Organizations. On June 7, 1999, bin Laden was added to the **Federal Bureau of Investigation**'s Ten Most Wanted list, with a $5 million reward offered for his capture. The U.S. government displayed his picture on wanted posters, matchbooks, and leaflets distributed worldwide in nearly a dozen languages. Unfortunately, this led many to believe that bin Laden was single-handedly taking on the most powerful country in the world, turning him into a popular hero in some places. In response to the embassy bombings in Africa, President Clinton ordered air strikes against a bin Laden camp in Khost, Afghanistan, as well as what was believed to be an al-Qaeda chemical weapons facility in Sudan.

Bin Laden evaded capture and continued his campaign of terror. Nineteen U.S. servicemen and women were killed when the USS *Cole,* a navy destroyer ship, was bombed in Yemen in October 2000. The bombing was eventually connected to al-Qaeda and is now seen as a forerunner of what was to come on September 11, 2001. On that day nineteen al-Qaeda members hijacked commercial airliners and flew them into the World Trade Center in New York, the Pentagon in Washington, D.C., and a field in Pennsylvania. It was the worst single terrorist attack on U.S. soil in the country's history, killing nearly three thousand people. Al-Qaeda links have been cited for most of the large terrorist acts worldwide since then, but other powerful and deadly terrorist organizations may be responsible for some of the violent deeds.

On the run?

After the attacks on September 11, a U.S.-led invasion of Afghanistan forced al-Qaeda into hiding in Afghanistan. Al-Qaeda's operations were damaged, but the organization remained powerful. In 2003, the United States invaded Iraq and deposed its dictator, Saddam Hussein (1937–2006). (See **Iraq Invasion**.) Iraq quickly grew unstable, partly due to differences between the two major Muslim groups, the Shiites and the Sunnis. As the Iraqi conflict grew, al-Qaeda operators apparently moved into the country and recruited Iraqi rebels into the organization, attempting to further destabilize Iraq by igniting sectarian conflict. A new terrorist group arose called al-Qaeda-in-Iraq.

In mid-2007 the location of al-Qaeda leaders bin Laden and al-Zawahiri remained unknown. Individual cells remained secret, and many financial assets were in the hands of al-Qaeda members. Political and social conditions around the world continued to produce anger and resentment against the West, resulting in a constant supply of new recruits for al-Qaeda and connected terrorist groups.

Alabama

Alabama became the twenty-second state of the Union on December 14, 1819. Located in the eastern part of the south central United States, it borders **Tennessee**, **Georgia**, **Mississippi**, **Florida**, and the Gulf of Mexico. Its capital is Montgomery, and the state motto is "We dare defend our rights."

During the sixteenth century, Spanish expeditions explored the region now known as Alabama. In 1702, two French naval officers established Ft. Louis de la Mobile, the first permanent European settlement in the region. It remained under French control until 1763, when it was turned over to the British.

The Spanish took control of Mobile in 1780 during the **American Revolution** (1775–83). American troops seized the city in the **War of 1812** (1812–15). West Florida, which included Mobile at the time, was the only territory added to the United States as a result of that war.

Native Americans still held most of present-day Alabama at the start of the nineteenth century. As American settlers began moving into the area, the Creek tribe was forced to sign a treaty giving about 40,000 square miles (103,600 square kilometers) of land to the United States. This opened up about three-fourths of the present state to white settlement.

Statehood and secession

Alabama fever took hold of Americans as they poured in from **Kentucky**, Tennessee, Georgia, **Virginia**, **North Carolina**, and **South Carolina**. Alabama became a territory in 1817 and adopted a state constitution on August 2, 1819. Four months later, Alabama became a state.

Alabama seceded (separated) from the Union in January 1861 and joined the Confederacy. Montgomery served as capital of the Confederacy until May, when the seat of government was moved to

Richmond, Virginia. Historians estimate that at least twenty-five thousand Alabamians were killed in the American **Civil War** (1861–65). The state was readmitted to the Union in 1868.

Industry

Alabama's economy was based on **cotton**. The abolition of **slavery** brought about an attempt by the state to help build a "New South" in which agriculture would be balanced by industry. Throughout the 1880s and 1890s, approximately twenty towns in Alabama claimed to be iron-working centers. Birmingham became the leading industrial center.

Alabama became home to industries such as coal and steel in the late nineteenth century, and other industries such as clothing, textiles, and wood products followed. Even with this diverse economic base, the state still fell behind in wage rates and per capita income in the early 2000s. Manufacturing grew at just over half the rate of all state goods and services in the years between 1974 and 1983. When recession (a significant decline in economic activity for an extended period of time) hit from 1980 to 1982, it affected Alabama harder than it did the nation as a whole. In the beginning of the twenty-first century, the nation entered another recession, and many people working in manufacturing and the textile industries lost their jobs.

Civil rights

Alabama was the backdrop to civil rights demonstrations during the 1950s and 1960s. One of the most famous events of the **civil rights movement** was the **Montgomery bus boycott** of 1955, begun when **Rosa Parks** (1913–2005) refused to give up her seat to a white man and move to the back of the bus. Some demonstrations and protests became violent, such as the 1963 **Birmingham Baptist Church bombing** in which four young African American girls were killed. Alabama's governor at the time was Democrat George Wallace (1919–1998), who served four terms. Like most traditional Southerners, Wallace was in favor of **segregation** (keeping races separate).

Alabama spent the last decades of the twentieth century trying to improve its educational system as well as its health care system. Widespread poverty worked against the state, and in the twenty-first century it remained one of the nation's poorest states. According to the

U.S. Census Bureau, Alabama had the fifth-lowest median (average) income ($38,783) in the nation in 2007. The median income for the United States as a whole was $48,451.

The Alamo

The Alamo was a mission, or religious compound, built by the Spanish in the early eighteenth century in what is now San Antonio, **Texas**. The four-acre walled compound was devoted to the agricultural and religious education of the area's Indians. By the early nineteenth century, the Alamo had been abandoned by the Catholic Church (see **Catholicism**) and taken over by Spanish soldiers. After Mexico won its independence from Spain in 1821, the Mexican army occupied the compound.

American rebellion

By the 1830s, Texas had a majority of U.S. residents, although the area belonged to Mexico. In 1835, these residents revolted against Mexico. The rebels in San Antonio were able to clear their area of Mexican soldiers, and they quickly took command of the Alamo compound. On February 23, 1836, three thousand to four thousand Mexican troops crossed the Rio Grande—a river that borders what is now Texas and Mexico—under the command of Mexico's dictator, General Antonio López de Santa Anna (1794–1876). Their intent was to recapture the fortification. A force of 145 Texans, under the joint command of colonels William B. Travis (1809–1836) and James Bowie (1796–1836), prepared to defend the Alamo.

The siege

Santa Anna and his forces approached the stout-walled Alamo mission and demanded that the rebels surrender. When Travis replied with a cannon shot, the Mexican army surrounded the fort, and a thirteen-day siege began. The rebels sent a message to the commander in chief of the Texas military, **Sam Houston** (1793–1863), with a plea from Travis for reinforcements. On March 2, thirty-two of Houston's men made it through Mexican lines into the fort. They joined the Alamo's defenders, an assortment of men from eighteen different states and several European countries, many of whom were relatively new to Texas. Among the rebels was the frontiersman and former U.S. congressman **Davy**

Mexican soldiers led by General Antonio López de Santa Anna stormed the Alamo and defeated Texas rebels trying to hold the compound. KEAN COLLECTION/GETTY IMAGES

Crockett (1786–1836) of **Tennessee**, who led twelve Tennessee volunteers. With the 32 newcomers, there were only about 187 men defending the Alamo against about 4,000 Mexican troops. During the siege, they suffered from lack of sleep and ran low on ammunition, but no one tried to flee.

At four o'clock in the morning of March 6, Santa Anna and his troops stormed the Alamo on all sides. The Texans fought against all odds. Their guns got hot from heavy firing, their ammunition was nearly gone, and men began dropping from exhaustion. Even when the Mexicans penetrated the walls of the Alamo, the defenders continued to fight, clubbing them with rifles and drawing knives. The last point taken was the church, where Crockett and his volunteers fell. By eight o'clock that morning, the last of the 187 defenders was dead, and about 1,500 of the Mexican troops were killed.

The fall of the Alamo sowed panic throughout Texas. Much of the civilian population and the government fled toward U.S. soil. Meanwhile, Sam Houston gathered an army. Six weeks later, marching to meet Santa Anna, Houston delivered an impassioned address to his troops, telling them to "Remember the Alamo!" With that cry, they defeated the Mexicans at a battle near the San Jacinto River, establishing the independent Texas Republic.

Alaska

Alaska entered the Union on January 3, 1959, to become the forty-ninth state. Its name means "great land," and its motto is "North to the Future."

Alaska lies in the northwest corner of North America and is separated from the contiguous (adjacent) forty-eight states by Canada. It is the largest of the fifty states, with a total area of 591,004 square miles (1,530,699 square kilometers). Alaska occupies 16 percent of all U.S. land.

The state has a number of offshore islands, including Saint Lawrence and others in the Bering Sea, Kodiak Island in the Gulf of Alaska, and the Aleutian Islands in the Pacific Ocean.

Between ten thousand and forty thousand years ago, America's aboriginal peoples crossed a land bridge connecting Siberia with America. These hunter-gatherers from Asia dispersed and became three distinct groups: Aleut, Eskimo, and Indian.

Russian voyagers landed in Alaska in 1741, and in 1784 the first permanent Russian settlement was established on Kodiak Island. Russia sold its Alaskan territories to the United States in 1867 for $7.2 million, or two cents per acre. It became known as the **Alaska Purchase**.

Economy

The gold rush in the late 1880s hastened Alaska's economic development. That progress was overshadowed in 1898, when gold was discovered in Canada's Klondike region. Hundreds of thousands of people hoping to strike it rich came to the Yukon River valley and other Alaskan regions, including the Arctic. When the Alaska Railroad was built in 1914, even the most remote wilderness area became accessible.

Alaska depends heavily upon oil for its economy; 85 percent of its revenue comes from oil. When overproduction in the Middle East drove down the price of oil late in the twentieth century, the state's revenue declined by two-thirds, and the state lost twenty thousand jobs between 1985 and 1989.

In March 1989 the oil tanker *Exxon Valdez* hit a reef and, in one of the worst pollution disasters worldwide, spilled nearly eleven million gallons of crude oil that contaminated 1,285 miles of shoreline. The affected areas included Prince William Sound and its wildlife sanctuary, the Gulf of Alaska, and the Alaska Peninsula. The Exxon Corporation was fined more than $1 billion in civil and criminal penalties.

Alaska's Arctic National Wildlife Refuge (ANWR) has been the subject of national debate since the 1990s. Some people have favored opening the twenty-million-acre wilderness to oil drilling, a move that failed to receive enough support from Congress to pass until 2005. At that time, both the Senate and the House of Representatives voted to approve drilling as part of a larger bill to reduce federal spending. Many Senate members remained committed to preventing any drilling, however, and they threatened a filibuster (a delay tactic used by a Senate minority to prevent the passage of a bill) if the text regarding drilling in the ANWR was not removed. The text was removed and, as of early 2008, drilling was still up for debate.

Unlike most states whose populations vote either Republican or Democrat, Alaska is overwhelmingly (59 percent) unaffiliated with either party. In spite of this, in presidential elections since 1968, the state has voted Republican ten consecutive times.

At the time of its statehood induction, Alaska was almost completely dependent upon the federal government for its economic stability. During the 1970s, its petroleum industry developed, and the construction of the Trans-Alaska Pipeline brought both money and people to the state. Other important industries include commercial fishing and tourism. Tourism brought in $1.5 billion in 2003, which was 5 percent of Alaska's gross state product.

Alaska Purchase

The Alaska Purchase was a treaty by which Russia sold territory to the United States in 1867. The area comprised present-day **Alaska** and contained abundant natural resources. Russia was motivated to sell the area because of financial concerns and its lagging interest in the region.

The region of Alaska, which had been part of Russian territory for years, had proved to be a drain on the Russian treasury. Years of neglect hampered the region's profitability, so Russia was interested in surrendering responsibility for it. With the American population increasing in California to the south, the Russians decided to open conversations to sell the area to the United States.

In March 1867, the U.S. secretary of state, William Seward (1801–1872), and Russian minister Eduard de Stoeckl (1804–1892) negotiated a treaty under which the United States would purchase Alaska for $7.2 million. As Alaska had nearly 586,400 square miles, the cost was only about two cents per acre. Alaska ultimately proved to be rich in natural resources of timber, coal, copper, gold, and oil as well as salmon and furs.

Americans mock purchase

While both governments thought they had negotiated the better deal, news of the treaty was not well received by Americans. Critics mocked the treaty with names like Seward's Folly or Seward's Icebox. They said the price was too high for a territory that would prove to be worthless. Supporters argued that the region's natural resources would help commerce in the region and assist in opening trade with Asia.

The treaty was presented to the Senate on March 30, but public outcry prevented its quick approval. The necessary two-thirds vote came only after an impassioned three-hour speech by Charles Sumner (1811–1874), chairman of the Senate Foreign Relations Committee. The treaty passed that day, April 9, and the two countries exchanged ratifications on June 20.

The formal transfer of Alaska occurred on October 18, 1867, before the United States had paid Russia the agreed price. Political squabbling delayed approval for funding by the House of Representatives. The appropriations bill was finally approved a year after ratification, and payment was made on August 1, 1868.

Gold was discovered in Alaska in 1881, and prospectors, merchants, miners, and explorers streamed into Alaska to seek a fortune. In 1884, Congress organized the territory by passing the Organic Act, which placed Alaska under a collection of federal laws and **Oregon** state laws.

A second Organic Act in 1912 provided for land ownership, mail service, and a civil government under the Territory of Alaska. Alaska became the forty-ninth, and largest, state in the union in 1959.

Alien and Sedition Acts

In March 1797, **John Adams** (1735–1826; served 1797–1801) entered office as the second president of the United States. His term was marked by challenges both internationally, with a war between France and Great Britain, and domestically as political differences grew between members of the **Federalist Party** and **Democratic-Republican Party**, the country's two main political parties. In 1798, both tensions culminated in the passage of the Alien and Sedition Acts by the Federalist-controlled Congress.

Conflict on the high seas

Great Britain and France were at war over issues related to colonization and commerce. The United States was officially neutral in the war. In 1795, however, the United States had signed a commerce and alliance treaty with Britain called **Jay's Treaty**. France believed Jay's Treaty was a breach, or violation, of treaties of commerce and alliance that America had signed with France during the **American Revolution** (1775–83).

In angry response, France began seizing American merchant ships bound for British ports. France forced the sailors on those ships to serve France in its war with Great Britain. American attempts to negotiate peace with France in 1797 resulted in the **XYZ Affair**. Diplomatic dispatches revealed that three French agents, referred to as X, Y, and Z in the reports, had demanded bribes from the American peace envoy before opening negotiations.

Party politics

Domestic reaction to these foreign affairs emphasized growing philosophical differences between the Federalists and the Democratic-Republicans. While the actions of the French were not popular, many Democratic-Republican Americans still distrusted England and sympathized with the ideals of the French Revolution, by which the people of France overthrew its monarchy in 1789.

Federalists, maintaining their history of antiforeign sentiment, became suspicious of the loyalty of the thousands of French West Indian refugees who flocked into the United States in an effort to escape revolutionary terror. The refugees often aligned themselves with the Democratic-Republicans.

Congress acts

Rallying behind the anti-French sentiment in the wake of the XYZ Affair, in June and July 1798 the Federalists of Congress passed four acts of legislation known as the Alien and Sedition Acts. The laws were intended to suppress both alien and domestic subversives, people who opposed the federal government. The Alien and Sedition Acts proved to be convenient tools for undermining the strength of the Democratic-Republican Party as well.

The first of the four laws, called the Naturalization Act, increased the length of residency required before an alien, or foreigner, could apply for American citizenship. Previously the probationary period had been five years. By increasing the period to fourteen years, the Federalists successfully suppressed immigrant citizenship and hence immigrant votes in America, which hurt mostly the Democratic-Republican Party.

Two of the acts were specifically aimed at removing aliens from America. The Alien Friends Act allowed the president to deport any alien suspected of threatening the peace and safety of the United States. The Alien Enemies Act authorized the president to seize, imprison, or deport any aliens, dangerous or not, who were citizens of a country at war with the United States. Neither act was ever enforced, and both expired in 1800.

The Sedition Act proved to be the most controversial and powerful of the acts. Aimed at citizens and aliens alike, the act made it illegal to write, publish, or speak anything of "a false, scandalous, and malicious nature" against the government or the president "with intent to defame … or to bring them into contempt or disrepute." Acting on behalf of the Adams administration, Secretary of State Timothy Pickering (1745–1829) brought more than a dozen indictments, or formal accusations, under the Sedition Act. Ten resulted in convictions, including those against Matthew Lyon (1749–1822), a Democratic-Republican congressman from **Vermont**, and the editors of eight major Democratic-Republican newspapers.

Backlash

With no public way to criticize the administration or to challenge the Sedition Act, its opponents turned to state legislatures for relief. **Thomas Jefferson** (1751–1836), who was then vice president, anonymously penned the Kentucky Resolutions as **James Madison** (1751–1836) drafted the Virginia Resolutions. Both documents emphasized the rights of the states to declare federal laws unconstitutional and to decide when the federal government had overstepped its proper bounds.

While no other states passed official statements of opposition, public support for the Sedition Act eventually began to wane. The trials under the Sedition Act marked an early American confrontation between the power of the federal government and the liberties and free speech that people expected to enjoy in their new nation.

Recognizing that the Federalists may have gone too far, President Adams fired Pickering by May 1800 and no longer urged prosecutions under the Sedition Act. Although he managed to secure peace with France by October 1800, the effects of the Alien and Sedition Acts were profound enough to affect public opinion of the Federalist Party. Vice President Jefferson, the Democratic-Republican candidate for president in the election of 1800, won and was inaugurated the day after the Sedition Act expired by its own terms, on March 3, 1801.

Alien Registration Act

In the early years of **World War II** (1939–45), some Americans were concerned that foreigners and subversive, or revolutionary, groups were plotting to undermine the U.S. government. Although the United States had not yet entered the war, Congress passed the Alien Registration Act in 1940 to address some of these concerns.

The Alien Registration Act was proposed by U.S. representative Howard W. Smith (1883–1976) of **Virginia**, so the law was also called the Smith Act. It was quite controversial, because it severely limited free speech aimed at criticizing the U.S. government. It also required all noncitizen adults to register with the United States, hence the name of the act. Section I imposed a $10,000 fine and time in prison for those who attempted to undermine the morale of U.S. soldiers.

Sections II and III imposed similar penalties for those who supported or encouraged the overthrow of the government. Merely teaching or advising such action was not allowed, even without taking active steps. The Smith Act also outlawed the publication and distribution of material that advocated a revolution or the organization of a rebellious group. The act prohibited attempts to violate any part of the law. A 1948 revision made conviction somewhat harder by requiring proof of overt acts to advocate or attempt the overthrow of the government. Merely harboring such beliefs was no longer prohibited under the act.

During the 1940s and 1950s, more than a hundred people were charged with violation of the Smith Act. Only twenty-nine served time in prison for their conduct. The government targeted enforcement activity at members of communist and socialist organizations. (Communism and socialism are both economic and political theories that advocate communal ownership of property, and support governments in which the means of production are owned and controlled by the state for the good of all citizens.) Cases were appealed to the U.S. **Supreme Court**. In 1951, the Court found that the act did not violate rights under the U.S. **Constitution**. In 1957, however, the Court decided that teaching or advocating the overthrow of the government is constitutionally protected free speech. After that decision speech had to be accompanied by subversive action in order to be a punishable offense.

Allies

The Allies were the countries united in an alliance in **World War II** (1939–45) to fight the **Axis** countries of Germany, Japan, and Italy. The countries that first declared war on Germany after its invasion of Poland in 1939 were the founding Allied forces. They were Poland, Great Britain, and France.

Many countries joined the Allied efforts over the course of the war. Twenty-six countries signed the Declaration by the United Nations on January 1, 1942, uniting them in the Allied cause. More nations would sign later.

The leading efforts of Great Britain, the Soviet Union, and the United States in the second half of the war earned them the distinction as "the Big Three." Prime Minister Winston Churchill (1874–1965) of Great Britain, Premier Joseph Stalin (1879–1953) of the Soviet Union, and President **Franklin D. Roosevelt** (1882–1945; served 1933–45) of the United States coordinated the military efforts of the Allies across the

Newspapers across the globe gave constant updates on the movement of Allied forces.
HULTON ARCHIVE/GETTY IMAGES

world. China and France, the latter when not occupied by Germany and its Nazi dictator, Adolf Hitler (1889–1945), played important leading roles as well.

The Allies managed to defeat the Axis powers even though their resources were stretched around the world. After the capture of Italy's dictator, Benito Mussolini (1883–1945), Italy switched sides to fight with the Allies in September 1943. The battles across Europe ended with the unconditional surrender of Germany on May 7, 1945. Battles around the Pacific Ocean against Japan continued until the United States used the **atomic bomb** for the first time to end the war. After suffering the devastation of the cities Hiroshima and Nagasaki, Japan agreed to surrender on August 10, 1945.

Amendments
See **Individual Amendments, e.g. First Amendment**

American Civil Liberties Union

The American Civil Liberties Union (ACLU) is an organization founded to defend equal rights and civil liberties for all Americans, including the rights to free speech, due process, and freedom of the press.

Founding in 1920

The ACLU has its roots in **World War I** (1914–18). ACLU founder and long-time president Roger N. Baldwin (1884–1981) strongly opposed the war. He joined the antiwar organization American Union Against Militarism (AUAM) in New York in 1917 and quickly became its most determined crusader. After the war, on January 20, 1920, Baldwin and some of his AUAM associates established a new group they called the American Civil Liberties Union.

Baldwin immediately changed the focus of the ACLU from antiwar issues to civil liberties. The ACLU's sole commitment was to the **Bill of Rights**, the amendments made to the U.S. **Constitution** regarding liberties, such as freedom of religion, speech, and press, and the right to privacy, to assemble peacefully, and to petition the government.

The ACLU was founded during a period known as the **red scare** of 1920, when an overwhelming fear of Communists was sweeping the nation. Communists are people who believe in an economic or political system in which property is owned collectively by all members of society, and labor is organized for the common good. In 1919, the U.S. government launched nationwide raids to round up and detain alleged radicals, who it claimed were part of a Communist plot to destroy the country. The ACLU, still a tiny new organization, worked tirelessly in the courts to stop the government from violating civil liberties, going to court to fight its deportation of foreigners for their political beliefs and its attempts to stop trade unions from organizing.

Famous cases

In 1925, Baldwin wanted to test the powers of his organization on the issue of free speech. He was particularly concerned about a **Tennessee** law that prohibited teaching the theory of evolution in schools. The theory of evolution is a scientific explanation of how changes may have happened in populations of animals, including human beings, from one

Roger Baldwin founded the American Civil Liberties Union (ACLU) and focused on protecting liberties, such as freedom of religion, speech, and press, and the right to privacy. © BETTMANN/CORBIS

generation to the next, due to genetic modifications. The people responsible for the anti-evolution laws believed that human development was the work of God and should not be explained to students in scientific terms. Baldwin believed the prohibition against teaching a scientific theory was a violation of the right of freedom of speech. He sought out a teacher willing to break Tennessee's anti-evolution law so ACLU lawyers could take the issue to court. John T. Scopes (1900–1970) volunteered, and thus began a trial that came to be called the **Scopes monkey trial**, because of the evolutionary theory that human beings evolved from apes. Although it lost the case, the ACLU gained notoriety and respect from the trial.

Since the Scopes trial, the ACLU has been involved in many of the most famous controversies in American history, playing a role in an estimated 80 percent of the landmark **Supreme Court** cases related to individual rights. During **World War II** (1939–45), the ACLU challenged the internment of Japanese Americans, who were forced to leave their homes and businesses and live in confinement in government camps simply because of their ancestry. (See **Japanese Internment Camps**.)

ACLU lawyers argued a case against religious prayers in public schools, resulting in the Supreme Court ruling that the practice was unconstitutional. The organization defended many protesters of the **Vietnam War** (1954–75). In 1977, it defended the right of the Nazi Party to hold a demonstration in the predominantly Jewish town of Skokie, Illinois.

ACLU and African American civil rights

From its beginnings, the ACLU made the issue of racial justice a major part of its program. It established a close working relationship with the **National Association for the Advancement of Colored People** (NAACP). In the 1940s, ACLU leaders developed a proposal for a broad legal attack on institutionalized **segregation**, which is the separation of blacks and whites in public places. It eventually became the basis for NAACP attorney **Thurgood Marshall**'s (1908–1993) successful legal fight against segregation and led to the landmark *Brown v. Board of Education* ruling in 1954. The ACLU was also a supporting force in the African American **civil rights movement** of the 1960s.

On a number of issues, however, the ACLU and African American civil rights activists have disagreed. On **First Amendment** (freedom of speech) grounds, the ACLU opposed measures designed to restrict the activities of racist groups such as the **Ku Klux Klan**. It also opposed efforts by the NAACP to have the racist film *Birth of a Nation* banned in a number of cities. Its position was that the First Amendment guaranteed freedom of speech and assembly to all groups and that authorities could not make distinctions between groups based on their personal beliefs.

The twenty-first century

In 2005, the ACLU had five hundred thousand members and handled about six thousand court cases. Supported through membership dues, tax-deductible contributions, and grants, the ACLU's program consists mainly of litigation (legal proceedings), lobbying (attempts to influence government activities and policies), and public education.

Throughout nearly ninety years of activism, the ACLU remains committed to the fundamental principle that the defense of civil liberties must be universal, or extend to everyone. At times this has resulted in harsh criticism and the loss of some core supporters. The ACLU's defense of the freedom of speech of racist and anti-Semitic groups, such as the Klansmen and American Nazis, deeply angered some of its supporters. The ACLU's position that civil liberties should not be suspended in the interest of civil defense was not popular in the first fearful days after the **September 11, 2001, terrorist attacks** on the United States. Most historians agree, though, that the ACLU's insistence on upholding the Bill of Rights has remained remarkably evenhanded and courageous amid the changing currents of public opinion.

American Colonization Society

In 1816, the American Colonization Society (ACS) was organized in **Washington, D.C.**, with the objective of encouraging, and paying for, free black Americans to establish and live in a colony in Africa.

Why colonization?

For a time, the colonization project seemed to appeal to everyone. Many of the first members of the ACS were Southerners who supported a gradual abolition (elimination) of **slavery**. (See **Abolition Movement**.) They promoted colonization as a means to deal with the growing numbers of free blacks that would result from abolition. Soon many Northerners joined the society, believing, like the Southerners, that free blacks and whites could not live together without conflict. Colonization appealed to Southern slave owners as a way to rid the South of troublesome free blacks, who they feared would incite rebellions among their slaves. It was also popular with some Northern antislavery advocates, who hoped it would make slaveholders more willing to free their slaves. Some African Americans also endorsed the idea in the belief that Americans would probably never treat them as equals and that they might have a better life in distant Africa.

Most black Americans, though, argued that the United States had been the home of their families for generations. They had a clear right to live there as equals and were willing to fight for that right. Most abolitionists came to strongly oppose the ACS.

Liberia

After a long search for a location for the new colony, the ACS bought a large area of land on Cape Montserado, in West Africa, about 225 miles south of Sierra Leone. There, in 1822, the society established the colony of Liberia. Liberia's capital, Monrovia, was named in honor of the fifth president of the United States, **James Monroe** (1758–1831; served 1817–25), who, along with Congress, gave the society close to $100,000 to transport black Americans to Liberia. In the project's first ten years, about 2,638 blacks migrated to Liberia.

To encourage the colonization of Liberia, the ACS published letters from blacks who had moved there and had good things to say about it. It also published *The African Repository and Colonial Journal*, which served as strong propaganda (the spreading of ideas or information, both true and otherwise, to promote or damage a cause) by painting a positive picture of Liberia for black Americans. The ACS also promised to provide colonists with land and economic support for six months. This promise was not always kept, and emigrants were at times left stranded on the Cape.

In 1838, the Commonwealth of Liberia was formed under the administration of a governor appointed by the ACS, and the ACS governed the country until it became a republic in 1847. By 1846, thirteen to fourteen thousand free black Americans had immigrated to Liberia under the plan. Joining these emigrants in Liberia were slaves rescued from illegal slave-trading ships off the coast of Africa. (See **Slave Ships and the Middle Passage**.)

Conflict

By the 1840s, the ACS was mired in controversy. Abolitionists, black and white, opposed the society's basic assumption that African Americans could not live and work in the same communities as white Americans. They argued that African Americans had worked hard in the United States and had earned the right to call it home. They thought the ACS was creating a distraction from what abolitionists considered the only reasonable course of action—the immediate abolition of slavery in the United States. Most Southern plantation owners did not approve of the ACS either. They did not want to see African Americans, a group they considered the region's labor force, shipped across the Atlantic.

The news from Africa was not much better. The native people of Liberia resented the newcomers from the United States. Armed conflict and bloodshed erupted in the colony. In 1847, the ACS went bankrupt (did not have enough money to cover its debts). The American Liberians took the opportunity to found the independent Republic of Liberia. Seizing power, they dominated the native groups as well as the Africans rescued from slave ships, creating a rigid class system in the new country. The ACS stopped promoting colonization as part of its agenda, and by the end of the century the group had disbanded.

American Federation of Labor–Congress of Industrial Organizations

The AFL-CIO is a voluntary federation of labor unions that represents workers in various industries. AFL-CIO stands for the American Federation of Labor and Congress of Industrial Organizations.

The AFL-CIO began as the American Federation of Labor (AFL) in 1886. At that time, America was in the midst of the **Industrial Revolution**. Factory workers were becoming a significant percentage of the country's labor force. Workers formed unions to help them bargain with employers for better working conditions.

The AFL was led at first by Samuel Gompers (1850–1924). Gompers believed that unions should focus on organizing skilled laborers, but not unskilled ones. Gompers preferred unions to organize based on the type of work members did, not the industries in which they worked. He also believed that unions should not be too involved in politics. Rather they should focus on strategies and tactics for bargaining with employers.

In the 1930s, the **Great Depression** (1929–41) made poor working conditions even worse for laborers. By then, the factory system had a large number of unskilled laborers in the American workforce. Some members of the AFL, including John L. Lewis (1880–1969), believed that unions should organize unskilled workers based on the industries in which they worked. Lewis also believed that unions had to be more political and work for laws that favored workers.

At the AFL's annual convention in 1934, Lewis and his friends helped pass a resolution that resulted in the AFL working to increase organization among industrial unions. The executive committee of the AFL disagreed with the resolution. It associated unskilled laborers with violent strikes and other radical organizing tactics. So the AFL did not do much to implement the resolution.

In November 1935, Lewis and others formed the Committee on Industrial Organizations. They intended to operate within the AFL as a separate committee. AFL president William R. Green (1872–1952) opposed the committee. The AFL ordered the committee to disband and then suspended it in 1936 and expelled it in 1937.

The AFL-CIO heavily recruited for members with posters and pamphlets. The organization works for favorable labor laws and helps workers bargain with their employers. THE LIBRARY OF CONGRESS

Unions and Race

Organized in 1886, the American Federation of Labor initially represented the interests of skilled, white, male, and immigrant workers from Europe. African Americans were typically excluded from the unions and related work with restrictions on membership, apprenticeship, and hiring practices. In response, black workers, particularly railroad porters, longshoremen, and plasters, formed all-black unions on their own. When the Congress of Industrial Organizations formed in 1938, it adopted more inclusive racial policies to strengthen its membership and its bargaining power with the federal government.

In 1938, Lewis and his supporters formed their own organization called the Congress of Industrial Organizations (CIO). The AFL and the CIO functioned separately for the next two decades. The CIO initially had great success, growing as industry boomed during **World War II** (1939–45). This forced the AFL to modify its recruitment efforts for its member unions.

After World War II, the federal government passed many laws to restrict the power of unions. By the 1950s, the AFL and the CIO decided they needed to work together for favorable laws and to organize workers for bargaining with employers. They merged into one federation in 1955, representing around sixteen million workers, about 35 percent of the American workforce. By the end of the century, the figure fell to around fourteen million, or 20 percent of the workforce, as factories began to move overseas, forcing Americans to find other types of work.

American Flag

The Marine Committee of the Second Continental Congress in Philadelphia, **Pennsylvania**, adopted a resolution on June 14, 1777, stating that the flag of the United States would have thirteen stripes, alternating red and white. (See **Continental Congress, Second.**) The union would be symbolized with thirteen white stars on a blue field. There was no direction as to how many points each star would have or how they would be arranged. As a result, the first American flags varied in pattern.

Popular legend has it that the first American flag was sewed by a Philadelphia seamstress named Betsy Ross (1752–1836). Ross knew General **George Washington** (1732–1799), who was the leader of the Continental army at the time. Historians have not been able to verify the Ross story, although it is known that Ross sewed flags for the Pennsylvania navy in 1777. Many various flags were sewn throughout the **American Revolution** (1775–83), but the flag commonly referred to as the Betsy Ross flag (with the stars arranged in a circular pattern) did not appear until the early 1790s.

The first unofficial national flag was called the Grand Union Flag or the Continental Colors, and it was raised at the request of Washington near his headquarters outside Boston, **Massachusetts**, on January 1, 1776. This flag had thirteen alternating red and white horizontal strips and, in the upper left corner, the emblem of the British flag of the time. The first official flag, known as Old Glory or the Stars and Stripes, was approved by the Continental Congress the following year on the day the flag resolution was adopted. The emblem of the British Union Flag was

Betsy Ross shows George Washington the first American flag she made in Philadelphia in 1776. A year later, the Continental Congress formally approved the 13-stripe, 13-star flag of red, white, and blue. AP IMAGES

replaced by thirteen white stars on a blue background, representing the **thirteen colonies**. No one knows with certainty who designed the flag, though many historians believe it was Francis Hopkinson (1737–1791), a member of the Continental Congress and signer of the **Declaration of Independence**.

In the twenty-first century, the American flag has thirteen horizontal stripes: seven red and six white alternating. The union of fifty states is represented by fifty white, five-pointed stars on a field of blue in the upper left quarter of the flag. President **Dwight D. Eisenhower** (1890–1969; served 1953–61) gave specific proportional measurements for each facet of the flag in August of 1959.

American Indian Movement

The American Indian Movement (AIM) was founded in Minneapolis, **Minnesota**, in the summer of 1968 by founders Dennis Banks (1937–) and Clyde Bellecourt (1939–). Modeling itself after the **Black Panther Party**, the organization initially focused on forming street patrols to stop police brutality and other violence in the local Indian community. A number of service programs ranging from alternative schools to low-cost housing followed within the next two years.

Expands to national goals

After 1971, with the recruitment of American Indian activists such as Russell Means (1939–) and John Trudell (1946–), the organization became national in character and shifted its focus to gaining recognition of American Indian treaty rights in **Indian reservations**. (Reservations are tracts of land set aside by the federal government for use by the American Indians, often as the result of major concessions on the part of American Indian communities.) Most of AIM's activity from late 1972 onward was based at the Pine Ridge Reservation in **South Dakota**.

Trail of Broken Treaties

For a time, AIM pursued a strategy of forcing confrontations with federal, state, and local authorities to gain national attention for the plight of American Indians. The most spectacular of these clashes was called the Trail of Broken Treaties.

Originating on the West Coast in the autumn of 1972, the Trail of Broken Treaties began as a car caravan of several hundred American Indians who traveled across the country to **Washington, D.C.** There they were prepared to carry out a week-long schedule of ceremonies, meetings, and peaceful protests. The protesters brought with them a list of twenty points for presentation to federal officials, calling for the restoration of treaty activity between federal and tribal governments, the recognition of existing treaties, the creation of a commission to review treaty commitments, and much more. The document forcefully asserted sovereignty (self-rule) for Indian people.

The road-weary protesters expected to find decent accommodations when they arrived in Washington. Instead, they found they had no assigned places to stay, no provisions, and no real acknowledgment from federal officials. Hundreds found themselves stranded in an unfamiliar city. On the morning of November 3, caravan participants sought shelter in the **Bureau of Indian Affairs** (BIA) building while the group's leaders met with federal officials. A confrontation between police and Native Americans soon erupted in the lobby of the bureau. Within minutes, the police were pushed out onto the street and the building was barricaded from within. The protesters officially occupied the BIA building for the next week.

The takeover of the BIA might have been interpreted by some as a bold act of political resistance. However, damage to the building and its contents, and the destruction and removal of important tribal documents, as well as those pertaining to individual Native Americans, resulted in notable negative press. As the main force behind the Trail of Broken Treaties, AIM had secured a reputation as a militant (war-like) organization capable of violence.

Wounded Knee II

AIM's membership grew in the early 1970s as many American Indians joined the movement for American Indians rights. Attention began to focus on the Pine Ridge Reservation in South Dakota when Richard Wilson was elected president of the Oglala Sioux tribal council in 1972. Wilson was accused of buying hundreds of votes in that election. His administration was charged with mishandling government funds and granting questionable contracts to whites. In response to these charges, Wilson had opponents beaten and their families threatened. He maintained a GOON squad—an acronym for Guardians of the Oglala Nation—to physically intimidate his opponents.

Investigators from the **Department of Justice** concluded later that Wilson had imposed a "reign of terror" on reservation residents and that federal authorities had funded him to do so. But Wilson won the support of the BIA by refusing to allow protests within the reservation. The BIA ignored complaints against him, funded his GOON squad, and sent its own agents to help him. Means, by then an AIM leader, vowed to run against Wilson in the next election for tribal chair, but that would not occur until 1974.

The residents of Pine Ridge voted to impeach Wilson as tribal chair in 1973, but at his hearing he managed to talk the tribal council into voting in his favor. Several hundred angry members of the Oglala Sioux tribe convened a meeting, asking AIM to attend. AIM's policy was to enter the reservation only on request. The Oglala Sioux Civil Rights Organization made the official request for AIM's help in overthrowing Wilson.

The occupation

On February 26, 1973, AIM members began to caravan to the Pine Ridge Reservation. As he tried to enter the reservation, two members of Wilson's police force beat Means. He later returned, leading a larger band of about 250 Indians. According to a police report, they broke into the reservation store at 7:55 PM and took weapons and ammunition. Then they took over the community of Wounded Knee, the site of the 1890 **Wounded Knee massacre**. Their original intent appears to have been a short occupation to negotiate for Wilson's dismissal and a traditional tribal government free of BIA interference. The various government forces, however, blockaded the roads and arrested anyone coming out of Wounded Knee who appeared to be implicated in the takeover. In response, the occupiers set up defenses and barricades of their own. A seventy-one-day armed standoff had begun.

Support for the occupation grew on other reservations. Other Indians made their way to Wounded Knee. During the occupation, there was regular gunfire between the federal agents and the occupiers. Hundreds of thousands of shots were fired into the village; two Indians were killed and another dozen badly wounded during the fighting. The occupation ended peacefully when federal officials agreed to discuss violations of U.S. treaty obligations with the Oglala chiefs.

The aftermath

In the aftermath of Wounded Knee, 562 federal felony charges were lodged against AIM members. Only fifteen of those resulted in convictions, but the expense of continuously posting bail and paying attorneys exhausted the movement's funds and diverted its members' attention for years.

From March 1973 to March 1976, at least 69 AIM members and supporters died violently on Pine Ridge, while some 340 others suffered serious physical assaults. In twenty-one of the AIM deaths, eyewitnesses identified the killers as known GOON squad members. Not one of these crimes was ever brought to trial as the result of a federal investigation.

The disagreement among the Oglala Sioux did not end, nor did friction between AIM and the government. A shootout at Pine Ridge in June 1975, which killed one Indian and two FBI agents, led in 1977 to a controversial trial and a life sentence for murder for AIM leader Leonard Peltier (1944–).

Later years

Despite the Wounded Knee trials and Peltier's conviction, AIM has remained active. The organization has drawn considerable national and international attention to the Peltier case. In 1978, AIM participated in the "Longest Walk," a national march on Washington, D.C., in the continued attempt to air Native American grievances. Three years later, AIM established Yellow Thunder Camp on federal land in the Black Hills of South Dakota. The establishment of the camp was the first step, according to AIM leaders, in reclaiming this sacred land for the Lakota, or Sioux, people. AIM has also protested against false and harmful images of Native Americans in the media and as sports team mascots, and against environmental abuses.

American Party

See **Know-Nothing Party**

American Red Cross

The American Red Cross was established on May 21, 1881, in **Washington, D.C.**, by a nurse named Clara Barton (1821–1912) and some of her acquaintances. Barton had visited Europe just after the

American **Civil War** (1861–65), where she learned of the International Red Cross Movement. Once she returned to America, she campaigned for an American Red Cross society, which would provide care to the wounded in time of war and disaster. Sixty-year-old Barton was the organization's first leader, and she remained so for twenty-three years.

Under Barton's leadership, the Red Cross conducted its first domestic and overseas disaster-relief efforts, assisted the U.S. military throughout the **Spanish-American War** (1898), and successfully campaigned for the inclusion of peacetime relief work as part of the International Red Cross Movement.

The Red Cross received its first congressional charter in 1900 and a second one in 1905. This charter outlined the purposes of the organization and remained in place into the twenty-first century.

With the onset of **World War I** (1914–18), the Red Cross grew from 107 local chapters in 1914 to 3,864 in 1918. Membership grew from seventeen thousand to more than twenty million adult and eleven million Junior Red Cross members. By the end of the war, the American public had donated $400 million in funds and materials. Twenty thousand registered nurses were recruited to serve in the military, and additional Red Cross nurses volunteered to fight the worldwide influenza epidemic of 1918.

Once the war was over and attention could be turned to peacetime activities, the Red Cross focused on service to veterans. It enhanced its programs in accident prevention, safety training, and nutrition education. Volunteers were on hand to help victims of the Mississippi River floods in 1927, those of the severe drought throughout the Great Plains states known as the **Dust Bowl**, and those of the **Great Depression** throughout the 1930s.

War, again

Once again the Red Cross was called upon in time of war, this time for **World War II** (1939–45). More than 104,000 nurses signed up for military service as the Red Cross prepared twenty-seven million packages for American and Allied (forces fighting alongside the Americans) prisoners of war. (See **Allies**.) The organization shipped more than three hundred thousand tons of supplies overseas and initiated a national blood drive that collected 13.3 million pints of much-needed blood to be used by the military.

With the end of the war came another refocus of priorities, and the Red Cross established the first nationwide civilian blood program, which eventually supplied almost 50 percent of the blood and blood products in America. In the 1990s, the organization expanded its role in biomedical research and began "banking" human tissue for distribution. As America entered other wars, the Red Cross provided services to members of the military. It has since expanded its services to include civil defense, HIV/**AIDS** education, training in CPR (cardiopulmonary resuscitation, an emergency medical procedure), and the provision of emotional care and support to disaster victims and survivors. The Red Cross played a key role in helping the federal government form the Federal Emergency Management Agency (FEMA) in 1979.

Controversy

After the **September 11, 2001, terrorist attacks** on the World Trade Center in New York City and the Pentagon near Washington, D.C., the Red Cross came under scrutiny and was criticized for its handling and management of donations. The organization established the Liberty Fund, to which Americans donated $547 million, all of which they assumed would go directly to victims of the tragedy. The fund was closed in October 2001 after meeting its donation goal. When it was revealed that only 30 percent of donations directly assisted victims and that the rest would go toward improved telecommunications, building a blood supply, and planning for future terrorist attacks, there was public outcry. The Red Cross then hired someone from outside the organization to handle the management of the fund, and it was promised that all monies would go to the victims, survivors, and their families.

Criticism and controversy followed the Red Cross into 2005, the busiest hurricane season on record. Hurricane Katrina, which hit **Florida**, **Louisiana**, and **Mississippi** in August, was the most devastating natural disaster the organization had ever dealt with. The Red Cross was criticized for its management of nearly $1 billion in donations and received allegations that it responded more efficiently and quickly to white victims and neighborhoods than it did to African Americans.

American Revolution

The thirteen British colonies in America fought the American Revolution (1775–83) to become independent from Great Britain. (See **Thirteen Colonies**.) As a result, a new nation was born, the United States of America.

Taxation without representation

By the 1760s, the British colonies in America had developed into thirteen individual territories with their own economic and political systems. For the most part, the British Parliament and monarchy had refrained from being involved in most aspects of colonial life since the early 1700s. The British maintained and managed their economic interests in the colonies, but they also allowed the colonies to govern themselves to a large extent.

The outbreak of the **French and Indian War** (1754–63) changed the status of the colonies in 1754. The British provided troops to support and protect the colonists in the conflict against the French and the Indians. The war lasted until 1763 and depleted the British treasury.

After the war, the British Parliament sought to replenish its treasury. Taxes had never been applied to the colonies, but Parliament decided it was necessary for the colonies to share the responsibility of paying war debts. Parliament enacted a series of tax measures over the next ten years that sparked outrage throughout the colonies. Although the vast majority of the colonial population was loyal to British rule, they had grown used to levying their own taxes through their own governments. As the colonists had no representation in Parliament, they felt they had no duty to pay taxes to Great Britain.

Parliament was firm about its decision to tax the colonies, however, and the series of acts placed on the colonies were strict. Parliament attempted to control colonial trade and passed restrictions on colonial money. It taxed imports in America through measures like the **Tea Act** (1763) and the **Sugar Act** (1764). Another set of laws included the **Stamp Act** (1765), the **Declaratory Act** (1766), and the **Townshend Acts** (1767). These laws placed duties (taxes on imports) on a wide variety of goods, such as legal documents, glass, and lead.

The American Revolution ended shortly after the surrender, shown here, of British General Charles Cornwallis to George Washington at the Battle of Yorktown in 1781. TIME & LIFE PICTURES/GETTY IMAGES

Tensions rise

The colonies had developed independently over time. Their governments, economies, and populations were noticeably different. As a result, the colonies often disagreed on policy matters and rarely united in a cause.

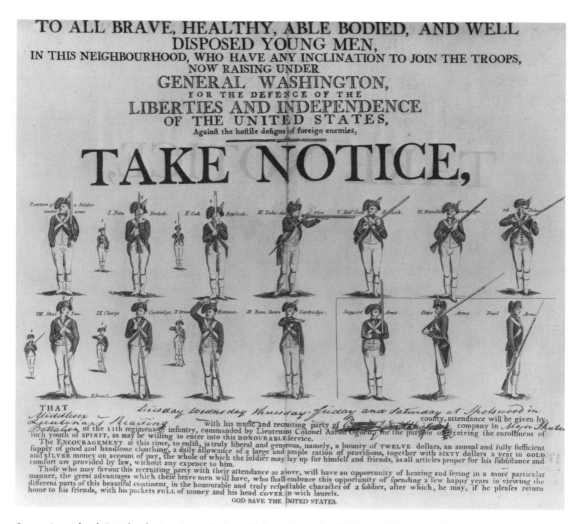

In reaction to harsh British rule, American colonists rallied together and called for enrollment into the U.S. Army at the start of the American Revolution. MPI/HULTON ARCHIVE/GETTY IMAGES

The actions of the British Parliament began to unite the colonies in common resentment of British rule. The Stamp Act particularly angered the colonists, as it seemed to affect everyone. Printers were among those most affected, however, and they aroused public opposition through the publication of newspapers, editorials, and pamphlets.

The colonists resisted Britain's actions in a variety of ways. Public criticism appeared in print over Parliament's taxation without the consent of colonial representatives. Merchants and laborers created the Sons of Liberty, a military-like club. Ordinary colonists harassed tax collectors, attended public protest meetings, and participated in boycotts of British goods. In protest, colonists dumped loads of tea into the Boston Harbor in December 1773, an event called the **Boston Tea Party**.

Increased colonial resistance led to enactment of the **Coercion Acts** in 1774, by which Parliament restricted the power of local governments. When Britain dissolved the **Massachusetts** legislature, closed Boston Harbor, shut down colonial courts, and quartered, or housed, British troops in private homes, the colonists were inspired to work together as they never had before. Reaction spread far beyond Massachusetts, and some Americans began to consider military resistance.

The colonies organize and fight

In 1774, delegates from the colonies gathered at the First Continental Congress to evaluate the level of discontent among all the colonies. (See **Continental Congress, First**.) The Congress sent a petition to the British government seeking a resolution of their complaints. Though not all Americans agreed that greater resistance was necessary, some colonists began to prepare for war.

Historians generally agree that prior to the outbreak of the Revolution, only one-third of the colonists actively supported military action and independence. The remaining two-thirds were either Loyalists faithful to British rule, or uncommitted either way.

Tensions between the colonists and the British turned hostile on April 19, 1775. British troops went to Lexington and Concord in Massachusetts to collect weapons and capture rebels. (See **Battle of Lexington and Concord**.) When the British met armed resistance from

---

Culpeper's Rebellion

During the colonial period in America, England passed dozens of navigation acts to control trade in the colonies. The acts placed heavy duties on goods imported into the colonies, and prevented the colonies from trading with other nations. Their purpose was to ensure that colonial trade enriched England.

In 1677, rebels led by John Culpeper (1644–1693) revolted against the colonial government in the Albemarle section of the colony of Carolina. Dissatisfaction with the Navigation Acts was at the heart of the rebellion. The rebels seized Thomas Miller, who collected import duties for England under the **Navigation Acts**. They also replaced the colonial government with their own government for two years, naming Culpeper governor.

The proprietors of the colony eventually resumed control and sent Culpeper to London to stand trial for treason. Culpeper escaped punishment with the help of the Earl of Shaftesbury. The rebellion, though it did not last, was an early indication of the trouble between England and the colonies that would lead to the American Revolution.

---

citizen militias, the conflict became violent, and the American Revolutionary War began.

The colonies united with a vote for independence at the Second Continental Congress in the summer of 1775. (See **Continental Congress, Second**.) Colonial delegates worked to establish an independent government under the **Articles of Confederation**. Although the document provided a unifying government, it proved to be weak: It was unable to supply the funds, supplies, and military staffing that could have made for a swifter war.

American victory was due in great part to the strength of command and leadership from General **George Washington** (1732–1799). Against the odds, Washington overcame problems posed by political squabbles, a weak federal government, inexperienced militias, and lack of supplies. Though it struggled at first, the Continental Army was transformed into a disciplined and effective force under Washington's supervision.

The other key to American victory was the vital support of France. In May 1779, France and America signed a treaty that provided an alliance and loans for the American cause. Spain and the Netherlands also joined the fight on behalf of the Americans. The combined efforts of these countries finally brought military victory in October 1781. At the Battle of Yorktown in Virginia, British General Lord Cornwallis (1738–1805) surrendered. The war formally ended with the **Treaty of Paris** in 1783.

Amistad Insurrection

In the 1830s, Africans were regularly kidnapped by slave traders and sold in an illegal slave trade. One group of Africans rose up in rebellion against their captors only to find themselves in a battle within the U.S. court system. Their story brought the concept of **slavery** into sharp focus in a country divided by its beliefs about slavery.

In 1839, a Portuguese slave ship brought a shipload of kidnapped Africans from present-day Sierra Leone to sell in Havana, Cuba. After crossing the seas in a cramped and filthy slave ship, a group of fifty-three Mende-speaking Africans, led by a man named Sengbe, who came to be called Cinque (c. 1817–1879), were sold to two Spaniards, Jose Ruiz and Pedro Montes. At this time slave trading was illegal in the United States, but the ever-growing demand for slaves had created a flourishing trade and colonial authorities did nothing to prevent it.

The mutiny

The Spaniards boarded the Africans on the *Amistad,* a ship heading toward their estates in northern Cuba. During the voyage, the Africans conversed in sign language with the ship's crew, asking what would happen to them. A seaman jokingly gestured that they would be killed and eaten. Soon after that, the African captives seized control of the ship, killing two crew members.

The mutineers (people who rebel) spared the lives of Ruiz and Montes and ordered them to pilot the ship to Africa. The Spaniards pretended to sail east by day, but secretly reversed course by night. After two months they brought the *Amistad* to the northern coast of the United States. The Africans were arrested and jailed in **Connecticut**, and charged with committing murder and piracy. Ruiz and Montes, backed by the Spanish government, pressed a claim for the return of the *Amistad,* including its cargo of slaves.

A divided public

While the Africans awaited trial, newspapers across the country carried their story. Many regarded them as curiosities, but Connecticut's aboli-

Death of Capt. Ferrer, the Captain of the Amistad, July, 1839.

Don Jose Ruiz and Don Pedro Montez, of the Island of Cuba, having purchased fifty-three slaves at Havana, recently imported from Africa, put them on board the Amistad, Capt. Ferrer, in order to transport them to Principe, another port on the Island of Cuba. After being out from Havana about four days, the African captives on board, in order to obtain their freedom, and return to Africa, armed themselves with cane knives, and rose upon the Captain and crew of the vessel. Capt. Ferrer and the cook of the vessel were killed; two of the crew escaped; Ruiz and Montez were made prisoners.

The slave mutiny onboard the Amistad *in 1839 divided the public as to whether the men should be freed.* MPI/HULTON ARCHIVE/GETTY IMAGES

The testimony of the slave Cinque about the terrible conditions on the Amistad *was an important factor in the Supreme Court upholding previous court decisions and declaring the Africans free and able to return to their native land.* NEW YORK PUBLIC LIBRARY PICTURE COLLECTION

tionists (people who oppose slavery and work to end it) eagerly took up the captives' cause. They organized an *Amistad* relief committee and hired respected attorneys to defend the Africans. Aside from sympathy for the Africans, the abolitionists viewed their case as a way to put the institution of slavery on trial.

Naturally, people from the southern slave states opposed the abolitionists and sided with the lawyers prosecuting (pursuing charges against) the Africans, demanding that they be returned to their "owners." Southerners wanted the courts to uphold what they believed to be the absolute rights of slaveholders. They feared slave rebellions and did not want the *Amistad* rebels to go unpunished, for fear their own slaves might follow their example. President **Martin Van Buren** (1782–1862; served 1847–41) also wanted to see the Africans deported to Cuba. For him, this solution would avoid diplomatic tension with Spain and keep voters in the South on his side at election time.

The trial

In the *Amistad* trial, the defense lawyers asserted that the Africans had the right to free themselves from the horrible conditions of slavery. They argued that returning them to Cuba meant certain death for them. In addition, since the captives had been kidnapped in violation of Spanish law, the abolitionists argued that the blacks were not legally slaves and therefore were not "property" belonging to Ruiz and Montes. In January 1840, Cinque, who had learned a little English, electrified the courtroom with his testimony about conditions on the *Amistad,* at one point shouting "Give us free! Give us free!"

The judge in the *Amistad* case ruled in favor of the Africans. He deemed them innocent of murder and piracy, since they had only acted to free themselves. He ordered the ship and its goods to be returned to Ruiz and Montes, but stated that the Africans were to be freed and allowed to return to their homes.

John Quincy Adams for the defense

The prosecution appealed, and the *Amistad* case went before the U.S. Supreme Court. At the time, five Supreme Court justices were Southerners who had owned slaves. The defense sought out former U.S. president **John Quincy Adams** (1767–1848; served 1825–29) to present its case, banking on his renown as much as on his legal ability. In his seventies and still an outspoken member of the U.S. House of Representatives, Adams had been following the *Amistad* case since the beginning. He enchanted the court with hours-long orations about the principles of American freedom and justice. Even as this was going on in court, though, President Van Buren had stationed a ship nearby with standing orders to carry the prisoners to Cuba. Abolitionists watched the ship night and day to ensure that the president did not overstep his powers and whisk the captives away.

In March 1840, the Supreme Court upheld the earlier court's decision. The Africans were free, though reduced in number to thirty-five owing to deaths in prison. It took almost another year for the *Amistad* relief committee to raise money to hire a ship to carry Cinque and the other Africans back to Sierra Leone. They are the only known Africans sold as slaves in the New World to return to their lands. Upon his return home, Cinque was unable to find his wife. He disappeared shortly after his return and little else is known of his life. In the United States, though, he remains a symbol of resistance to the Atlantic slave trade.

The *Amistad* decision did not condemn slavery. It simply held that Africans who were not legally slaves could not be considered property. If the *Amistad* rebels had been slaves by U.S. law, or if the abolitionists had not intervened on their behalf, the decision would have been very different. As it happened, though, the case provided the nation with a rare perspective on the human rights of kidnapped African people. Abolitionists viewed this as a victory, whereas slave owners of the South generally viewed the decision with contempt.

Antebellum Period

Antebellum is a Latin word that means "before the war." In American history, the antebellum period refers to the years after the **War of 1812** (1812–15) and before the **Civil War** (1861–65). The development of separate northern and southern economies, westward expansion of the nation, and a spirit of reform marked the era. These issues created an unstable and explosive political environment that eventually led to the Civil War.

Separate economies

After the War of 1812, England finally acknowledged American independence and began to establish a relationship with the young nation. With the last of the military threats gone, the United States turned its attention to building a strong nation. Its economy was strong and diverse, and Americans had a lot to offer other countries.

In colonial times, the southern and northern areas of the country had diverse economies. Each, however, soon established areas of specialization that reflected regional differences. The North, with its great port cities, began to focus on industry. A constant stream of immigrants provided cheap labor for the variety of businesses. The South, with its fertile lands, focused on agriculture. By 1815, **cotton** was the primary crop in the South. The invention of the **cotton gin** helped the region serve a growing worldwide demand for the crop. The institution of **slavery** provided the labor to harvest large plantations for greater profits.

As a result of the very different businesses in the North and the South, their economies developed differently. In Congress, politicians engaged in heated debates as they tried to serve the needs of their own region. The institution of slavery was a particularly difficult issue. As the nation gained territory and **westward expansion** began, politicians argued over whether slavery would be allowed to expand into the new areas.

Expansion and the slavery question

Under President **Thomas Jefferson**, the United States had made the **Louisiana Purchase** in 1803, and the lands began gradually to organize into states. After the War of 1812, the nation expanded even more rapidly. **Florida** Territory was ceded by Spain in 1819. The **Oregon** Treaty and the Mexico Treaty added lands farther west. By 1848, the U.S. territory stretched from the Atlantic Ocean all the way to the Pacific Ocean. In 1821, there were twenty-four states in the Union. By 1861, when the Civil War broke out, there were thirty-four.

Rapid growth caused growing pains for the young nation. With every addition of a state, politicians in Congress had to confront the differences between North and South. Slavery was always a point of conflict. According to the **Constitution**, slaves were counted as three-fifths of a citizen for purposes of federal representation and taxation. If slavery continued to expand, the Northern politicians would begin to lose influence in policy decisions. In the interest of economic security, Northern politicians argued against the expansion of slavery. Southerners supported the expansion.

Social reforms

The antebellum period was also marked by increased public activism. During the Second **Great Awakening** (from 1800 to the 1830s), Christian morality found energetic expression in religious revivals, mass meetings where people sought salvation. The spirit of reform also motivated organizations working toward social change. Temperance organizations hoped to eliminate social ills caused by alcohol consumption. Others hoped to improve society through education reform and increased literacy. Abolitionists focused on ending slavery everywhere. Americans debated these issues as the young nation struggled to improve itself.

Some aspects of the antebellum period, particularly in the South, have been presented in a positive light in popular **movies** and books. For instance, plantation life in the South is sometimes portrayed with nostalgia. Such presentations, however, ignore the evil of slavery and the difficult political and social realities of the times. The antebellum period came to an end with the outbreak of the Civil War in 1861.

Susan B. Anthony

Susan B. Anthony's Quaker upbringing greatly influenced the role she played in nineteenth-century America. **Quakers**, properly known as the Religious Society of Friends, had founded their religion on the belief that priests and places of organized worship are not necessary for a person to experience God. In the Quaker view, all people have an "inner light" that can guide them to divine truth. Quakers do not believe in armed conflict or **slavery**, and they were among the first groups to practice equality between men and women. Anthony led a crusade to ensure that all women were granted the rights she herself had come to expect.

Susan B. Anthony was born on February 15, 1820. Her father, a cotton-mill owner, instilled in his children the ideas of self-reliance, self-discipline, and self-worth. Both her parents were strong supporters of the abolitionist (antislavery) and the temperance (avoidance of alcohol) movements. (See **Abolition Movement** and **Prohibition**.)

Protests inequality

After completing her schooling at the age of seventeen, Anthony began teaching in schools in rural **New York** state. Teaching was one of the few professions open to women at the time, but wages for men and women differed greatly. Anthony's weekly salary was equal to one-fifth of that received by her male colleagues. When she protested this inequality, she lost her job. She then secured a better position as principal of the girls' division of a private school.

In 1849, after teaching for over ten years, Anthony found her professional future bleak. She joined the local temperance society but was denied the chance to speak at a meeting because she was a woman. Unwilling to be silenced, she founded the Daughters of Temperance, the first women's temperance organization. She began writing temperance articles for the *Lily*, the first woman-owned newspaper in the United States. Through the paper's editor, Amelia Bloomer (1818–1894), Anthony met women involved in the recently formed women's suffrage (right to vote) movement. (See **Women's Suffrage Rights**.)

Works for women's suffrage

In 1851, Anthony met women's rights leader **Elizabeth Cady Stanton** (1815–1902). They formed a deep personal friendship and a political bond that would last for the rest of their lives. From that point on, Anthony worked tirelessly for women's suffrage. She lectured on women's rights and organized a series of state and national conventions on the issue. She collected signatures for a petition to grant women the right to vote and to own property. Her hard work paid off in 1860 when the New York state legislature passed the Married Women's Property Act. It allowed women to enter into contracts and to control their own earnings and property.

During the **Civil War** (1861–65), Anthony and most other members of the women's movement worked toward the emancipation of the slaves. In 1863, she helped form the Women's Loyal League, which supported the policies of President **Abraham Lincoln** (1809–1865; served 1861–65). After the war, Anthony and others tried to link women's suffrage with that of the freed slaves. They were unsuccessful. The **Fifteenth Amendment**, finally adopted in 1870, extended voting rights only to black men—not to women. Anthony and Stanton continued to fight, forming the National Woman Suffrage Association.

Brought to trial for voting

The **Fourteenth Amendment**, adopted in 1868, had declared that all people born in the United States were citizens and that no legal privileges could be denied to any citizen. Anthony decided to challenge this amendment. Saying that women were citizens and the amendment did not restrict the privilege of voting to men, she and fifteen other women voted in the presidential election of 1872. All sixteen women were arrested three weeks later, but only Anthony was brought to trial. The presiding judge opposed women's suffrage and wrote his decision before the trial even had started. Refusing to let Anthony testify, he ordered the jury to find her guilty and then sentenced her to pay a $100 fine. She refused, and no further action was taken against her.

Susan B. Anthony led a movement to try and bring equality between men and women. THE LIBRARY OF CONGRESS

Anthony continued to campaign for women's rights. Between 1881 and 1886, she and Stanton published a three-volume collection of writings about the movement's struggle. Through Anthony's determined work, many professional fields became open to women by the end of the nineteenth century. Nevertheless, at the time of her death in 1906, only four states—**Wyoming**, **Colorado**, **Idaho**, and **Utah**—had granted suffrage to women. Fourteen years later, in 1920, Congress adopted the **Nineteenth Amendment**, finally giving women throughout America the right to vote.

Antietam, Battle of
See **Battle of Antietam**

Anti-Federalists

A loose organization of delegates to the **Constitutional Convention** of 1787 who shared political goals became known as the Anti-Federalists. They opposed the policies for a strong central government supported by a larger group of delegates, members of the **Federalist Party**. The presence of the Anti-Federalists forced some compromises during the writing of the **Constitution**. The government created by the Constitution, however, was stronger than the Anti-Federalists desired.

Anti-Federalists worked during the writing of the Constitution to preserve the power of state government. Mindful of their experience under an overbearing English government, they sought to limit the power of a single national government. Some Anti-Federalists believed that state government was important for maintaining control over local affairs and keeping power in the hands of the people rather than an elite ruling class. Other Anti-Federalists simply wanted most governmental power to come from the state rather than from a central national government. Still others were concerned that a strong central government could too easily violate individual rights to liberty (freedom). Although they often spoke in terms of democratic governance by the people, the Anti-Federalists generally did not favor political rights or civil liberties for women, slaves, and similar groups.

Although the Anti-Federalists managed to work out some compromises during the Constitutional Convention, many opposed the final draft of the Constitution. They felt that, on balance, it gave too much power to the federal government. When **Alexander Hamilton** (1755–1804), **James Madison** (1751–1836), and John Jay (1745–1829) wrote the *Federalist Papers* to support the ratification (acceptance) of the Constitution, Anti-Federalists wrote articles to encourage the defeat of the Constitution.

The Anti-Federalists failed to defeat the Constitution, which was ratified in 1788. They generated enough political pressure, however, to force the Federalists to agree to incorporate a **Bill of Rights** into the Constitution. Containing the first ten amendments to the Constitution, the Bill of Rights protects individual liberty from unfair conduct by the federal government. The bill also says that any power not granted to the federal government is reserved to the states and the people.

The Anti-Federalists never organized themselves into a political party. As a group, they faded under the first installation of the federal government in 1789. The aggressive economic policies of Hamilton, who was the secretary of the Treasury under President **George Washington** (1743–1826; served 1801–9), stirred more opposition to the Federalists. Many who had aligned with the Anti-Federalists organized under **Thomas Jefferson**'s leadership to oppose the Federalists as Democratic-Republicans. The **Democratic-Republican Party** survived well into the nineteenth century.

Antiwar Movement (Vietnam)

In every war the United States has fought, there have been protesters. The antiwar movement during the Vietnam War (1954–75) is particularly memorable because it played out at a time when there were actually two other strong movements taking place: the student movement and the **civil rights movement**.

The civil rights movement, led by **Martin Luther King, Jr.** (1929–1968), began in the mid-1950s and attracted not only blacks but also the era's young white middle class. These young people saw the civil rights movement as part of a larger social movement that questioned the status quo (the existing state of affairs) in general. Racial **segregation** and inequality were two of society's ills, as was an economy sustained by war and the exploitation of smaller and poorer countries. Even the quality of education was in question: Students believed that the system promoted conformity over creativity and individuality.

Reform-minded student organizations and societies formed across the country in the early 1960s. Some focused on women's rights, others on educational reform or civil rights. By 1965, however, the protest against U.S. involvement in the Vietnam War eclipsed all other concerns.

Early protests

Although the war had begun in 1954, the United States's involvement was not significant until 1965. The first antiwar protests were loosely organized student demonstrations in which protesters gathered to share their concerns. In April 1965, teachers at college campuses across the country began hosting "teach-ins," forums in which U.S. foreign policy was explained and criticized. Before the month was over, a national event in **Washington, D.C.** was broadcast to more than one hundred colleges. April also saw the first major demonstration: **Students for a Democratic Society** (SDS) organized the event, which attracted around fifteen thousand participants to Washington, D.C.

Many opponents of the Vietnam War were protesting the draft. The draft is a means of building up the military. Males eighteen and older had to register with the government's Selective Service, and if their names were drawn in a lottery, they were required by law to join the military and serve in the Vietnam War. The draft, also known as conscription, was first used during the American **Civil War** (1861–65). (See also **Conscription Acts**.) The first public draft protest of the Vietnam War took place in October 1965 in New York City. David Miller broke the law when he burned his draft card, and for his act of protest he was arrested, found guilty, and served two years in jail. Meanwhile, the antiwar movement gained momentum as it stretched across the globe. Antiwar protests were held simultaneously in the United States; Paris, France; Rome, Italy; and London, England.

Focused and determined

By 1967, the antiwar movement had grown so widespread that those who were only moderately opposed to the war marched alongside those with more extreme perspectives. The days of a handful of protesters standing on a street corner waving signs were gone, and in their place were groups numbering in the thousands. On October 21, 1967, the National Mobilization Committee to End the War in Vietnam organized a rally in Washington, D.C. More than one hundred thousand people participated in the rally, and thirty-five thousand continued in the planned march to the steps of the Pentagon.

Protest music played a major role in the antiwar movement. Folk music was at the height of its popularity, and performers such as **Bob Dylan** (1941–), John Lennon (1940–1980), and Peter, Paul, and Mary loaned their voices to the movement at demonstrations and press statements. Dylan's 1963 hit "Blowin' in the Wind" became a theme song of the movement.

Although most peace activists embraced nonviolence, emotions ran high, and antiwar slogans such as "Make love, not war," and "Hell no, we won't go!" offended parents, spouses, and friends whose loved ones

Thousands of antiwar protestors demonstrate in front of the United Nations in 1967. AP IMAGES

were fighting overseas. Battles sometimes broke out between protesters and police, counterprotesters, and armed troops.

Seasons of violence

The violent protests peaked in 1968. The most famous protest of the year took place in August, just months after the assassination of U.S. senator **Robert F. Kennedy** (1925–1968) of **New York**. The Democratic National Convention was being held in Chicago, **Illinois**, that year, and when it became clear that Vice President Hubert H. Humphrey (1911–1978) would emerge as the **Democratic Party**'s presidential nominee, a coalition of extremist antiwar organizations showed up in Chicago intent on disrupting the convention.

What they found there were twelve thousand police officers, almost six thousand Illinois National Guardsmen, and five thousand federal troops. On the night Humphrey was nominated, rioting broke out all over Chicago. Some eyewitnesses reported that the authorities provoked the demonstrators to violence. By the time the riots had subsided, more than one thousand people were wounded and almost seven hundred had been arrested.

In the most notorious confrontation between protesters and police, on May 4, 1970, at Ohio's Kent State University, a peaceful protest ended in tragedy when four demonstrators were shot and killed by National Guardsmen who opened fire on the protesters. (See **Kent State Shooting**.) Nine other students were wounded. The nation was shocked, and eight million students protested by going on strike from their colleges and high schools. Five days after the shooting, one hundred thousand people marched in Washington, D.C., to protest the senseless deaths of the unarmed students. Singer Neil Young (1945–) wrote a song, "Ohio," about the tragedy, and the event is referenced in numerous other songs.

From the margins to the middle

As violence increased within the antiwar movement, there was a shift in public opinion: Older Americans and prominent public figures became more vocal in their criticism of the continuing war. Politicians spoke out against the government's actions, and even some veterans of the war organized to bring an end to what had become the longest-running war in U.S. history. The Republican candidate, **Richard M. Nixon** (1913–1994; served 1969–74), won the presidential election in 1968 with a campaign platform to end the war.

Nixon had no great plan to bring home the troops, but he did try to bomb the North Vietnamese into submission. When that failed, he put into action a plan that eventually turned over responsibility for the ground war to South Vietnam. This was known as "Vietnamization," and it did allow U.S. troops to gradually withdraw, although U.S. air fighters were still standing by to deploy at a moment's notice.

Days after the Kent State shooting in 1970, state police opened fire on student protesters at

As the Vietnam War continued, protests grew increasingly confrontational and violent between demonstrators and police.

Jackson State College in **Mississippi**. Twelve students were injured and two were killed. One student at a New York school responded to the Kent State shooting by hanging a banner out a dormitory window that read "They Can't Kill Us All." Nixon's response was seen as callous by members of the antiwar movement. He met with about thirty student protestors at the **Lincoln Memorial** in Washington, D.C., just five days after the shooting, but his attempts at reaching out were condescending and clumsy.

With the 1971 publication of the Pentagon Papers—a top-secret, seven-thousand-page government report on the planning and policy making before and during the war—most Americans began to support total withdrawal of troops from Vietnam. The report uncovered lies, illegal actions, and other unethical behavior on the part of the president, the government, and the military. By the time the war officially ended in 1975, nearly all of the United States was a part of the antiwar movement.

Appomattox Courthouse

Appomattox Courthouse, Virginia, is the American **Civil War** site at which the Confederate army, led by General **Robert E. Lee** (1807–1870), surrendered to **Union** general **Ulysses S. Grant** (1822–1885) on April 9, 1865. The surrender is commonly viewed as the end of the Civil War, although afterward the **Confederate States of America** government briefly attempted to maintain its rebellion.

Confederate surrender came after a series of encounters between the forces under Lee and Grant. Eighty thousand Union soldiers forced thirty-five thousand Confederate soldiers out of Petersburg, Virginia, in the end of March 1865. Grant continued pushing the rebels south and eventually managed to cut them off and surround them.

On April 9, realizing the position the Confederates were in, Lee sent a flag of truce to Grant. The two generals met that afternoon to arrange the surrender. By all accounts, Grant was generous with the terms. He allowed the officers to keep their side arms (weapons kept by the belt; hand guns and swords) and the soldiers to keep their horses for working their farms. He also issued rations to the starving Confederates. In all, 7,892 infantrymen surrendered with arms to Union forces at

Appomattox. A total of twenty-eight thousand Confederate troops were paroled (released after promising not to fight) by the agreement.

Appomattox Courthouse became a national historic site in 1954.

Arizona

Nicknamed the Grand Canyon State, Arizona entered the Union on February 14, 1912, as the forty-eighth state. It is the sixth-largest state in terms of size, with a total boundary length of 1,478 miles (2,379 kilometers). Arizona lies in the Rocky Mountains region of the United States and is bordered by **Utah**, **Nevada**, **California**, **New Mexico**, and Mexico.

It is believed that the region now known as Arizona was inhabited by several cultures by 500 C.E., including the Anasazi, Mogollon, and Hohokam. These cultures were in decline by the fourteenth century for reasons unknown even in the twenty-first century. When the first Europeans arrived in the sixteenth century, they found native populations—the oldest of which were the Hopi—living a hunter-gatherer lifestyle in the river valleys.

Arizona was a largely peaceful territory, even when Mexico revolted against Spain in 1810. When the **Mexican-American War** (1846–48) broke out in 1846, two U.S. armies marched across the Arizona region. The **California Gold Rush** in 1849 also brought thousands of Americans through the region. In 1863, President **Abraham Lincoln** (1809–1865; served 1861–65) signed the Organic Act of Arizona, which created the new Territory of Arizona.

Arizona is largely desert and has a dry, hot climate. The northern region of the state includes the Grand Canyon, a vast gorge more than 200 miles (320 kilometers) long, up to 18 miles (29 kilometers) wide, and more than 1 mile (1.6 kilometers) deep. This same region boasts the Painted Desert, the Petrified Forest, and Humphreys Peak, the highest point in the state at 12,633 feet (3,853 meters).

Although Phoenix has air quality poorer than most other U.S. cities, most of the state is known for its clear air, open lands, and breathtaking forests. Arizona works hard to protect these resources in the wake of a growing population and tourist industry.

Population and economy

Arizona once was considered a "retirement" state, where people moved in their sixties. This is no longer true; only 13 percent of the population in 2006 was age sixty-five and older. The majority of the population (28 percent) was age twenty-five to forty-four. By far, the largest concentration of the state's residents (nearly 1.5 million) lived in the capital city of Phoenix. The next most populated city was Tucson, home to just over five hundred thousand people.

By the 1970s, Arizona's agricultural economy had been replaced by manufacturing, with centers in Phoenix and Tucson. The state's primary industries included wood products, computer and electronic equipment, and transportation equipment. Still, Arizona ranked twenty-ninth in the nation in terms of agricultural output value in 2005. The state led the nation in copper and molybdenum production in 2004.

Tourism and travel accounted for more than $13.76 billion in direct sales in Arizona in 2004, and 27.8 million Americans and another 900,000 international tourists visited the state that year. The state's twenty-two national parks and monuments, the most popular being Grand Canyon National Park, attract millions of visitors annually.

Arkansas

Nicknamed the Natural State, Arkansas was the twenty-fifth state to enter the Union (June 15, 1836). It is located in the western south-central United States, bordered by **Missouri**, **Oklahoma**, **Texas**, **Louisiana**, **Mississippi**, and **Tennessee**. Arkansas ranks twenty-seventh in size among the fifty states, with a total area of 53,187 square miles (137,754 square kilometers).

The first Europeans to explore Arkansas were Spaniards, led by **Hernando de Soto** (c.1496–1542), in 1541. Prior to their appearance, the region was inhabited by Quapaw, Caddo, Osage, and Choctaw as well as Cherokee tribes.

In 2006, Arkansas ranked thirty-second in the nation's population, with an estimated total of 2,810,872 residents. Its capital city, Little Rock, was home to just under 185,000 people. Although much of Arkansas's population was once African American, the state lost a substantial portion of its farm population during the **Great Depression** (1929–41; a worldwide economic crisis), and many African Americans migrated to industrialized states to look for work. Modern Arkansas is predominantly white.

Although Arkansas has a diverse manufacturing economy ranging from textiles to bicycle production and including a major woodworking industry, its economy continues to be enhanced by the **cotton** industry. Other major agricultural industries in the state include soybeans, poultry, and fish farming. Arkansas is home to more than fifty Fortune 500 firms, including Tyson Foods and Wal-Mart Stores.

Arkansas is a poor state. In 2004, 17.9 percent of its population lived below the poverty line, which made Arkansas the fifth poorest state in the nation. In 2003, 18 percent of the state's total population had no health insurance. Of that population, 47 percent had family members who worked full time, year-round.

In 1957, the Little Rock school system became the site for public controversy when the school board announced its voluntary compliance with the **Supreme Court**'s 1954 *Brown v. Board of Education* decision, which called for the **desegregation of public schools**. On September 5 of that year, nine African American students attempted to enter Central High School. (See **Little Rock Central High School Desegregation**.) Governor Orval Faubus (1910–1994) ordered the National Guard to take over the school to prevent these children from attending. Guardsmen were removed via court order later that month. By 1980, Central High was one of the most racially balanced schools in the South.

Arlington National Cemetery

Arlington National Cemetery is comprised of 624 acres and sits on the **Virginia** bank of the Potomac River, opposite **Washington, D.C.** It was originally part of the estate of President **George Washington** (1732–1799; served 1789–97) and was passed along to his adopted son, G. W. Parke Custis. Custis's daughter, Mary Ann, who inherited the estate, married Confederate general **Robert E. Lee** (1807–1870).

Military hospital erected

The United States seized the estate upon the outbreak of the American **Civil War** (1861–65). The military built a fort and a hospital on the site and the grounds were used as a cemetery. In 1882, the U.S. **Supreme Court** declared the property be returned to the Lee family. The family accepted $150,000 payment for the land and it became one of the most important historical sites maintained by the U.S. government.

The soldiers of every war since the **American Revolution** (1775–83) are buried in Arlington National Cemetery, as are distinguished statesmen, including Presidents **William Howard Taft** (1857–1930; served 1909–13) and **John F. Kennedy** (1917–1963; served 1961–63). Also in the cemetery is the Tomb of the Unknowns (also known as the Tomb of the Unknown Soldier), which commemorates the dead of both world wars and the **Korean War** (1950–53). This shrine sits on top of a hill overlooking Washington, D.C., and was opened to the public in 1932. The tomb is guarded twenty-four hours a day, seven days a week, by the U.S. Army.

Includes ceremonial facilities

The Tomb of the Unknowns is part of the Arlington Memorial Amphitheater, which seats fifteen thousand people and is host to Veteran's Day and Memorial Day services. It was completed in 1921 and sits on the site where Robert E. Lee once had his gardens.

There are other sites on the cemetery grounds that attract hundreds of thousands of tourists each year. One of these is a memorial to the members of the crew who died in the ***Challenger* Space Shuttle explosion** in January 1986. There is also a Pentagon memorial, dedicated to the 184 lives lost during the **September 11, 2001, terrorist attack** on the Pentagon.

Army

The U.S. Army was officially established on June 14, 1775. **George Washington** (1732–1799) was commander in chief of the first national army, which included around 8,000 men. In October 1776, Congress voted to increase the army to include 88 battalions of infantry, or 60,000 men, each of whom would serve for three years, or if they enlisted during wartime, for the duration of the war. Two months later, Congress voted to establish 22 more battalions, for a total of 110. There were approximately 75,000 soldiers in the Continental army until 1781, when Congress reduced the number of battalions to 59, a more realistic and manageable number.

The original army consisted mainly of infantry (foot soldiers) and artillery, but it also had a small cavalry (mounted soldiers), a small corps of engineers, and a few maintenance personnel to repair and maintain equipment. The army disbanded almost completely after the **American Revolution** (1775–83), but some remained to help protect the frontier settlements.

The army has participated in every war in U.S. history since the Revolution. After the **War of 1812** (1812–15), Secretary of War **John C. Calhoun** (1782–1850) established a peacetime army that remained intact until the start of the **Mexican-American War** (1846–48). In 1820, that army included about ten thousand troops, but it reduced its ranks by half later that year and maintained that level until 1835, with intermittent increases to total up to twelve thousand men.

The **Spanish-American War** (1898) was the first overseas war for the U.S. Army. By the end of the war, more than 274,000 men had joined the army, but most of them never left their training camps in the United States. After the war, the Army War College was founded and the school system modernized. Between 1900 and 1916, the army numbered from 65,000 to 108,000 officers and soldiers. Their duties extended overseas and included building the **Panama Canal** from 1907 to 1914.

In 1903, the army recognized the National Guard as part of its ranks during emergencies; in 1916, the National Defense Act added a reserve corps and began to provide officer training in colleges.

World wars

Even with the reforms in place, the army was not ready when **World War I** (1914–18) began. The government implemented the selective service system, or draft, by which all young men had to register, and if their names were chosen by lottery, they had to join the military. Some were exempted because of physical or mental illness, but healthy men who were called to duty had to serve. Within eighteen months, the army grew from 210,000 to 3,685,000.

The draft was used again during **World War II** (1939–45). Numbers reached a peak of around 8.3 million officers and men during the war, 5 million of whom were deployed overseas to fight. The army was divided into three commands: Army Air Forces, Army Ground Forces, and Army Service Forces. The **Air Force** eventually became its own independent military branch; the service forces were responsible for keeping operations running smoothly on the homefront.

After the war, the United States gained new ground in world affairs, and with it, added responsibility. A peacetime draft was enacted, and for most of the next twenty-eight years the army was comprised of both volunteers and draftees. During the **Korean War** (1950–53), the army was desegregated, and soldiers all were given equal opportunity for advancement. Before this time, although African Americans had served in the army since the **Civil War**, they always had been grouped into units separate from whites, and were never promoted to officer levels.

The draft continued almost through the **Vietnam War** (1954–75); it ended on July 1, 1973, when American troops withdrew from combat. The army once again became voluntary, and it remained so in the twenty-first century.

War in Afghanistan and Iraq

The Army participated in wars during the twenty-first century. The United States attacked Afghanistan in October 2001 in response to **al-Qaeda**'s involvement in the **September 11, 2001, terrorist attacks** on U.S. soil. In 2008, that war was still in progress. In March 2003, a coalition of troops led by the United States invaded Iraq. (See **Iraq Invasion**.)

Peacetime activities

The army has served the nation in peacetime, too. During the nineteenth century, soldiers helped survey the lands for the transcontinental railroad lines, keep peace during **Reconstruction** (the time of rebuilding in the South after the Civil War), and explore the West. Army doctors have contributed to the advancement of modern medicine, and in times of natural disaster, army personnel provide assistance to victims.

Benedict Arnold

Benedict Arnold was a patriot during the **American Revolution** (1775–83). Although he fought heroically for the American cause and earned the rank of brigadier general, he is most remembered for his acts of treason.

Early life

Arnold was born in Norwich, **Connecticut**, in 1741. His parents, Benedict and Hannah King Arnold, were well established, and young Arnold had a good education. The household was strict and religious, and he was a bit rebellious against the constraints of home. He twice ran away from home to join a militia fighting in the **French and Indian War** (1754–63).

In 1762, Arnold's parents died. He moved to New Haven, Connecticut, where he became a druggist and bookseller. He was quite successful and began another business trading between Quebec, Canada, and the West Indies. In February 1767, he married into a prominent family from New Haven. He and his wife, Margaret Mansfield, would have three sons between 1768 and 1772.

Military career

Arnold became a captain in the Connecticut militia in 1775 and participated in the siege of Boston. It was the beginning of a notable army career. When his wife died while he was on a mission, Arnold devoted himself entirely to the Revolutionary cause. He served with distinction and earned the rank of major general.

Arnold's military career was plagued with inadequate recognition for his performance and accusations of misconduct. He prepared his resignation several times, but the personal pleas of General **George Washington** (1732–1799) prevented him from actually resigning. The American cause had many victories as a result of his bold and determined leadership.

Change of sides

In May 1778, Arnold was assigned to be the commander at Philadelphia after the British evacuation from that city. He met and fell in love with a socialite, Margaret Shippen. Over time they would have four sons and one daughter.

In attempting to entertain and live as an aristocrat, Arnold fell deeply into debt. Soon after his marriage, Arnold began the treasonous relationship with the British for which he is so well remembered. It is assumed that a combination of his need for money and resentment of the authorities responsible for his difficult career motivated him to sell military information to the British.

In 1780, Arnold obtained a command at West Point. This was a strategically important military base, and Arnold offered to turn the fort over to the British for a financial reward. The plot was foiled when his contact, Major John André (1750–1780), was caught on September 20 with incriminating documents. André was executed, but Arnold managed to flee to the British in New York. He was received into the British Army and given the rank of brigadier general of provincial troops. He continued to fight in the war, though now opposite his countrymen.

End of life

In 1781, Arnold sailed with his family to England. His personality and reputation for treason made him quite unpopular in England. Although he attempted to continue military service and a number of business ventures, he had little success. He failed as well to gain sufficient recognition and compensation for the services he rendered to the British during the war. It proved to be difficult to establish himself socially as well as economically in the new country. The time until his death in London in 1801 was unhappy.

Chester A. Arthur

Chester A. Arthur was the twenty-first president of the United States, serving from 1881 until 1885.

Climbs the political ladder

Chester Alan Arthur was born to an Irish minister and his wife on October 5, 1829, in Vermont. He graduated from college in 1848 and went on to study law. To support himself, he worked in education as a teacher and a principal. To complete his formal training, Arthur moved to New York City, where he passed the bar exam in 1854. Two years later, he opened his own law firm.

Arthur quickly became active in politics in an effort to make contacts and find clients. The **Republican Party** benefited from the young lawyer's knowledge and efforts, particularly **New York** governor Edwin D. Morgan (1811–1883), whose 1860 reelection was due in large part to Arthur's tireless promotion. As thanks, Morgan appointed Arthur to

Chester A. Arthur was the twenty-first president of the United States. THE LIBRARY OF CONGRESS

the position of state engineer-in-chief. Within a year, the outbreak of the American **Civil War** (1861–65) caused Arthur to be reappointed as the state assistant quartermaster general. His duties included supplying housing, food, and equipment for New York's militia (volunteer civilian fighting troops). By 1862, he was promoted as the state quartermaster general.

Arthur returned to his law practice in 1863 when Democrat Horatio Seymour (1819–1886) was elected governor. He kept close ties with the Republican Party and with U.S. senator Roscoe Conkling (1829–1888) of New York in particular. Conkling was a corrupt politician with a great amount of power, and he helped secure Arthur a position as collector for the port of New York. As collector, Arthur was responsible for all paperwork filed on imports and exports as well as for collecting import taxes on goods coming in from other countries. In such a powerful position of authority, Arthur gave thousands of jobs to fellow Republicans based solely on their political affiliation. Whether they were qualified to perform these government jobs was not important. This was known as the spoils system, and American politics relied heavily on such strategy.

In 1877, President **Rutherford B. Hayes** (1822–1893; served 1877–81) had the Customs House investigated. Arthur was held accountable for the poor management of the organization and lost his job in 1878.

Enters vice presidency

Arthur ran as vice president on the **James A. Garfield** (1831–1881; served 1881) ticket (list of candidates) in the 1880 election and the duo won, despite Arthur's past. Just four months into the Garfield presidency, Charles J. Guiteau (c. 1840–1882), an enraged attorney who had unsuccessfully sought a government position, shot Garfield. The president lingered for ten weeks before dying in September. Arthur took over the presidency.

While vice president, Arthur had not joined Garfield in his battle against Conkling and other supporters of the spoils system. Once he reached the presidency, though, he wanted to prove himself trustworthy. He stopped spending time with friends who knew him before his change of heart, and he began to support civil service (government workers) reform.

Arthur was responsible for passing the first federal immigration law in 1882. The law barred criminals, lunatics, and paupers (extremely poor people) from entering America. That same year, Congress passed the Chinese Exclusion Act, which put severe restrictions on Chinese immigrants. (See **Asian Immigration**.)

In 1883, Congress passed the Pendleton Act, which established a Civil Service Commission that required that applicants to government agency positions pass a test. No longer would a friendship with a politician influence who was hired. The act also protected government employees from being fired for reasons other than job performance. The Pendleton Act angered Republicans because it allowed members of the **Democratic Party** to secure powerful positions in the civil service.

Angering his own party did not concern Arthur. He also sought to lower taxes so that the federal government did not have an embarrassingly high surplus of revenue each year. Republicans were traditionally in favor of high taxes, and they were furious over the signing of the Tariff Act of 1883. The law brought a gradual reduction in import taxes over the next decade.

A year after he became president, Arthur learned that he had a fatal kidney disease. He kept this information private, and in 1884, he sought reelection to avoid the appearance of being afraid of getting beat. He failed to receive his party's nomination, however, and died in 1886.

Articles of Confederation

The Articles of Confederation, written in 1776, became the first constitution adopted by the rebelling American colonies to unite them under a common government. The Articles bridged the gap between the time the **thirteen colonies** broke from Great Britain in 1776 and adopted the **Constitution** of the United States of America in 1788.

Prior to the revolutionary period, the American colonies functioned separately. By standing together against the imperial conduct of Great

Britain during the 1760s and 1770s, the colonies began to feel a sense of unity. As talk of independence spread, revolutionaries turned their thoughts to establishing a new nation.

Beginning in May 1775, delegates from the colonies gathered at the Second Continental Congress to discuss independence from Britain and to define an independent government. (See **Continental Congress, Second**.) While one committee produced the **Declaration of Independence**, another sought to create a document that would bring the independent states together under a central government.

A first draft of the Articles of Confederation was presented as early as July 12, 1776. Congress approved a final draft and sent it to the states on November 15, 1777. Every state was required to ratify, or accept, the document before it became official. The **American Revolution** (1775–83) and political differences between the states delayed ratification (acceptance) for nearly five years. Congress started to function as defined by the Articles as soon as a majority of states had accepted it, but the document was not fully ratified until March 1, 1781.

The Articles of Confederation reflected the conflicts between the colonies and the imposing rule of the British government. State independence was well protected under the Articles. States maintained control over imposing taxes, regulating commerce, and enlisting troops. States were to support national efforts through participation of their delegates at Congress and contributions of their troops and money to the central government.

Under the Articles, there were no balanced branches of government; Congress was the national government. Congress held power over war, foreign policy, foreign loans, regulation of money, and Indian trade. Each state sent two to seven delegates to Congress annually, but each state had only one vote. A simple majority of states normally decided issues, although for the most important ones the consent of nine states was required. Amendments to the Articles of Confederation required unanimous support.

The national government established by the Articles struggled to assert enough control to accomplish its tasks. Dependent on the generosity of the states for war expenses, soldiers, and military supplies, Congress had trouble managing the Revolutionary War. The politics of congressional committees, constantly changing delegates, and the nine-state requirement for approving some changes further hampered Congress's ability to function.

In spite of the difficulties presented by the Articles of Confederation, Congress functioned well enough to carry the new nation through its first years. Congress successfully organized a federal government and raised an army that waged an eventually victorious war. Congress took charge of negotiating foreign alliances and loans with France and other nations, as well as a peace treaty with Great Britain in September 1783. Congress worked to bring national stability and unity with such institutions as a national bank and a standard currency.

Eventually, however, the men who controlled the national government wanted it to have greater powers. With support from influential men such as **George Washington** (1732–1799; served 1789–97), the states called for a national constitutional convention in 1787. The Constitution written at that convention was ratified by the states in 1788, turning the Articles from a functional document into a historical one.

Asian Immigration

Asian immigrants to the United States arrived from many different countries, at different times, and for different reasons. There is no single historical background for Asian Americans, but a wide range of histories.

In 2000, the U.S. Census reported a population of 11.9 million people of Asian descent, making up 4.2 percent of the total U.S. population. The number of Asian Americans had soared since 1960, when there were only 878,000 people of Asian descent in the nation. The national backgrounds had changed significantly as well. In 1960, 99 percent of Asian Americans came from three national backgrounds: 52 percent were Japanese, 27 percent were Chinese, and 20 percent were Filipino. In 2000, Chinese and Filipino Americans were the largest groups, followed by Asian Indians, Koreans, and Vietnamese. Japanese Americans were the sixth-largest group.

Early Chinese immigration

The Chinese were the first Asian immigrants to come to the United States in significant numbers. A few Chinese seamen and merchants had arrived on the East Coast of the United States by the end of the eighteenth century, but it was not until the discovery of gold, or **California**

Gold Rush, in 1848 that large numbers began the long journey to the Americas. The 1850 census counted only about 750 Chinese in **California**, but by 1852 more than 10,000 aspiring Chinese gold miners had passed through the Customs House in San Francisco.

Spurred on by a harsh economy at home, an estimated 322,000 Chinese people, mostly men, entered the United States between 1850 and 1882. A majority came from the rural provinces of Kwangtung and Fukien and spoke Cantonese. Although some paid their own way, most were very poor and financed their passage by the "credit-ticket" system; that is, they borrowed money from Chinese middlemen, which they were to repay with interest out of their earnings in America.

The Chinese workers formed urban clusters within larger cities. These clusters were called Chinatowns, and they operated independently of the larger cities around them. The Chinese found strength in numbers, and they relied upon each other to create a cultural identity that would protect them against the harsh attitudes of Americans.

The Chinese not only lived in Chinatowns, they also shopped and socialized there. The culture of Chinatowns was much like that of the homes the immigrants had left behind. Although these cities-within-cities were originally overcrowded slums full of crime and violence, many turned into tourist attractions by the mid-1900s.

Chinese immigrants were treated badly in the United States. They were subject to discrimination, often violent. They could not become American citizens, for a 1790 law reserved citizenship for white persons. Even so, Chinese immigrants journeyed throughout the West, seeking gold or job opportunities in **Nevada**, **Oregon**, **Idaho**, **Colorado**, and **South Dakota**.

Thousands of non-Chinese travelled from the eastern United States in search of instant wealth from gold. But most miners were disappointed; they did not find gold simply lying around in streams and gulches. Mining was hard work, and many men gave up after weeks or months of finding nothing. Disappointment led to resentment, as Americans considered their Chinese peers competition for the gold. Soon the Chinese were accused of stealing the Americans' wealth.

One other aspect of the Chinese workers frustrated Americans: They would not fight back. They were a peaceful group of immigrants and accepted their fate in America. Whereas other groups might respond with violence, the Chinese instead drew strength from each other. Having developed Chinatowns as their home base, they lived largely separate from the larger cities around them. By limiting their interactions with non-Chinese, they did not often confront racial hatred face-to-face.

After the Gold Rush, thousands of Chinese went to work in the **railroad industry**. Construction of the Central Pacific—the western half of the transcontinental railroad—was accomplished largely because of the skill, dedication, and hard work of some twelve thousand Chinese workers. But most Chinese were publicly denied any credit for their years of labor. A famous photo taken at Promontory Point, **Utah**, records the celebration over the last spike being driven into the Transcontinental Railroad in 1869. That golden spike connected the east and west by railway. Not one Chinese worker appears in the photo.

After the railroad work was completed, in California in particular, Chinese labor became an important part of the economy. Chinese laborers converted the swamps of the San Joaquin and Sacramento deltas into rich farmland. Half of the labor force in San Francisco's four key industries—shoes, woolens, tobacco, and garments—was Chinese. Even with these contributions, the Chinese increasingly became the target of white resentment and racism.

The first restrictions on immigration

Succumbing to pressure from anti-Chinese groups, in 1882 Congress passed the Chinese Exclusion Act, the first major restriction on immigration to the United States. The act prohibited Chinese laborers from entering the United States; it also prohibited them from becoming U.S. citizens. Another act six years later banned the reentry into the United States of Chinese laborers who had gone back to China to visit. Thus, Chinese men could not visit their families or even go home to marry. These immigration restrictions permanently separated untold numbers of Chinese families who would never see one another again.

The Chinese Exclusion Act marked the beginning of an illegal immigration movement that involved an **"underground railroad,"** much like the one used by African American slaves earlier in the century to flee north to non-slave states. People secretly worked together to smuggle Chinese citizens into the United States via **Texas**. The Chinese would be safely hidden and transported by various men and women on their journey to the United States. Once in Texas, these aliens attended a secret school that taught them enough English to help them find work.

Chinatowns became even more important to the immigrants, as they needed to find shelter and steady work.

In spite of the Chinese Exclusion Act, the illegal immigration movement caused the Chinese population in America to increase. It peaked in 1890 at around 107,488 people. The number decreased after that, mostly because the majority of Chinese immigrants were travellers who had never planned to stay. Using the Chinese underground railroad, they returned to their native land.

The Chinese were legally forbidden to immigrate to the United States until 1943, when China became America's ally (partner) in **World War II** (1939–45). At that time, the Chinese fell under regular immigration law. Most Chinese immigrants who entered the United States after the war were women, many of them the wives of Chinese men already in America.

Early Japanese immigration

Japan had been an isolated country until the 1860s, when it embarked on a program of industrialization and modernization. This program involved imposing heavy taxes on already impoverished peasants (land

Japanese laborers were first recruited to work on sugar plantations in Hawaii and later also did agricultural work throughout California. © BETTMANN/CORBIS

workers), many of whom, encouraged by stories of the "land of money trees," left Japan for America.

Japanese laborers were at first recruited to work on the sugar plantations of the independent kingdom of **Hawaii**, beginning around 1868. By 1890, some 12,000 Japanese had settled in Hawaii and 3,000 in the United States. In the 1890s, some 50,000 more Japanese came to Hawaii and 22,000 to North America. In 1910, the Japanese population in the United States, by then including the territory of Hawaii, was 153,000.

The Japanese government, unlike the Chinese, was able to regulate emigration. Wishing to avoid the problems of gambling, prostitution, and drunkenness that had beset the predominantly male Chinese immigration population, Japan actively promoted the emigration of women. From the end of the **Civil War** (1861–65) through the early twentieth century, the Japanese were the largest group of Asians to immigrate to the United States.

Filipino immigration

In 1903, the United States annexed (took control of) the Philippines, which had been a Spanish colony for four hundred years. The Filipinos were assigned unclear status as U.S. nationals—something between a foreigner and a citizen. As colonists, they were free to immigrate to the United States, and many arrived during the period from 1906 to 1934. Many came as laborers for farms and industry, and a significant number of Filipino students came to study at American universities on government-funded scholarships. These students were expected to return to the Philippines when they had finished their studies to provide the colony with their professional skills, but many stayed in the United States.

Further regulation of Asian immigration

The Barred Zones Act of 1917 and the Immigration Act of 1924 effectively ended Asian immigration to the United States. The 1917 law barred immigration from most of Asia, while the 1924 legislation established immigration quotas (a proportional number) for each country; the quotas for most Asian countries were set at zero. For a time, Filipinos could enter the United States as U.S. nationals, but in 1935 Congress passed legislation that imposed a quota of fifty Filipino immigrants per year. Immigration from Asia virtually stopped.

The McCarran-Walter Act of 1952 opened immigration to specially skilled Asians, thus increasing Asian immigration. In 1959, Hawaii became a state. Hawaii's population was strongly Asian, with people of Filipino, Japanese, Chinese, and Korean descent. **Native Hawaiians** are of Polynesian descent. Hawaiian statehood added significant numbers of Asian Americans to the U.S. population.

Asian immigration, 1965–2000

It was not until 1965 that large numbers of Asians were able to immigrate to the United States. The Immigration and Nationality Act of 1965 abolished the national origins quotas and ended policies that discriminated against Asian nations. It provided 170,000 visas (documents allowing a person to legally enter the country) for people emigrating from countries in the Eastern Hemisphere, with no limit for any one country. The act gave special preference to family members of people already in the country.

The act dramatically changed U.S. immigration. From only 3 percent of the total of immigrants in 1960, Asians made up 34 percent of all immigrants to the United States in 1975. The nations of origin began to change as well.

After the Immigration and Nationality Act of 1965 abolished stricter restrictions on immigration, many people were able to send for their families to join them in the United States. © BETTMANN/CORBIS

Chinese were the largest group of immigrants. In 2000, there were more than 2.4 million Chinese Americans, making up about 21 percent of Asian Americans, and recent Chinese immigrants made up the fourth-largest group of foreign-born U.S. residents. In 2002, the U.S. Census Bureau reported that the Chinese language ranks second (after Spanish) among foreign languages spoken in the United States. The Filipino American population soared as well, from 176,130 in 1960 to 1.8 million in 2000.

Immigration by Asian Indians rose from 300 in 1965 to 14,000 in 1975; in 2000 there were 1.9 million Asian Indian Americans. Asian Indians immigrated to the United States mainly because of widespread unemployment in their home country. They have settled throughout the nation. One of the country's fastest growing ethnic groups, they are also one of its wealthiest.

In little over a century, the Korean American population has grown from a small group of political exiles and immigrant laborers in Hawaii and California to become one of the fastest-growing ethnic groups in the United States. According to the 2000 U.S. Census, Americans identifying themselves as of Korean descent numbered 1,228,427.

Southeast Asian immigration

There were less than four thousand Vietnamese Americans in 1970. The **Vietnam War** (1959–75), a war between the communist North Vietnamese and the anticommunist South Vietnamese, changed that dramatically. Despite U.S. participation on their side, the South Vietnamese were defeated in 1975. On the day the capital city of Saigon fell, at least sixty-five thousand South Vietnamese fled the country.

The first wave of about 130,000 Vietnamese arrived in the United States in 1975. That year, the United States passed the Indochina Migration and Refugee Act, which gave 200,000 Vietnamese refugees special status and permission to enter the United States. The situation in Vietnam deteriorated in the following years, and hundreds of thousands more fled. In the period between 1983 and 1991, 66,000 Vietnamese entered the United States legally, and 531,310 more arrived between 1991 and 2000.

In 1975, neighboring Cambodia was taken over by the Khmer Rouge, a radical and brutal revolutionary group under the leadership of

Pol Pot (1926–1998). The Khmer Rouge aimed to turn Cambodia back into a farming country and began by forcing Cambodians to move from the cities to the country, where many starved. The government then began killing educated and professional Cambodians and anyone connected with Americans. The death toll ran into the millions. When Vietnam invaded Cambodia in 1979, hundreds of thousands of Cambodians took advantage of the situation to flee to Thailand. From there, tens of thousands eventually immigrated to the United States. In the 1990s, Cambodia's political situation improved, and emigration from the country slowed down. In 2000, there were an estimated three hundred thousand Cambodian Americans.

In 1975, communist forces took over Laos as well as Vietnam. Thousands of Laotians fled to the United States, entering the country as refugees. In 2000, there were 198,000 Laotian Americans.

Other groups of Asian descent, such as Thai, Hmong, Pakistani, and Taiwanese Americans, have also developed significant populations since the 1970s.

John Jacob Astor

John Jacob Astor, one of the richest and most powerful men of his time, was an entrepreneurial wizard who made his fortune from the western fur trade and urban real estate. Astor played a central role in **westward expansion** in the nineteenth century. He created a complex business structure that spanned the continent and reached out to markets in Europe, South America, and Asia. In many ways, his business practices were the forerunners of the large industries of the late nineteenth century.

Astor was born on July 17, 1763, in the city of Walldorf in present-day Germany. At the age of sixteen, he moved to London, England, to help his brother sell musical instruments. At twenty, he immigrated to New York City, where he established a prosperous business purchasing furs in Canada for resale in Europe and the United States. He expanded his interest in furs and entered the profitable China trade, trading furs for tea and silk. (See **Fur traders and mountain men.**) Astor was extraordinarily successful, becoming a millionaire by 1807. According to many historians, he was the first millionaire in the United States.

The American Fur Company

In 1808, Astor established the American Fur Company and set out to command the fur trade from the Great Lakes to the Pacific. To accomplish this, he had to challenge the powerful British fur companies in the West. He hired traders to set up Astoria, a trading post in **Oregon**, in 1811. From Astoria, the traders were to obtain furs from the Indians and then ship the pelts directly to China. As promising as the scheme first seemed, Astor's timing was poor. In 1812, the United States went to war with Great Britain in the **War of 1812**. In 1813, the British Northwest Company surrounded Astoria and forced Astor's agent to sell out the entire post for far less than it was worth. A furious Astor was forced to abandon his Oregon trade.

Although the American Fur Company was unable to capture the Pacific trade, it nonetheless became the largest American fur trading firm in the West as Astor expanded his interest in the Great Lakes region. In 1821, the American Fur Company invaded the Upper **Missouri** fur trade. By either combining with competitors or buying them out, Astor's company managed to capture much of that market as well. But by the early 1830s, Astor realized that American beavers were rapidly being depleted (over-hunted until there were few left). Beaver hats, once all the rage in Europe, had gone out of style. He sold the American Fur Company in 1834, getting out before the market dried up.

Land speculation

Astor had long invested his profits from furs in New York City real estate. After 1834 and until his death fourteen years later, he continued to buy, improve, and sell land on Manhattan Island. He owned at least $5 million in land when he died. Even as he grew wealthier, his greed seemed to increase. According to those around him, over the years Astor's personality changed. Earlier, he had a reputation as a cunning but fair employer and an honest dealer. In later life, he became known as a harsh, selfish, and greedy man.

Astor speculated in land elsewhere, including in the West. (The town of Astor, **Wisconsin**, for example, later became Green Bay.) He bought stock in railroads and canals, purchased government bonds, and was involved in various banks. When Astor died in 1848, his estimated worth was $20 million, making him the wealthiest person in the nation. He left $400,000 to found a library, which became the heart of the New

York Public Library, today one of the largest in the world. He left most of the rest of his wealth and businesses to his son William, establishing one of the great family fortunes of the early United States.

Atlantic Charter

The Atlantic Charter was signed August 14, 1941, four months before the United States officially entered **World War II**. It was a joint statement by President **Franklin D. Roosevelt** (1882–1945; served 1933–45) of the United States and Prime Minister Winston Churchill (1874–1965) of Great Britain. The charter reflected their countries' eight common objectives for a postwar world. The objectives emphasized the different philosophies of the two democracies and the other main Allied power, the Soviet Union. President Roosevelt hoped the charter would encourage support in the United States for entering the war alongside the **Allies**.

The Atlantic Charter was written during a secret meeting between Roosevelt and Churchill when the United States was still technically a neutral country. It was becoming clear to Roosevelt that the United States would probably enter the war soon, so the meeting covered many issues concerning the war. Churchill was not convinced of the need for a joint declaration, but he introduced ideas in a draft statement. A number of points proved to be controversial, but at the end of the meeting a final statement was formed. The ideas it contained would prove to be highly important in guiding Allied initiatives throughout the war and in establishing postwar peace.

The Atlantic Charter included eight basic points. It set forth the concept that each country should have the right of self-determination. This meant that territorial changes would happen only with the approval of the people concerned. Furthermore, each country would be allowed to establish the government of its choosing. Both powers declared that they sought no territorial gains from the war. Other points reflected their hopes for a world in which all nations would have access to trade and prosperity. They included thoughts on a new system of international security that would allow freedom of the seas, encourage fewer arms, and reduce fear in the world.

The Atlantic Charter was welcomed in both countries. Its importance, however, became clear only after the United States entered the war. The Charter helped define Allied goals when it was included as part of the Declaration by the United Nations in January 1942. Twenty-six nations embraced the aims of the Atlantic Charter when they signed the Declaration by the United Nations. That number eventually doubled.

The Atlantic Charter had a significant impact on the postwar world. The notion of an international system of security prompted the formation of the United Nations (UN), created in 1945. By grounding itself in the declaration of 1942, the UN embraced the principles of the Atlantic Charter. The right of self-determination thus became a guiding principle in international politics. In the thirty years following the war, important transfers of political power happened throughout the world. With encouragement from the Atlantic Charter, many countries were motivated to establish their independence from outside rule.

Atlantic Slave Trade

In 1502, Spanish colonists asked the king of Spain for permission to bring African slaves to the New World to provide labor for their large farms, or plantations. The colonists occupied the West Indies, the islands in the Caribbean Sea on which explorer **Christopher Columbus** (1451–1506) had first landed ten years earlier. In their first decade in the West Indies, the Spanish colonists had forced Native Americans to do their labor, but the native Caribbean people were dying in large numbers from overwork and from the infectious diseases brought to the New World by the Spanish. The Spanish king gave his approval for the colonists to import Africans, and the Atlantic slave trade began.

Trade on the African coast

The Portuguese, who claimed the exclusive right to trade on the west coast of Africa, had started the African slave trade in the early fifteenth century. While they were trading other goods with the Africans, the Portuguese noticed that **slavery** was an accepted part of life there. The most common form of slavery occurred when one tribe forced prisoners of war from other tribes to become their domestic slaves. Portuguese traders soon learned to buy slaves from the African coastal rulers. They also rented land from the local rulers and built a series of great forts that looked like castles along the coast of Africa. These forts, called barracoons, were designed to temporarily confine the Africans who had been purchased by the Europeans and were awaiting transport to Europe.

One of the African coastal kingdoms from which Portugal obtained slaves was Benin, located in the forests of Nigeria. Benin was a large empire with a powerful army. Like many other coastal kingdoms, Benin came to accept the slave trade as a fast way to increase its wealth and maintain its status with Europeans. The Portuguese slave traders later developed a slave trade in southern Africa in Kongo, virtually destroying the once-powerful civilization by taking so many of its people into slavery. When profits failed there, they moved on, turning their attention to Angola, farther south. Using black mercenaries (paid soldiers) equipped with firearms, they began a long war in Angola, capturing many Africans in battles that were truly slave hunts. The Portuguese slave traders then found sources for more captives in the prosperous Swahili coastal cities of East Africa.

The Atlantic slave trade thrived as the plantations of the New World grew. By the eighteenth century the actual slave catching was done mainly by inland groups, such as the Ashanti and the Dahomey, while the coastal tribes acted as middlemen between the slave catchers and the European slave traders. The captives usually came from regions 200 to 300 miles inland, often much farther. African slave traders marched the captives in coffles, or gangs, to the coast. To prevent escape, two slaves were often linked together by means of a stick with a fork at each end into which the slaves' necks were fastened. Once they reached the coast, the captives were kept in a barracoon. When enough people had been collected, they were ferried out by canoe to the ships waiting offshore.

British slave trade

The Portuguese claim on the slave trade was soon challenged by French, Dutch, Swedish, Danish, Prussian, and English slave traders, or slavers. By 1713, England had a virtual monopoly (exclusive right to the trade) on the slave trade north of the equator. Around that time, there was a great boom in the slave trade due to the increasing demand for slaves in the West Indies, where large tobacco and sugar plantations demanded a tremendous amount of physical labor.

Unfortunately for the slaves, the profits on the Caribbean plantations were so high that many people were worked to death within a year or two of arriving. With profits made from the work of one slave in less

After slaves were caught, they were marched to the coast. To prevent escape they were often yoked together by means of a stick with a fork at each end into which the slaves' necks were fastened. ENGLISH SCHOOL/THE BRIDGEMAN ART LIBRARY/GETTY IMAGES

than a year, the plantation owners were able to purchase another person to replace one who had died. The English city of Liverpool was built largely on money made from this inhuman, but booming, trade. The people of Africa became convinced that white men were cannibals who ate nothing but human flesh, as they could think of no other explanation for the enormous demand for African people.

Slave trade begins in the colonies

In the early days, English colonies in North America depended on European indentured servants for labor. Indentured servants were individuals who were committed to working for someone for a fixed number of years, usually in exchange for the price of their passage to the colonies. Indentured servants had few rights during their period of service, but after it was over they were free. By the seventeenth century, the supply of indentured servants began to run short, and the colonists sought African slaves to meet labor demands.

The first black slaves landed in **Jamestown, Virginia**, in 1619. They were treated as indentured servants. Although they were not treated as well as their European counterparts, at least some of the early African slaves gained their freedom at the end of their contract. Some went on to become property owners and professionals. But within a few decades African slaves in the colonies had come to be considered human property rather than indentured servants.

Initially all the original **thirteen colonies** had slaves. Small farms in New England, however, had much less use for physical labor than the plantation system in the South, which relied heavily on slave labor. When demand grew for sugar, tobacco, rice, and **cotton**, the number of slaves in the South grew as well, and slaves became concentrated there. (See **Slavery in the Antebellum South**.) Slavery was abolished in most northern colonies at the end of the eighteenth century, but the New England colonies continued to take an active part in the slave trade itself by providing ships and crews and selling the slaves in the South.

Triangular trade and the Middle Passage

The Atlantic slave trade developed into a triangular, or three-legged, trade in the mid-eighteenth century. A captain in Europe or New England would load up with rum and other goods to trade and sail to Africa, where the goods would be exchanged for slaves. He would then take his slaves to the West Indies or the Americas and sell them, taking on a cargo of molasses, which he would transport to New England to be made into rum. In this way, a captain was never forced to sail with an empty hold and could make a profit on each leg of the voyage.

The base of the triangle, the two- to five-month voyage in which the African captives were transported across the Atlantic Ocean to the Americas, became known as the Middle Passage. (See **Slave Ships and the Middle Passage**.) The captives were packed into tiny spaces and forced to live in unbearable conditions for the voyage. Many died on the way.

Scholars believe between twelve and fifteen million Africans were brought across the ocean during the four-hundred-year history of the African slave trade between 1500 and 1900. The great majority of them went to the West Indies and Brazil. By comparison, what became the United States imported relatively few slaves, about five hundred thou-

African American slaves work the land on a plantation in the South, which relied heavily on slave labor. HULTON ARCHIVE/GETTY IMAGES

sand people. Many of the slaves who came into the United States were purchased from the West Indies, not directly from Africa.

Prohibiting foreign slave trade

By the end of the eighteenth century, opposition to the slave trade grew strong in Europe and the United States. Great Britain abolished the trade in 1807, and the United States did the same in 1808, prohibiting the import of slaves from foreign countries but continuing to allow the sale of slaves between states. (See **Abolition Movement.**)

The Atlantic trade continued to increase despite the prohibitions against it. The invention of the **cotton gin** in 1793 and the development of the power loom created an almost unlimited demand for cotton and resulted in fresh demands for slaves. The value of a prime field hand rose from $500 to $1,500. The records of one slave smuggler showed that on a single successful trip he made a net profit of $41,439. Two or three such voyages could make a man wealthy for life.

The illegal slave trade

The slavers started using fast ships that were rarely caught by the much-slower British patrol ships on the African coast. As slavery was still legal in Africa, the native rulers continued to erect barracoons along the coast and await cruising slavers. Arriving slave traders would signal from their ships, usually by flags, that they were in the market for a certain number of slaves. The captives were then ferried out and quickly loaded onto the slave ships; the slaver would then sail for the West Indies at high speed. Unless a frigate (a type of warship) was able to catch a slaver in the act of loading, capture was highly unlikely.

In 1840, the British Navy, tired of seeing the barracoons packed with slaves along the coast, finally burned them after freeing the captives. As a result, the barracoons had to be relocated far inland, which made loading the slaves onto ships much more difficult. Meanwhile, slaves continued to be run into southern ports of North America.

The end of the slave trade

With the abolition of slavery in the United States and the end of the American **Civil War** (1861–65) in 1865, the Atlantic slave trade largely came to an end. (Brazil continued its trade in slaves until 1888, when it became the last country in the Western Hemisphere to outlaw slavery.) For Europeans and Americans, the Atlantic trade and slave labor had resulted in prosperity, at least for a time. For Africans, the slave trade was decimating. It bled dry great sections of the continent, leaving communities so weak that they could not harvest crops. The slave trade also encouraged local wars and discouraged the development of Africa's resources because the trade was so enormously profitable that nothing else could compete with it.

Atomic Bomb

The scientific discovery that would enable the creation of the atomic bomb occurred on the eve of **World War II** (1939–45). In 1934, experiments with uranium by Italian physicist Enrico Fermi (1901–1954) led to the discovery of nuclear fission. Scientists found that each fission of a uranium-235 nucleus releases 100 million times more energy than is released in a chemical reaction.

Most of the scientists who worked on nuclear fission experiments were German or Italian. They fled their native countries as German dictator Adolf Hitler (1889–1945) and the Nazis began their ascent to power. Had these men not emigrated to America, it is quite likely that Hitler would have been the one to control the use of the atomic bomb.

In the late 1930s, scientist **Albert Einstein** (1879–1955) wrote a letter to President **Franklin D. Roosevelt** (1882–1945; served 1933–45), encouraging a national effort for the development of an atomic bomb. The government did not move quickly. It was not until mid-1942 that a program, authorized by Roosevelt, began to build the bomb. The **Manhattan Project** was the name given to the work by a division established within the Army Corps of Engineers. The sole purpose of this project was to develop the atomic bomb.

The first nuclear bomb test was conducted on July 16, 1945, in **New Mexico**. The test was a success, detonating a bomb as powerful as 20,000 tons of TNT explosives. Within a month, two such bombs were dropped on Japan, killing an estimated 110,000 to 150,000 people and injuring another 200,000 or more. On August 15, six days after the second bomb was dropped, Japan announced its surrender, bringing World War II to an end.

By 1962, two thousand nuclear weapons existed across the globe. The Soviet Union and the United States owned 98 percent of them. By the end of 2007, there were still 26,000 nuclear warheads in existence; more than 95 percent belong to Russia and the United States.

Stephen Austin

Stephen Fuller Austin was the chief colonizer of **Texas**. He carried out his father's dream of creating an agricultural society in the remote Spanish-held region. He was largely responsible for founding the state of Texas.

Early years

Stephen Austin was born on November 3, 1793. His father, Moses Austin, was a mine owner. In 1798, the Austin family moved to the province of Spanish **Louisiana**, where Moses established and operated a lead mine south of St. Louis. In 1804, young Stephen Austin began school in **Connecticut** and then entered Transylvania University in

Kentucky. In 1810, he returned to **Missouri**, which had become part of the United States because of the **Louisiana Purchase** (1803). Austin worked at a bank in St. Louis, and in 1814 he was elected to the Missouri Territorial Legislature.

In 1820, Austin moved to the **Arkansas** Territory, where he established a farm on the Red River. He was appointed district judge that same year. It was obvious that Austin had natural leadership ability. In 1821, he went to New Orleans to study law.

Moses Austin's dream

Around this time, events set in motion by his father changed the course of Austin's life. Moses Austin decided to found a farming colony in the unsettled land in the Spanish province of Texas. In 1821, Moses secured a grant from the Spanish authorities that permitted him to settle three hundred families in Texas. These families would agree to become Spanish subjects in return for grants of land. Moses Austin, however, died before he could begin his colonization venture. As he lay dying, he asked Stephen to carry out his dream of founding a colony in Texas.

Founding the colony

Austin had just secured his father's colonization grant from the Spanish authorities when Mexico became independent from Spain in 1821. The grant was no longer valid. Austin traveled to Mexico City to speak directly with the new Mexican government. He could not immediately secure a grant for his Texas colony and ended up staying in Mexico City for a year. While there, he learned to speak and write in Spanish and made many friends among the Mexican leaders. The Mexican government finally approved the grant in early 1823.

Austin returned to Texas and assumed direction of the colony, which grew rapidly. By the end of 1824, almost all three hundred colonists

Stephen Austin set up the Austin colony and was largely responsible for founding the state of Texas. THE LIBRARY OF CONGRESS

permitted by the colonization charter had received land grants. The Austin colony was centered along the rich land of the Brazos River. The small town of San Felipe became its chief settlement.

Texas, Mexico

In 1824, the Mexican government approved additional colonies of Anglo-Americans (white, non–Hispanic Americans) in Texas. Austin was able to bring hundreds more families into Texas, and by 1830 he had attracted some five thousand. Among this population was a significant number of African American slaves.

By the 1830s, the Mexican government was concerned that too many Anglo-Americans had immigrated to Texas. As a result, it passed the law of April 6, 1830, which (among other restrictions) ended all future immigration into Texas from the United States. Austin worked hard to secure a repeal of this law. He once again went to Mexico City to lobby for measures favorable to Texas. Although he failed to secure all the concessions he wanted, he did convince the government to repeal some of the most objectionable aspects of the law.

Rebelling

By the time Austin returned to Texas in late 1831, Anglo-Texans had grown impatient. The town council of San Felipe called for a convention of Anglo colonists to discuss the abuses of the Mexican authorities in Texas. The Convention of 1832 drafted a long list of terms the Anglo-Texans wanted the Mexican government to grant. A year later, a second convention met and drafted a provincial constitution for Texas as a separate state within Mexico. Austin was chosen to deliver this document to the Mexican government, and he left for Mexico City in May 1833.

After Austin presented the proposed Texas constitution to government officials in Mexico City, he wrote a letter to the town council in San Antonio describing the political situation in Mexico. A Mexican government official got hold of this letter and claimed that Austin's desire for Texas to form its own government constituted treason. Arrested in early January 1834, Austin remained in prison until December of that year. He was not able to return to Texas until July 1835. Confinement in the harsh Mexico City prison permanently ruined his health.

The revolution

During Austin's absence from Texas, many Anglo-Texans had come to favor a complete break with Mexico. The Texas Revolution began on October 2, 1835, with a skirmish between Anglo and Mexican troops near Gonzales, Texas. Austin was named commander of the revolutionary army, a position he held for only a few months. The Texas government then appointed him as an agent to the United States, charged with finding materials and supplies for the revolt. Austin spent much of the Texas Revolution seeking help in the United States.

Austin returned to Texas during the summer of 1836 after the Texas Revolution had ended in an Anglo-American victory. **Sam Houston** (1793–1863), the commander-in-chief of the Texas armed forces during the revolution, was elected president of the new Republic of Texas. Austin, who lost to Houston in the election, became secretary of state but served only a few months until his death on December 27, 1836.

Automobile Industry

When industrialist Henry Ford (1863–1947) introduced his now-famous Model T automobile in 1908, he changed the lives of millions of Americans.

Ford did not invent the automobile; the Model T was not Ford's first car. His contribution to the automotive industry was designing a car that was so simple and affordable that the average American could own one. The Model T was that car. In 1908, more than ten thousand of them sold for $825 (the equivalent of about $19,000 in 2007 using the Consumer Price Index), each in the first year of production. Because of innovative production techniques that eventually included the moving assembly line, the price dropped to $575 (about $12,000 in 2007) within four years, and sales skyrocketed. By 1914, Ford owned 48 percent of the automobile market. His new car-manufacturing plant was turning out one Model T every ninety-three minutes. By 1927—years after the perfection of the assembly line—Ford was producing one car every twenty-four seconds. The price dropped to $300 (about $3,500 in 2007).

Ford made more than cars. He made it possible for Americans to live in the country and work in the city. For those who did not like city life, he allowed for the development of an entirely different lifestyle: the sub-

Henry Ford sits in his invention, the Quadricycle. The vehicle had four large bicyclelike wheels, was steered with a system like that in a boat, and had two forward speeds.

urbs. His innovations created jobs and allowed for mobility on a scale never before known. Suddenly, distances between loved ones did not seem so great, and families could visit relatives or take summer vacations. Tourism became a major American industry. Weekend jaunts to the country became a popular pastime, whereas before, the farthest one could hope to travel in one trip was fifteen miles or so. Horses pulling wagons or carriages could not be expected to go farther than that.

It can be argued that the introduction of Ford's economical Model T had the greatest effect on the lives of women. Where once their lives centered around the home, if for no other reason than that they had no

This production assembly line puts together Ford's Model T, a car affordable enough for most Americans to own. AP IMAGES

means of transportation at their disposal, they now could travel conveniently. Rural women could visit their neighbors miles away without having to leave an entire afternoon open for the walk or horse ride. They could shop at their local merchants or venture farther to stores where selection and price were more consumer friendly. The car made women more visible in towns and society in general, giving them an independence and power they had never had.

Thanks to affordable cars, more people could attend colleges and universities, and hospitals were now more accessible. More cars meant the development and maintenance of new roads and **highways** that connected one region to the next. By the 1950s, interstate highways were built, connecting one end of the country to the other.

America was not the only producer of automobiles, but **World War II** (1939–45) bombs had destroyed factories in Japan. Recovery was

Henry Ford

The world of industry was forever changed in 1913, the year Henry Ford invented the assembly line. As is often the case with inventions, one might wonder why it took so long for anyone to come up with the idea of the assembly line. It is a logical way to build something.

Henry Ford was born July 30, 1863, in Michigan. Although he was born into a farming family, he showed an early interest in all things mechanical. He left home at the age of sixteen to work as an apprentice (student assistant) for a machinist in Detroit. In 1888, he married and supported his family by running a sawmill.

Ford took a job with the Edison Illuminating Company in Detroit in 1891. He began as an engineer and was promoted to chief engineer just two years later. During this time, he began spending his free hours experimenting with internal combustion engines. In 1896, he invented the Quadricycle. This vehicle had four large bicyclelike wheels, was steered with a system like that in a boat, and had two forward speeds.

Pleased with his progress, Ford established the Ford Motor Company in 1903. He was the company's vice president and chief engineer. Ford introduced the Model T car five years later. Only two or three cars were made each day at the Ford plant. Small groups of men would work on each car using components purchased from outside manufacturers. It was not an efficient way to build vehicles.

The Model T changed the way America lived. Ford's cars were selling faster than he could build them, so he moved his factory to a bigger plant in the Detroit suburb of Highland Park in 1910.

Ford was the first industrialist to manufacture interchangeable and standardized parts. He eventually made many models of automobiles, but many of the parts in each model were the same as those in other models. By making one part to fit all cars, Ford was able to lower the cost of his autos, thus making them more affordable for more consumers.

In keeping with that efficient spirit, Ford invented the assembly line. Workers stood in one place while a moving belt carried each car along. Every worker was responsible for incorporating one part onto the automobile. Parts were delivered to each worker by a carefully timed conveyor belt so that assembly was smooth and efficient. Again, this invention allowed Ford to lower the cost of his cars because it now took less time to assemble each one. Soon, he was the largest car manufacturer in the world.

slow, but Japan produced 1,070 passenger cars in 1949. Throughout the **Korean War** (1950–53), Japan served as a supply depot for United Nations troops—just as the major U.S. automakers had done during World War II. They manufactured trucks for them, and in addition, produced 1,594 cars in 1950. In 1955, automobile production increased to 20,220, still not enough to pose a threat to America.

Japanese automobile companies realized that most Asians could not afford vehicles, and if they wanted to stay in business, they would need to export. In 1957, Toyota sold 288 cars in the United States. The following year was better, with sales at 821. Nissan also chose to export and sold 1,131 cars and 179 trucks in 1959; another 1,294 cars and 346 trucks sold the following year. In the mid-1960s, Nissan and Toyota bought some of the smaller Japanese manufacturers, and Mitsubishi partnered with Isuzu.

Japanese autos were not the only exports to the United States; German cars, led by Volkswagen, outsold Japanese vehicles throughout the 1960s and into the 1970s. In fact, Volkswagen opened the first foreign-owned U.S. auto manufacturing plant in 1978 (and closed in 1987 due to increasing Japanese presence). Regardless of where the cars were made, all the exports were compact. America, meanwhile, continued to produce larger cars. This proved to be its downfall. When gas prices skyrocketed in 1973, Americans demanded more fuel-efficient cars. In 1975, 695,000 Japanese cars were sold in the United States, and sales only increased for the remainder of the decade. In 1980, Japan manufactured 7 million automobiles compared to 6.4 million produced by the United States. Nearly 2 million of those cars were exported, and for the first time, Japanese car production exceeded that of America and became the number one manufacturer in the entire world.

In the last decade of the twentieth century, automobile companies turned to innovation in hopes of revitalizing the market. Automakers developed the sport utility vehicle (SUV), a lighter type of truck that could be driven on and off the road. As the end of the first decade of the twenty-first century approached, high gas prices forced automakers to reduce SUV and truck production in favor of smaller, less gas-guzzling cars.

In 2006, Toyota continued to be the industry leader in manufacturing, followed by General Motors (once the largest U.S. corporation), Ford, Volkswagen, and Honda.

Aviation

The **Wright Brothers**—Wilbur (1867–1912) and Orville (1871–1948)—were the first men to successfully fly an airplane. They did it in Kitty Hawk, **North Carolina**, on December 17, 1903. They flew 120 feet (37 meters) in twelve seconds. The brief flight was the result of years of experimentation, research, and sheer determination. And it was the dawn of mechanical flight.

Before the Wright brothers took to the air in their powered airplane, the only means of air transportation was the hot air balloon. The first human flight in a balloon took place in Paris, France, in 1783. Ballooning became a favorite pastime in Europe in the late eighteenth century, but those balloons were not steerable, so passengers were at the mercy of the weather and wind. Gliders followed, and then the Wright brothers made their famous first airplane flight. They used the research and experiments of their predecessors to build the first aircraft that could sustain flight.

Military aviation

Airplanes proved a major asset in time of war. Bulgaria was the first country to use airplanes for military service, in the First Balkan War (1912–13). Both sides fighting in **World War I** (1914–18) relied heavily upon airplanes as weapons. In 1914, the French attached a machine gun to the front of one of their planes, thus allowing aircraft to shoot at one another. Pilots of such planes were known as aces, and they were publicized as modern-day knights. One German ace, Manfred von Richthofen (1892–1918), became known as the Red Baron. He shot down eighty planes in air-to-air combat.

Technological advancements led to improved aircraft for use in **World War II** (1939–45). This era of advancements is known as the Golden Age, and it was during this time that **Amelia Earhart** (1897–1937) became the first woman aviator to cross the Atlantic Ocean on a solo flight. The zeppelin, a hydrogen-filled airship, named *Hindenburg* crashed and burned in **New Jersey** in 1937, killing thirty-five people and bringing an end to the airship.

One of the most impressive achievements of the Golden Age was the development of instrument flight, for which aviator Jimmy Doolittle (1896–1993) is credited. He was the first pilot to use nothing but instruments to guide him in taking off, flying, and landing. Prior to that, aviators relied on sight.

Aircraft production increased during World War II, and a German aviator flew the first jet plane in 1939. Germany also led the way in developing the first cruise missile, ballistic missile, and manned rocket. By the end of the war, America had produced more than 160,000 aircraft of various types.

Commercial aviation

Once World War II ended, military aircraft were used to transport people and goods. Soon many airlines were established, with routes that crossed North America and other continents. The first American airliner took to the skies in 1949. In 1956, the Boeing 707 was introduced, raising the level of comfort, speed, and safety. As passengers began to consider flying as commonplace as driving a car, the military continued making progress in aviation technology. The sound barrier was broken in October 1947, and soon the **space race** was in full swing as America and the Soviet Union competed to be the leader in space exploration.

The space race resulted in the first men landing on the moon. American astronauts Neil Armstrong (1930–) and Buzz Aldrin (1930–) made their lunar landing in 1969, the same year Boeing announced its 747, the largest aircraft ever to fly. Even in the first decade of the twenty-first century, the 747 is one of the largest planes, and it transports millions of passengers each year.

Britain unveiled the first supersonic passenger airplane in 1976. The Concorde remained in service for twenty-seven years before it was retired. It remains an icon of success for the aviation industry.

Modern aviation

The Federal Aviation Act was passed in 1958, thereby establishing the Federal Aviation Administration (FAA). The major roles of the FAA include regulating U.S. commercial space transportation and civil aviation, promoting safety, and encouraging new aviation technology. One of the FAA's first tasks was to develop an air traffic control system to prevent in-air collisions.

The industry was deregulated throughout the 1980s, which resulted in an influx of smaller airlines and the merging of larger airlines. In order to compete, airlines dropped their ticket prices in the 1990s as the number of cities served increased.

After the **September 11, 2001, terrorist attacks**, airline security became top priority as regulations were tightened and strict airport security procedures were implemented.

Axis

The Axis powers were the countries that unified against the Allied coalition (which included Poland, Great Britain, France, and, later, the United States and the Soviet Union) in **World War II** (1939–45). Germany, Japan, and Italy were the founding powers of the Axis alliance. Later it included Bulgaria, Romania, Slovakia, and Hungary, among others. Military planning was led by German dictator Adolf Hitler (1889–1945), Italian dictator Benito Mussolini (1883–1945), and Prime Minister Hideki Tojo (1884–1948) of Japan.

The Axis powers concentrated efforts to conquer territory in two parts of the world. Germany led efforts in Europe while Japan led efforts in the Pacific. This strategy forced the Allied troops to split their resources between two areas of the world. At the height of their expansion, the Axis powers dominated large parts of Europe, Africa, Asia, and the Pacific Ocean. In the end, however, they were completely defeated by the **Allies**.

The Axis alliance began to evolve in 1936 when Italy and Germany signed a pact of friendship. The term *axis* stems from a statement Mussolini made at the time that all of Europe would revolve around the Rome-Berlin axis resulting from the friendship. The Tripartite Treaty that officially established the Axis powers as a military threat was signed by Germany, Italy, and Japan on September 27, 1940. The three countries wanted to build empires and establish a new world order. The treaty recognized a sphere of interest for each country and contained promises that they would help each other attain their economic, political, and military goals. Other countries later joined the Axis efforts.

The Axis powers were defeated in World War II. In a twist of politics, Italy's Mussolini was imprisoned, and Italy entered into a pact with the Allies in September 1943. Germany continued to fight intensively until it was pushed back across Europe. It surrendered unconditionally on May 7, 1945. The Allies, however, continued to fight in the Pacific arena against Japan until August 1945. Japan surrendered only after the United States dropped the **atomic bomb** on the cities of Hiroshima and Nagasaki.

B

Baby Boom Generation

After **World War II** (1939–45), American soldiers returned home from their victory ready to take advantage of a prosperous economy. Whereas the economic depression of the 1930s led to a drop in marriage and birth rates, the 1940s told a different story. There were nearly 2.3 million marriages in 1946, an increase of more than six hundred thousand over 1945. This was the first year of what became known as the baby boom, which lasted throughout most of the 1950s and into the early 1960s. Between 1948 and 1953, more babies were born than had been over the previous thirty years. Those born between 1946 and 1964 are called baby boomers.

The U.S. population increased from 150 million in 1950 to 179 million in 1960. This was the largest ten-year increase in population to date. By the middle of the next decade, baby boomers themselves reached childbearing age and birthrates again increased.

Effects

By 1958, children aged fifteen and younger comprised almost one-third of the American population. Toy sales that year capped at $1.25 billion, and diaper services were a $50-million enterprise. Many businesses profited from the baby boom, including school furniture companies, car manufacturers, home builders, even road and highway construction and paving companies. The **suburbanization** of America, in which large areas of homes were built on the outer edges of a city, developed at an amazing rate as growing families increased the demand for housing outside urban areas.

Baby boomers were the first generation to be raised with televisions in their homes. This technology gave boomers a sense of generational identity not available to those who came before them. Boomers' lives have been defined by events such as Woodstock (a rock music festival that took place in Woodstock, **New York**, in 1969), the **Vietnam War** (1954–75) and the accompanying **antiwar movement**, the assassination of President **John F. Kennedy** (1917–1963; served 1961–63), the **civil rights movement**, and experimental use of recreational drugs and alcohol.

"Overcrowding" is a term directly related to the baby boom generation. First it was the maternity wards of hospitals, which had a difficult time keeping pace with the upsurge of births. As boomers grew, schools became overcrowded. The 1950s and 1960s also saw an increase in the number of children and young adults entering the juvenile justice system. The term "juvenile delinquent" was given to those who did not fit into the societal norms, and juvenile institutions filled to overflowing. By the 1970s, colleges and universities experienced twice the number of students entering as in the previous generation. As boomers graduated, the job market became saturated, and graduates had trouble finding jobs in their fields. By the 1990s, housing prices skyrocketed as boomers reached middle age and thus began to settle down. Owning a home—a big home, if possible—was part of that goal.

The drastic increase in population placed a burden on education, healthcare, and other social service systems in the United States. Larger sums of public money were required to maintain these systems and keep them running smoothly. According to the U.S. Census Bureau, 330 baby boomers turned sixty every hour throughout the year 2006.

The first baby boomer filed for early retirement in October 2007, thus becoming the first to begin collecting Social Security. Social Security is a government system into which workers pay a certain amount, depending on their income level. In return, they can collect monthly payments once they retire and until they die.

Bacon's Rebellion

In the spring of 1676, Nathaniel Bacon Jr. (1647–1676) led a revolt against the governor of **Virginia** and local Indian tribes. Over the course of months, events unfolded into a significant uprising known as Bacon's

Rebellion. The immediate events that sparked the rebellion concerned a political disagreement between Governor William Berkeley (1606–1677) and Bacon, who was a member of Berkeley's council. It remains uncertain what other factors caused Bacon to take such drastic actions.

Unfolding of events

During the summer of 1675, there were several Indian raids against the colonists of Virginia. When a group of Virginians took revenge by murdering some Indians, the tribes increased their attacks. Governor Berkeley refrained from sending troops to counter the attacks and opted instead to build a chain of forts along the frontier.

A group of angry planters persuaded Bacon to lead a band of volunteers against the Indians, aggressive and friendly alike. Bacon petitioned the governor for a commission to organize the volunteers. Afraid of a full-scale war, the governor declined and warned Bacon that further action would define him as a rebel.

Governor Berkeley's warnings went unheeded, and in May 1676 Bacon set off with a force of three hundred men to the southern frontier. There they slaughtered and plundered a friendly tribe. Governor Berkeley declared Bacon a rebel for his actions and demanded that he be captured.

Bacon was imprisoned temporarily. He confessed his error and received a pardon from the governor. Days later, he slipped back to his home. He returned to the government in June with five hundred armed men. He forced Berkeley and the **House of Burgesses** (Virginia's legislative body) to grant him a formal commission to fight the Indians.

When Governor Berkeley attempted to raise forces to assert his own authority, Bacon turned on him. Civil war ensued. Berkeley was driven to the eastern shore of Virginia, leaving Bacon in charge of the western border. Bacon proceeded against another friendly tribe as Governor Berkeley took control of the capital, **Jamestown**. When Bacon arrived in Jamestown in September with six hundred men, he forced the governor's retreat and burned the town. A little more than a month later, Bacon suddenly fell ill and died. Governor Berkeley was able to return to confront Bacon's forces and suppress the rebellion. By February 1677, Governor Berkeley had reestablished his authority over Virginia.

In January 1677, royal commissioners (justices conducting an investigation on behalf of England) and one thousand English troops arrived in Virginia to investigate the uprising and to restore order. They arrived with royal pardons for the rebels, but Governor Berkeley rejected them. He ordered the execution of twenty-three rebels. The commissioners viewed the governor's actions as cruel, and they removed him from his post. Berkeley returned to England in May to defend himself but died before seeing the king.

Aggravating factors

While historians argue over the exact causes of Bacon's Rebellion, a few factors are considered to be particularly important. Virginia was a rapidly growing, but unstable, society at the time. Competition for political and social positions increased in the midst of such instability.

Social instability was further complicated by a slow economy. Overproduction of inferior **tobacco** and high taxes led to financial difficulties and hardships. Governor Berkeley's leadership was ineffective, and many were generally dissatisfied with the government. The known disagreement between Berkeley and Bacon over the governor's Indian policy was probably exaggerated by each of these factors.

Banking Crisis of 1933

A nationwide panic ensued in 1933 when bank customers descended upon banks to withdraw their assets, only to be turned away because of a shortage of cash and credit. The United States was in the throes of the **Great Depression** (1929–41), a time when the economy worsened, businesses failed, and workers lost their jobs. Bank customers did not have the benefit of government protection during the panic. The crisis led to government reform to protect bank deposits.

President Hoover and the Great Depression

The Great Depression began in October 1929, when the value of stocks traded on the stock market in New York fell tremendously. In only a few weeks, investors lost a sum of money that approached the national cost of fighting **World War I** (1914–18). At the time, banks opened as they always had, five weekdays plus Saturday mornings. Despite the severity of the stock market crash, within months political leaders announced brightly that the country was recovering and business was healthy. Financial panics in the past had usually come and gone quickly after speculators absorbed their losses. This time, however, the economy did not recover quickly.

In 1932, President **Herbert Hoover** (1874–1964; served 1929–33) took steps to improve the economy. He created the Reconstruction Finance Corporation, a government project for lending billions of dollars to various enterprises, including banks. The injection of money did not help enough. Shantytowns of tin and wood spread across the country and became known as **Hoovervilles**. Homeless people on park benches tried to keep warm with newspapers, known as Hoover blankets.

Bank runs

When depositors rushed to withdraw their money from a bank, the incident was called a bank run. Bank runs were spurred by fears that banks would go bankrupt, taking the savings of depositors with them. The mere hint of a bank closing often was enough to send depositors scrambling to withdraw their money. This resulted in banks, which do not keep enough cash on hand to cover all of their deposits, often collapsing.

Bank runs had serious effects because of unsound banking practices. During the 1920s, many banks had not acted in a responsible fashion. Some had lent money for poor investments. Others extended dangerously large credit to financial speculators. When the stock market crashed, many banks saw their assets evaporate. Creditors who had lent money to the banks liquidated what remained, and individual depositors were left with nothing.

Because few companies in the 1920s provided pensions for workers, many used the banks as a place to deposit a lifetime's worth of savings in anticipation of retirement. When the banks went under, many of these people, old and unable to work, lost everything. More than fourteen hundred banks collapsed in 1932, taking with them $725 million in deposits. The public scrutinized the remaining banks. At the first sign of trouble, a run on the banks occurred, and the banks usually ended up closing, many permanently.

President Franklin D. Roosevelt had numerous "fireside chats," or radio broadcasts, with the American public to try and reassure people that banking was safe.
AP IMAGES

Bank holidays

By March 1933, before President **Franklin D. Roosevelt** (1882–1945; served 1933–45) took office, about nine million people had lost their savings. It was clear that some action was necessary. State after state declared banking "holidays" that month, briefly closing local banks to prevent nervous depositors from creating bank failures with bank runs.

The day after his inauguration, President Roosevelt called Congress into a special session and announced a four-day nationwide banking holiday. While the banks were closed, the president introduced the Emergency Banking Act of 1933, which Congress passed the same day. During this bank closure, many people ran short of cash. In an era before credit cards, people without hard currency were unable to purchase groceries or attend public events.

These short-term and relatively minor hardships were offset by the fact that the federal banking holiday worked. In his first radio "fireside chat," broadcast three days after the banks were closed, President Roosevelt reassured the public that the banks had been made safe. The president's personal charm and his fondness for decisive action were apparent in this first **New Deal** success. The New Deal was a series of legislative and administrative programs initiated by President Roosevelt as a way to combat the effects of the Great Depression. Within the month, banking deposits had grown by more than a billion dollars.

The Pecora investigation

While the Roosevelt administration was busy restoring public confidence in banks, Congress was punishing bankers for old violations of the public trust. In 1933 and 1934, sensational hearings were held that detailed theft and fraud on the part of many bankers and other members of the business community. This introduced the term "bankster" to the cultural vocabulary.

The Senate Banking and Currency Committee, led by appointed New York legal counsel Ferdinand Pecora (1882–1971), revealed that the brokerage house of Lee, Higginson, and Company had defrauded the public of $100 million. National City Bank head Charles E. Mitchell (1877–1955), with a salary of $1.2 million, paid no income tax and had issued $25 million in Peruvian bonds that he knew to be worthless. Former secretary of the treasury Andrew Mellon (1855–1937) and banker **J. P. Morgan** (1837–1913) had also managed to avoid taxes, and twenty of Morgan's partners had paid no taxes in 1931 and 1932.

Throughout the hearings, the public was introduced to such Wall Street tactics as selling short, pooling agreements, influence peddling, insider trading, and the wash sale. By using such techniques, traders artificially inflated the worth of their stocks or gained financial advantage over other traders. National City Bank, for example, took bad loans, repackaged them as bonds, and sold them to unwary investors. Although such actions were technically legal, many viewed them as unethical and immoral, and the public reputation of bankers and financial businesspeople fell to a new low.

Banking regulation: the FDIC

The first reform to result from the Pecora investigation was the Glass-Steagall Act of 1933. It was a law sponsored by U.S. senator Carter Glass (1858–1946) of **Virginia** and U.S. representative Henry Steagall (1873–1943) of

Senator Carter Glass sponsored the Glass-Steagall Banking Act, which regulated many of the unstable practices that led to the Great Depression. AP IMAGES

Alabama amid a rash of bank failures. The law regulated many of the unsound practices that contributed to the Great Depression, including making it illegal for banks to deal in stocks and bonds.

The act created the Federal Deposit Insurance Corporation (FDIC) to insure small depositors against the loss of their savings if a bank went under. The FDIC initially guaranteed deposits to a maximum of $5,000.

Bataan Death March

During **World War II** (1939–45), the United States had to fight battles in two parts of the world. German troops were aggressively taking over Europe while Japanese troops were seizing control of the Pacific Islands and China. As a result, American troops and resources were spread between the two places. Most American attention, however, was focused first in Europe. U.S. troops in the Pacific faced battles with fewer resources and little backup.

U.S. troops trapped

Soon after the attack on the **Pearl Harbor** naval station in **Hawaii** in December 1941, American troops were fighting to defend an airfield in the Philippines. By the end of December, the American and Filipino forces were forced to retreat to the Bataan peninsula. By February, the Japanese attack had been defeated. The Japanese, however, had cornered the American troops with their backs to the sea. A large blockade isolated the Philippine Islands, preventing the Americans from escaping and receiving supplies. As a result, food, medicine, and ammunition ran dangerously low. Soldiers were starving and suffering from malaria and dysentery.

After four months of holding the Japanese back without additional resources, the American troops were seriously weakened. On April 3, 1942, the Japanese attacked again. This time they easily cut through American defenses. On April 9, more than seventy thousand American and Filipino soldiers surrendered. It was the largest American army ever to surrender.

Prosecuted for war crimes

The Japanese brutality that followed was eventually judged a war crime. The starving and sick troops were forced to walk over sixty miles to the prisoner of war camp. It is now known as the Bataan Death March, because it is estimated that between five thousand and ten thousand men did not survive the march. Intense heat, little food or water, and random acts of violence caused their deaths. Some managed to escape, but for the fifty-four thousand who made it to Camp O'Donnell, the brutality of the march was only the beginning.

Battle of Antietam

The Battle of Antietam was an American **Civil War** (1861–65) battle that happened along Antietam Creek near Sharpsburg, **Maryland**, on September 17, 1862. Confederate general **Robert E. Lee** (1807–1870) had undertaken an invasion of the North. He hoped to gain the loyalty of people in Maryland and boost the strength of the **Confederate States of America** (or Southern) cause in the border state. He also hoped to lure federal troops away from **Virginia** to relieve the area temporarily from the ravages of war. Lee's advance north was a great threat to the **Union** and its capital, **Washington, D.C.** Union general George B. McClellan (1826–1885) learned of some of Lee's plans and pursued the Confederates.

On the night of September 13, Lee heard that McClellan had learned of his plans. Rather than retreating in the face of an army twice as big as his, Lee decided to face the federal troops, so he paused in Sharpsburg. McClellan advanced on the evening of September 16 and carefully moved his men into position.

The battle that ensued the following day marked the bloodiest single day of the war. McClellan launched a series of uncoordinated attacks on three sectors of Lee's forces. The Confederate forces were pushed back but avoided complete disaster with the arrival of troops from Harper's Ferry, Virginia (now part of **West Virginia**) under Confederate general A. P. Hill (1825–1865). Fighting only paused with the dark of night.

On the following day, Lee stood fast, but McClellan did not renew his attack. Lee recognized that a renewed attack was futile and so ordered a retreat to Virginia. His troops withdrew across the Potomac River on September 19. McClellan's forces were badly crippled as well, so he decided not to pursue Lee's forces.

The battle's dead, wounded, and missing totaled over twelve thousand for each side. The battle, however, is remembered for more than its casualties. Many historians regard it as the turning point of the war. The stunning victory by the Union provided U.S. president **Abraham Lincoln** (1809–1865; served 1861–65) with military progress for which he had been waiting.

Lincoln followed the victory with an announcement of his **Emancipation Proclamation**. The proclamation declared freedom for slaves in the rebelling states. It changed the war from a political crusade to preserve the Union into a crusade to free the slaves and end **slavery**. The addition of a moral element to the North's cause impassioned supporters, made it a difficult war to abandon, and swung foreign support to the Union's side. All of this contributed to the eventual Union victory.

Battle of Bunker Hill

The Battle of Bunker Hill was fought on June 17, 1775. It was the first major battle of the **American Revolution** (1775–83). It is also called the Battle of Breed's Hill for the actual site of the clash.

The Battle of Bunker Hill had its roots in the colonial siege of Boston, **Massachusetts**. In an effort to get British soldiers out of the area, the colonists took control of the city. When they learned of a British plan to use troops to regain control, the colonists acted to stop them. Nearly fifteen hundred troops marched to Charlestown, just across the Charles River from Boston. There they embedded themselves on Breed's Hill, just below Bunker Hill, in the dark of night.

War Slogans

The Battle of Bunker Hill is the source of the famous war slogan, "Don't shoot [or fire] until you see the whites of their eyes." Historians debate who was the speaker of the command. Some say it was American General Israel Putnam (1718–1790), while others say it was Putnam's second-in-command, Colonel William Prescott (1726–1795). It also could have been an unidentified person lost in history.

Barriers saved colonists

When the British discovered the colonists, they set out to displace them with an army of twenty-two hundred men. The colonists, however, were well protected behind barriers they had made. The colonists successfully defended themselves during two of the three British advances. During the first two, the British suffered great losses. During the third advance, the colonists were running out of ammunition and retreated.

The colonists suffered approximately 450 soldiers captured, wounded, or killed. Though the British pushed back the rebelling colonists, they suffered nearly 1,000 casualties, about half of their army. The British claimed victory, but the great number of casualties gave the colonists encouragement to continue fighting for their cause.

Battle of Gettysburg

The Battle of Gettysburg is one of the most famous events of the American **Civil War** (1861–65). It took place from July 1 to July 3, 1863, in Gettysburg, **Pennsylvania**. Gettysburg is about thirty miles south of the state capital of Harrisburg. The battle was part of the attempt by the army of the **Confederate States of America** to invade the northern states and discourage **Union** support. The clash at Gettysburg was the deadliest of the war. Union victory ended the Confederate march north, forcing its army to retreat.

Confederate general George E. Pickett's charge during the Battle of Gettysburg in 1863. The Union victory at Gettysburg is considered by many as a major turning point in the American Civil War. HULTON ARCHIVE/GETTY IMAGES

By May 1863, the Confederate Army had defeated the Union Army in several important battles. The Northern population was growing more dissatisfied with the lack of Union progress, and a peace movement was growing. The Southern population, particularly in **Virginia** where most of the fighting occurred, was struggling to support the armies. Essential provisions like food were running low.

A bold strategy

Hoping to relieve Virginia from his armies, find provisions in the fields of Pennsylvania, and stir up antiwar sentiment in the North, Confederate general **Robert E. Lee** (1807–1870) decided to invade the North and perhaps capture Harrisburg. His troops numbered seventy-five thousand men organized into three corps.

Union troops met the Confederate invasion at Gettysburg on July 1, 1863. Nearly ninety thousand troops under the leadership of Union general George C. Meade (1815–1872) fought bitterly for three days to block the Confederate march. With great losses on both sides, General Lee retreated to Virginia on July 4. His army was severely weakened, with more than twenty thousand captured, wounded, or killed. The Union Army suffered approximately twenty-three thousand similar losses.

The Battle of Gettysburg was a major Union victory and is often considered the turning point of the Civil War. Though General Meade was criticized for not pursuing Lee's army in its retreat, Meade's army earned praise for its success in stopping the invasion.

Battle of Iwo Jima

Iwo Jima is an island in Japan's Volcano Islands, 750 miles (1,207 kilometers) south of Tokyo. During **World War II** (1939–45), its location was of strategic importance, and it became the site of a bitter battle between American and Japanese forces in February 1945.

By early 1945, the American campaign in the Pacific had pushed the Japanese back from their aggressive takeover of many islands. The Americans were close enough to begin attacking Japan itself, but the

Japanese base on Iwo Jima was able to detect the American bombers on their way to Japan, providing warning of approaching raids. The base on Iwo Jima was also able to launch planes that harassed the American bombers.

The capture of Iwo Jima became more important to the Americans. Under Lieutenant General Holland M. "Howlin' Mad" Smith (1882–1967), American marines mounted an attack to seize the island. The Japanese, however, were very well protected. Miles of tunnels, rocky volcanic terrain, and twenty thousand soldiers made the Japanese position difficult to overcome.

On February 16, 1945, American forces assaulted the island defenses from the air and the sea. Three days later, marines landed on the beaches. After four days, the American marines held the most terrain, but the Japanese were well entrenched and fought strongly. American forces secured the island on March 17, but resistance did not end for another nine days.

The battle left nearly five thousand Americans and twenty thousand Japanese dead. Many more were wounded. American control of Iwo Jima proved to be immensely important in the American push to end the war with Japan. Controlling a safe place for airplanes and troops so close to Japan allowed the Americans to be more aggressive and helped to force a Japanese surrender by August.

The Photograph and the Monument

The Battle of Iwo Jima quickly became symbolic of the strength and determination that the soldiers possessed to protect American liberty and freedom, regardless of the cost. Associated Press photographer Joe Rosenthal (1911–2006) captured the moment in an unforgettable picture that showed the emotion of the hard-fought victory. On February 23, 1945, after days of bitter fighting, thousands of American soldiers paused to watch forty marines scale Mount Suribachi to plunge an **American flag** into the volcanic rim. To protect the first-raised flag from souvenir hunters, it was replaced three hours later during a second flag raising. Rosenthal's memorable moment captured this raising as six soldiers, five marines, and a naval corpsman planted an immense, 8 x 4.5-foot flag. More than sixty years later, the photograph remains inspirational and meaningful to the American public.

On November 10, 1954, the Marine Corps Memorial was unveiled near Arlington, **Virginia**. At its heart is an immense bronze sculpture inspired by Rosenthal's photograph. Designed by Felix de Weldon (1907–2003), the Iwo Jima Monument rises 110 feet from the ground and weighs one hundred tons.

Battle of Lexington and Concord

The Battle of Lexington and Concord was the first battle of the **American Revolution** (1775–83). It was fought in the towns of Lexington and Concord, **Massachusetts**, and the roads in between on April 19, 1775.

The Battle of Lexington and Concord was the first battle of the American Revolution and considered a victory for American colonists. AP IMAGES

In the years leading up to the war, Great Britain had imposed a series of laws that displeased the colonists. In 1774, the colonists gathered in the First Continental Congress to explore how to react to Britain's colonial policies. (See **Continental Congress, First**.) The Congress and various colonial communities passed resolutions telling Great Britain that they would not continue to accept British policies unchallenged.

In 1775, Great Britain prepared to respond to possible rebellion in America. Ministers in London imposed embargoes on (blocked) the shipment of arms and ammunition to America. General Thomas Gage (1721–1787), who was governor of Massachusetts and commander-in-chief of British forces in America, made plans to seize gunpowder supplies held by the colonists.

Midnight rides

After nightfall on April 18, 1775, Lieutenant Colonel Francis Smith (1723–1791) and Major John Pitcairn (1722–1775) assembled British troops in boats at their fort in Boston to cross Boston Harbor. Their destination was a colonial gunpowder storage in Concord. Colonists monitoring British movements saw the British troops, triggering the famous midnight warning rides of men like **Paul Revere** (1735–1818) and William Dawes (1745–1799) to assemble colonial forces.

As Smith's men marched on a road toward Lexington, Smith realized the colonists were aware of their movements. He sent a message back to Gage asking for reinforcements while sending Pitcairn ahead with a small force of men to take control of a bridge over the Concord River.

Pitcairn and his men reached Lexington in the early morning hours of April 19, 1775. A group of colonial militia men led by Captain John Parker (1729–1775) was assembled on the village green, off the main road. Pitcairn diverted his men to the green, where they fired on the colonists, killing eight and wounding ten more. According to an account by American printer Isaiah Thomas (1770–1802) published on May 3, 1775, the colonists were dispersing as ordered by the British when the British fired on them.

The British troops continued to Concord to destroy the gunpowder supplies. They arrived around eight o'clock in the morning. The colonists had managed to remove some of their supplies to safety. After destroying some supplies, flour stores, and buildings, the British retreated toward Lexington around noon as a crowd of four hundred militiamen approached. The British suffered many casualties throughout the day as they marched through Lexington back to Charleston, Massachusetts, where they crossed the bay back to Boston. Colonial militiamen hiding along the road fired upon the British during the retreat.

At the end of the day, the British had 273 casualties out of 1,800 men who had been involved in the day's activities. American casualties totaled 95 men. Americans considered it an early victory in what became a war for independence.

Battle of Midway

The Battle of Midway was a naval battle between Japan and the United States during **World War II** (1939–45). It occurred around the atoll (island) of Midway, in the central Pacific Ocean, from June 3 to 6, 1942. It is remembered as an astonishing American victory that marked a turning point in the war in the Pacific.

Until the Battle of Midway, the Japanese fleet had great successes. It caused great damage to the American naval force and conquered islands across the Pacific with little challenge. When the Japanese decided to take Midway from American occupation, they were confident of another victory.

Japanese admiral Isoroku Yamamoto (1884–1943) assembled the largest fleet ever put together by the Japanese navy. There were 185 warships, including 4 aircraft carriers. Part of the fleet was deployed to the Aleutian Islands, southwest of the **Alaska** mainland, to strike American forces there. The bulk of the fleet spread out to move with stealth toward Midway.

The Japanese intended to make a surprise attack, but American intelligence learned of the plans. Because they had cracked certain Japanese codes, the Americans were able to learn where, when, and in what strength the Japanese forces would appear. With little notice and immense effort, the American fleet prepared to meet the greater Japanese fleet. Although they were outnumbered, the Americans carried the advantage of surprise.

The battle began on June 3 when American bombers took off from Midway and attacked the approaching Japanese. They caused no significant damage. The following morning, unaware that the American fleet was present, the Japanese admiral sent only half of his planes out to attack. The Americans launched all of their planes and, while suffering significant losses, managed to slow the Japanese attack considerably.

Before Japan could launch a second air attack, the Americans countered with an air attack on the Japanese carriers. No direct hits were made, but they managed to force the carriers to scatter to avoid the attacks.

During the raids, the Japanese learned of the American fleet's presence. Admiral Yamamoto called all planes to return for refueling and rearming. In the process, the carriers' decks were littered with fuel and bombs. Another wave of American planes arrived when the ships were highly flammable, and the Americans easily sank three Japanese carriers. The fourth Japanese carrier escaped to inflict crippling damage to a U.S. carrier, but it also was disabled and sunk the following day.

On June 5, the Japanese began to retreat. Further scuffles brought more losses to both sides over the next two days, but most of the damage was complete. The Japanese fleet had lost four carriers and its aircraft. Unlike the industrially prepared United States, Japan could not recover quickly from the losses. As a result, the superior Japanese fleet was severely weakened and lost the advantage in the Pacific Ocean. The Battle of Midway was an important victory that enabled the American forces to begin pushing the Japanese back from their aggressive occupations.

Battle of the Bulge

On December 16, 1944, the German army mounted a surprise attack on Allied forces in **World War II** (1939–45). Now known as the Battle of the Bulge, it was the last desperate offensive made by the Germans. Though the element of surprise initially gave the advantage to the German army, the Allied troops managed to regain ground and force a German retreat by the end of January 1945.

Nazis hoped to divide Allies

By December 1944, the plan to conquer Europe launched five years earlier by Nazi German leader Adolf Hitler (1889–1945) was losing on all fronts. From Italy, France, and the Soviet Union, Hitler's armies were being forced back to Germany. To prevent an Allied invasion of the homeland along the western border, Hitler organized a surprise attack. Hoping to split the **Allies**, he planned to push them back, capture Antwerp, and thus be in a position to negotiate peace. With few men available for such an attack, Hitler assembled his remaining reserves and relied on surprise to accomplish his goals. They secretly gathered more than two hundred thousand men and twelve hundred tanks near the Ardennes region of Belgium and Luxembourg, where the Allied presence was weakest.

The German forces waited for the weather to worsen to prevent Allied air support. On December 16, snow and fog presented the ideal opportunity to strike. German armies attacked along a sixty-mile front of the Allied lines. They drove forward hoping to separate the Allied armies. With the Allied armies being pushed back in this region, a bulge of German pressure formed in the Allied front. This bulge of German presence into the Ardennes region gives the battle its name.

December skies cleared

The German army had some success, including the capture of Bastogne and the isolation of some American troops. The weather cleared on December 23, however, enabling Allied planes to attack the Germans and to drop supplies to Allied ground forces. Though the battle began to turn at this point to favor the Allied counteroffensive, it would not end quickly. Bitter fighting continued until January 28, when the last of the bulge was eliminated and the Allied forces had recovered all the ground lost.

The Battle of the Bulge is remembered as the last major German offensive. It was a large-scale attack that left many casualties on all sides. Over six hundred thousand Americans were involved in the fighting, and nearly ninety thousand were captured, wounded, or killed. The Germans had nearly eighty-five thousand similar casualties. Hitler used the very last of his reserves in the offensive. Germany was severely weakened and fell to Allied forces just a few months later.

Battle of Little Bighorn
See **Custer's Last Stand**

Battles of Bull Run

During the American **Civil War** (1861–65), only one hundred miles separated the Confederate capital of Richmond, **Virginia**, from the **Union** capital of **Washington, D.C.** There were many violent encounters between the two sides within this stretch of land during the war, including two Battles of Bull Run. Bull Run is the name of a small stream near the site of the battles. Manassas, Virginia, was the closest town, so the battles are also called the Battles of Manassas.

The First Battle of Bull Run

The First Battle of Bull Run (Manassas) took place on July 21, 1861. It was the first major battle of the Civil War. Although the war had started in **South Carolina** in April, the two sides had only engaged in small skirmishes before Bull Run. Public opinion, however, called for greater action. The Union army was still gathering volunteers and trying to train its men, but President **Abraham Lincoln** (1809–1865; served 1861–65) faced pressure to suppress the rebellion. Under orders from Lincoln, Union general Irvin McDowell (1818–1885), who was posted near the nation's capital with thirty-five thousand men, advanced southward.

Two forces from the **Confederate States of America** waited to the south in Virginia. General Pierre Beauregard (1818–1893) had nearly twenty-two thousand men in his command along the line of Bull Run Creek, across the main highways to Washington. General Joseph E. Johnston (1807–1891) had nearly twelve thousand posted nearby in the Shenandoah Valley. When the Confederates became aware of the attack, they gathered along Bull Run Creek. General Johnston and his forces arrived to support General Beauregard on July 20, 1861, despite Union attempts to interfere with Beauregard's movement.

Union general McDowell attacked the Confederate forces on the morning of July 21. At first, his well-planned assault drove the Confederates back. The continuing arrival of fresh men from General Johnston's troops, however, gave the Confederates an advantage. The Union began a retreat. Though orderly at first, the retreat gave way to confusion when a bridge was destroyed. As Union troops continued to retreat to Washington, the Confederates abandoned their pursuit at Centreville, Virginia. They were too exhausted and disorganized to persist.

While the Confederates seemed to win the battle, it proved to be indecisive, like so many Civil War clashes. Neither the North nor the South won a great advantage, but many men lost their lives. A total of nearly 900 were killed (481 Union, 387 Confederate) and 2,500 wounded (1,011 Union, 1,582 Confederate). Over 1,000 were reported missing (1,216 Union, 12 Confederate). The battle foreshadowed the brutal toll that the Civil War would take.

The Second Battle of Bull Run

The Second Battle of Bull Run occurred in the same area as the first one, near Manassas, Virginia. The battle took place from August 29 to August 30, 1862, following the siege of Richmond by the Union. Confederate general **Robert E. Lee** (1807–1870) intended to shift the battles to the north towards Washington, D.C., to relieve pressure on Richmond.

Confederate soldiers launched a successful series of attacks on the Union troops, who were under the direction of Major General John Pope (1822–1892) of Virginia. Forcing a retreat back to Washington, the Confederates improved their position for an invasion into **Maryland**. The cost was high for both sides. The Union army had 1,747 killed, 8,452 wounded, and 4,263 missing or captured. The Confederates had 1,553 killed, 7,812 wounded, and 109 missing. General Pope was relieved of his command to hold him responsible for the defeat.

Bay of Pigs
See **Cuban Missile Crisis**

Beat Movement

The Beats were writers who formed an artistic protest movement from 1950 to 1959. Declaring themselves nonconformists, this small group of poets and novelists had a great deal of influence on the culture of their day. They became American antiheroes.

Who they were and what they did

The term "beat" has never been clearly defined. **Jack Kerouac** (1922–1969), largely considered the leader of the Beat Movement, is said to have coined the term Beat Generation when he said that he and his friends were beaten down in frustration at the difficulty of individual expression at a time when most artists were conforming to society. On another occasion, Kerouac said "beat" was derived from "beatific," suggesting the Beats had earned intellectual grace through the purity of their lives.

Other prominent members of the movement were Allen Ginsberg (1926–1997), William S. Burroughs (1914–1997), and Neal Cassady (1926–1968). They inspired each other to turn away from materialism to lead lives of adventure in search of meaning, and proposed that others follow their lead. In reality, the movement was very much an experiment with controlled substances, characterized by rampant drug and alcohol abuse and a fascination with the criminal world, especially drug dealers. A drunken Burroughs accidentally killed his second wife while trying to shoot a glass off her head. In another incident, Kerouac and Burroughs were charged as criminal accessories after Lucien Carr, a member of the Beat circle, killed a man, possibly in self-defense, who was obsessed with him.

Media attention

Life magazine covered the Beat Movement closely, describing the Beats in 1959 as "sick little bums" who were unwashed, uneducated, unmotivated, and unprincipled. The magazine helped establish the stereotype of the beatnik as a character who wears a goatee, sandals, blue jeans, and a dirty sweatshirt and answers to the name "Daddy-o." Beat women, called chicks, were depicted wearing black leotards, short skirts, heavy black eyeliner, and pale lipstick. As depicted in the media, beatniks hung around in coffeehouses, listening to jazz, and "hip" and "far out" were the catchphrases of the day. Many Americans saw the Beat influence as a threat, fearing it would spread from the East Coast and San Francisco into the heartland.

Prominent member of the Beat movement Allen Ginsberg reads poetry to a crowd. Ginsberg's book Howl *became one of the top-selling volumes of American poetry ever published.* AP IMAGES

Beat writing

The literary establishment was as critical of the Beats' writing as the popular media was of their attitudes. Many dismissed Beat writing as immature and uninteresting. Literary historians generally regard poet Ginsberg as the most credible figure of the movement. Unlike other Beats, he graduated from college and therefore had a literary tradition on which to draw. He wrote just one book during the Beat heyday, but it became the cornerstone of the movement. *Howl*, with its famous first line, "I saw the best minds of my generation destroyed by madness, starving hysterical naked, " was published in 1956 by Lawrence Ferlinghetti (1919–), a San Francisco publisher.

The book was soon banned for obscenity, and Ferlinghetti was arrested for printing obscene material. The media pounced on the trial, bringing Ginsberg's lament over the state of American culture into the spotlight. By the time Ferlinghetti was acquitted and the ban lifted, ten thousand copies of Ginsberg's book had sold. By 1980, more than a quarter million had sold. *Howl* remains one of the top-selling volumes of American poetry ever published and a major influence on American poetry.

Kerouac is arguably the most popular of the Beat writers. His novel *On the Road* (1957) became the definitive statement of Beat principles. Published just one month after the *Howl* obscenity trial, *On the Road* gained popularity through incessant media coverage of the Beat Movement. In the novel, characters based on the author, Ginsberg, and Cassady take a road trip in search of the meaning of life. It struck a chord with students of the era who wondered what life after college would hold.

Cassady was a key figure not for his own writing but for the influence he had on other Beats, who admired his wildness and spontaneity. Raised in the slums of Denver, **Colorado**, by fifteen a prostitute and petty thief, he met Kerouac in 1945 and began traveling with him. Their travels were the basis of Kerouac's *On the Road*, which turned Cassady into a symbol of Beat virtue.

Burroughs was considered by the others as more of a father figure. He published his first novel, *Junkie,* in 1953, at a time when he felt his life unraveling. His drug abuse problem, in fact, turned into a lifelong heroin addiction. The novel that brought him fame was published in 1959 in France. *Naked Lunch*, written in experimental style, was not published in America until 1962. The work was highly controversial for its use of sensitive material and obscene language. The book was banned in many regions; in a censorship trial in 1966, the book was found not to violate any obscenity statutes.

End of an era

By the late 1950s, the Beats had done and said what they had set out to do. Kerouac eventually faded from the literary scene. He died in 1969, at the age of forty-seven, from internal bleeding brought on by cirrhosis of the liver, a disease associated with alcoholism. Ginsberg broadened his horizons and remained a key figure in the avant-garde movement of the 1960s and 1970s. He died in 1997, at age seventy, of liver cancer brought on by hepatitis, a disease usually caused by drug and alcohol use. Burroughs continued to write and died at the age of eighty-three from a heart attack. Cassady became the unofficial mascot of the hippie movement of the 1960s. He died in Mexico at the age of forty-one of mysterious causes.

Beatlemania

The most influential and famous musical group to emerge in the 1960s was a quartet from Liverpool, England, known as the Beatles. Members included John Lennon (1940–1980), Paul McCartney (1942–), George Harrison (1943–2001), and Ringo Starr (1940–). The band's first recording was the tune "Love Me Do," and it was released in Britain in October 1962. By 1963, the Beatles were a sensation in England and adoring fans followed them everywhere. In early 1964, all of their one-night performances had to be cancelled due to rioting.

The Beatles first visited America on February 8, 1964, to appear on the popular television variety program *The Ed Sullivan Show.* Seventy million viewers tuned in, and a new record was set for the most-watched television appearance. It helped that America's media publicized the event. Magazines and newspapers carried photographs, reports, and in-depth articles chronicling the lives of the band nicknamed the Fab Four.

The Beatles took America by storm. Seemingly overnight, teenage boys were sporting long hair just like the Beatles, and teenage girls plastered their bedroom walls with posters and magazine pages of their favorite Beatle. Concerts sold out in record time, and police were required to keep the frenzy of female fans under control; it was not uncommon for hysterical teens to faint during a concert. In both Britain and America, Beatles tunes such as "I Want to Hold Your Hand" sold millions of copies, and the sound of the group could be heard in nearly every household that included teenagers.

While teens across the country raised the Beatles to a godlike status, parents and other adults feared the influence the Fab Four wielded over the younger generation. John Lennon did not help dispel the idea that his band's music was an evil influence when he made the comment that the Beatles were more popular than Jesus. That one statement led to record-burning throughout the nation, and adults were more determined than ever to squash Beatlemania.

The Beatles were an unstoppable force throughout the 1960s, however. Their cross-country tour in 1964 only cemented their place in American culture, as did the five movies they made, the most popular of which were *A Hard Day's Night* and *Help!* Their appeal lay in more than just their music. For millions of young people, the Beatles represented freedom from authority and convention. Each member was charismatic, and together, they were irresistible to a young America that was embroiled in the unpopular **Vietnam War** (1954–75). The Beatles, their music, and their charm provided American youth a much-needed escape from the harsh realities of the era.

The Beatles stopped touring in August of 1966. They focused exclusively on recording in the studio. In 1970, the Beatles broke up, and members began to pursue solo projects and careers.

Alexander Graham Bell

Alexander Graham Bell is remembered as the inventor of the telephone. He was also an outstanding teacher of the deaf, an inventor of many other devices, and a leading figure in the scientific community. Bell invented the graphophone, the first sound recorder, as well as the photophone, which transmitted speech by light rays. Among his other innovations were the audiometer, a device used to measure hearing; the induction balance, used to locate metallic objects in the human body; and disc and cylindrical wax recorders for phonographs.

Early life

Bell was born in 1847 in Edinburgh, Scotland, to a family of eminent speech educators and musicians. His father, Alexander Melville Bell, taught speech to the hearing and speech impaired and wrote textbooks on correct speech. Bell's mother was a portrait painter and an accomplished musician.

Bell received his early education at home. He graduated at age fourteen from the Royal High School in Edinburgh. Bell then enrolled as a student teacher at Weston House, a nearby boys' school, where he taught music and speech and, in return, received instruction in other subjects.

Experiments with harmonic telegraph

Bell's father had invented "visible" speech, a code of symbols for all spoken sounds that was used to teach deaf people to speak. Bell studied at Edinburgh University in 1864 and assisted his father at University College, London, from 1868 to 1870. During these years, he became deeply interested in the study of sound, especially as it affects hearing and speech. Bell followed this interest throughout his life, inspired in part by the acoustic experiments of German physicist Hermann von Helmholtz (1821–1894), which gave Bell the idea of telegraphing speech.

Inventor Alexander Graham Bell was a prominent figure in the scientific community. U.S. NATIONAL AERONAUTICS AND SPACE ADMINISTRATION

Bell's interest in speech and communication led him to investigate the transmission of sound over wires. With financial assistance from Gardiner Hubbard and Thomas Sanders, grateful fathers of two of his deaf pupils, Bell experimented with developing the harmonic telegraph, a device that could send multiple messages at the same time over a single wire. Using vibrating membranes and an actual human ear in his tests, Bell also investigated the possibility of transmitting the human voice by wire.

Invention of the telephone

Early in 1874, after having emigrated to the United States a few years earlier, Bell met Thomas A. Watson (1854–1934), a young machinist and technician with expertise in electrical engineering. Watson became Bell's indispensable assistant and the two spent substantial time together experimenting with transmitting sound.

In the summer of 1874, Bell developed the basic concept of the telephone using a varying but unbroken electric current to transmit the sound waves of human speech over a wire. At the urging of his financial backers, however, who were more interested in the potential of the harmonic telegraph, Bell did not pursue the telephone idea for several months. He resumed work on it in 1875 and, by September, began to write the required patent specifications.

Bell received his patent on March 7, 1876, and on March 10, the first official message transmitted by telephone passed from Bell to Watson in their workshop: "Mr. Watson, come here, I want you!"

Founds Bell Telephone

After a year of refining the new device, Watson and Bell, along with Hubbard and Sanders, formed the Bell Telephone Company in 1877. The Bell Company built the first long-distance line in 1884, connecting Boston and New York. Bell and others organized the American Telephone and Telegraph Company in 1885 to operate other long-distance lines. By 1889, when insulation was perfected, 11,000 miles of underground wires travelled through New York City.

Bell's claim to the invention of the telephone was challenged in more than six hundred lawsuits. The courts eventually approved Bell's patent, and the Bell Company's principal competitor, Western Union Telegraph, agreed to stay out of the telephone business. The Bell Company, in turn, ceased work on the telegraph. In 1899, with the sale of the Bell Company to a group of investors, Bell's financial future was secure and he could devote the rest of his life to working as an inventor.

Bell's later interests

The magazine *Science* (later the official organ of the American Association for the Advancement of Science) was founded in 1880 because of Bell's efforts. As National Geographic Society president from 1896 to 1904, Bell fostered the success of the society and its publications. In 1898, he became a regent of the Smithsonian Institution in **Washington, D.C.** He was also involved in sheep breeding, hydrodynamics (the dynamics of fluids in motion), and aviation projects.

Bell died in Nova Scotia, Canada, in 1922.

Irving Berlin

Irving Berlin was born Israel Baline in Temun, Siberia, on May 11, 1888. He fled with his family to **New York** in 1893 to escape the Russian persecution of Jews. Berlin's family settled in Manhattan's Lower East Side, a section of the city in which most Jewish immigrants resided.

Because his family was so poor, Berlin did not go to school but worked instead. He made money singing on street corners, and later he held a job as a singing waiter. It was during this period that he began writing songs. In 1907, he published "Marie from Sunny Italy" and signed his work I. Berlin. He would become famous with that last name.

The road to fame

Berlin held various odd jobs in the music industry in a neighborhood known as Tin Pan Alley. He eventually worked as a lyricist for music publisher Waterson & Snyder. His tune "Alexander's Ragtime Band" became an instant hit in 1911 and earned him the title King of Tin Pan Alley.

Berlin's musical talent was natural; he never received any formal training. He developed his style by playing only the black keys on the piano, so most of his early songs were written in the key of F-sharp.

Berlin was one of America's most successful songwriters by the 1920s. He began to stage his own music revues and comedies. Although he suffered through the **Great Depression** (1929–41) and lost his fortune like so many others, he managed to rebuild his career.

Although **Broadway** had been good to Berlin, he wanted to try his talents in Hollywood. He wrote the scores for many hit musical **movies**, including the 1942 musical *Holiday Inn*. One of his songs from that musical, "White Christmas," remains the best-selling song ever recorded, even in the twenty-first century.

Sound of a nation

Berlin's musical abilities bolstered the nation through two world wars. He wrote patriotic songs that kept hope alive during some of the most frightening and difficult times America had known. His most famous patriotic song, "God Bless America," was written during **World War I** (1914–18) but was sung in public for the first time in 1938.

Berlin was responsible for some of the most popular love songs of the twentieth century. By the time of his death on September 22, 1989, he had received numerous awards and become an icon of American popular music. His tunes helped shape the genre of pop music as he experimented with a variety of styles. More than that, however, Berlin became America's voice. Whether hopeful or fearful, he embodied a nation's collective soul and put its thoughts to music.

Bilingual Education

The United States has always been home to significant numbers of non-English speakers. Sometimes the language differences have been tolerated by English-speaking Americans, but not always. In the first half of

A little girl reads a book in Spanish in a dual language first grade classroom in Dodge City, Kansas. The city has the highest bilingual enrollment in the state. AP IMAGES

the nineteenth century, for example, the most prevalent language next to English was German. In the 1850s, bilingual schools (schools in which two languages were taught) teaching in German and English were operating in Baltimore, **Maryland**; Cincinnati and Cleveland, **Ohio**;

Indianapolis, **Indiana**; Milwaukee, **Wisconsin**; and St. Louis, **Missouri**. Similarly, **Louisiana**, with its large French-speaking population, allowed bilingual instruction in its schools. (See **New France**.) Several states in the Southwest had Spanish as well as English instruction. Hundreds of thousands of children in the United States were educated in a language other than English.

Anti-immigrant movement

Around 1900, anti-immigrant sentiments in the country increased. Several states passed laws against teaching in other languages. Immigrant children who did not speak English began to have a hard time in the public schools. In 1908, only 13 percent of the immigrant children enrolled in New York City schools at age twelve were likely to go on to high school, as opposed to 32 percent of native-born students. This trend was mirrored across the country as non-English-speaking immigrant children, not understanding the language spoken in their classrooms, fell further and further behind.

During **World War I** (1914–18), an intense wave of nationalism (pride and loyalty to one's own country, sometimes in an excessive way) swept the country. It reinforced the negative reaction of many Americans to the large number of immigrants entering the country. By 1925, thirty-seven states had passed laws requiring instruction in English regardless of the dominant language of the region. This opposition to bilingual education continued into the 1950s. Many children whose native language was not English received a very poor education in the public school system.

Federal government support

After the Cuban revolution of 1959, waves of Cubans fled to South **Florida**. Florida's Coral Way school district established the first state-supported program in decades to instruct students in Spanish, their native language, thereby easing their transition to English. The bilingual program provided all students, Anglo and Cuban, instruction in both Spanish and English with excellent results. With the success of the Coral Way project, state and local government involvement in language education became accepted.

The federal government soon took up the cause, starting with the **Civil Rights Act of 1964**, which prohibited discrimination in education, and the Elementary and Secondary Education Act of 1965, which funded schools and provided help for disadvantaged students. In 1968, after considerable debate, Congress passed a bill that amended (modified) the Elementary and Secondary Education Act. Under the amendment, the federal government would provide funding for bilingual education to school districts with a large proportion of non-English-speaking students who lived in poor neighborhoods. To receive funding, districts would be required to provide instruction in a student's native language until the child could demonstrate competence in English. The federal government put hundreds of millions of dollars into bilingual education programs nationwide by the mid-1970s.

Supreme Court support

In 1974, the **Supreme Court** gave its support to bilingual education in *Lau v. Nichols.* The ruling states that school districts with a substantial number of non-English-speaking students must take steps to overcome the students' language differences. After that ruling, the federal government was able to force school districts to initiate bilingual education plans. These *Lau* plans greatly expanded the number of bilingual programs across the country. They set standards to determine which students qualified for inclusion in a program and when they could be allowed (or forced) to exit. During this period, test scores repeatedly showed that non-English-speaking students who participated in well-designed bilingual programs consistently performed at the same level as their English-speaking classmates.

English immersion

None of the new acts or policies clearly addressed the goals of bilingual programs. Should the programs aim to send the student quickly back to regular English-language classes, or should they take a slower approach, allowing the student to maintain good grades and stay up to standard with his or her age level in school? Different programs addressed these questions in their own ways, and the lack of clarity contributed to a conflict that lasted into the 2000s. By the 1980s, a growing number of opponents of bilingual education believed that, rather than speeding immigrants into the English-speaking mainstream, bilingual education was causing them to hold onto their native languages and cultures. The critics considered this undesirable. Studies showed that some bilingual programs were allowing students to remain in bilingual classes longer than three years and were not teaching them sufficient English to function in mainstream classrooms. In the early 1980s, the federal government quietly withdrew its support for native-language instruction programs.

In 1984, the government began providing funding for English immersion programs—programs that placed non-English-speaking students in all-English classes, forcing them to learn English in a hurry or be left behind. Several studies in the mid-1980s showed that the performance of the limited-English students in the English immersion programs declined. Meanwhile, public attitudes in **California**, with its rapidly growing foreign-born population, became increasingly hostile to bilingual programs. In 1998, California adopted an English-only requirement for instruction in all its schools. **Arizona** and several other states followed.

Bilingual education remained controversial in the 2000s. Advocates contended that non-English-speaking children will receive little or no education unless they are taught in their own language during the years when they are first learning English. With a poor start due to language difference, students are much more likely to drop out of school and consequently face low-paying jobs and poverty in the future. Opponents argue that students in bilingual programs may not be motivated to learn English as well as they should and will therefore not be able to secure good jobs later in life. They argue that the government should not use its funds to help non-native people preserve their cultures in the United States.

Bill of Rights

The **Constitution** of the United States of America is the document that created the federal government. The first ten amendments, or changes, to the Constitution are known as the Bill of Rights. The Bill of Rights was inspired by suggestions from members of the state legislatures that approved the Constitution in 1788.

The first ten amendments to the Constitution, known as the Bill of Rights, contain rights and freedoms that the U.S. government must not violate. MPI/HULTON ARCHIVE/GETTY IMAGES

Concerns about the Constitution

The Constitution was written by the **Constitutional Convention** in Philadelphia, **Pennsylvania**, in 1787. The Convention contained delegates from twelve of the original **thirteen colonies**, later states. The delegates gathered at the Convention to improve the national government that existed under an agreement called the **Articles of Confederation**, which had been adopted in 1781.

After writing the Constitution through the summer of 1787, the Convention delegates sent it to the thirteen states for ratification, or approval. The Constitution stated that it would become effective upon ratification by at least nine states. The Constitution had strong support from influential politicians who wanted the United States to have a powerful central government. These people were known as Federalists; they were members of the **Federalist Party**.

Many Americans had great concerns about creating a strong federal government. Called **Anti-Federalists**, these people preferred that state governments have more power than the national government. While the Anti-Federalists objected to several parts of the Constitution, they focused their opposition on the absence of a bill of rights. In doing so, they hoped to gather enough popular opposition to prevent the Constitution from being ratified by the states.

A bill of rights is a document that specifies the rights of citizens that cannot be violated by a government. A bill of rights was not a new idea in 1787. Several states had a bill of rights in their state constitutions, including the **Virginia** Declaration of Rights and the **Massachusetts** Bill of Rights. There were older examples from English history: the **Magna Carta** (1215), the Petition of Right (1628), and the Bill of Rights (1689). Supporters of the idea found inspiration in the writings of philosophers John Locke (1632–1704), John Milton (1608–1674), and Thomas Paine (1737–1809).

Most Federalists either did not believe or were not too concerned that basic rights could be violated by the government set forth in the Constitution. They pursued the ratification of the Constitution as written by the Constitutional Convention, without a bill of rights. As the state conventions met to discuss ratification after the summer of 1787, however, it became apparent that the Anti-Federalists had mustered support for the notion of a bill of rights.

To convince the Anti-Federalist delegates to vote for ratification, the Federalists agreed to seek a federal bill of rights. As the state conventions began to approve the Constitution, they proposed more than one hundred amendments for the protection of individual liberties. By the time the Constitution was ratified by the required nine states in 1788, it was obvious that a bill of rights would have to be adopted.

Writing a bill of rights

The first U.S. House of Representatives assembled early in April 1789 with the Federalists in control of the government. (See **Legislative Branch**.) **James Madison** (1751–1836), a Federalist and the primary author of the Constitution, assumed leadership for creating a bill of rights. His personal plan was to write a bill of rights that would appease the Anti-Federalists without detracting from the powers of the federal government.

On June 8, 1789, Madison proposed that the House begin consideration of eight resolutions on amendments to the Constitution. The amendments were sent to a committee of ten members, including Madison, on July 21. Eventually the committee recommended a total of fourteen amendments to be considered by the full House of Representatives. After lengthy debate, the House voted that the amendments should not be written into the existing Constitution but should be added as a supplement. On August 24, the House proposed seventeen amendments to be sent to the Senate for its consideration.

The Senate began its debate the following week. Senate concerns prevented the passage of the amendments, so a committee of three U.S. senators and three U.S. congressmen gathered in September. They worked out a compromise agreement consisting of twelve amendments. Both the Senate and the House of Representatives passed the amendments and forwarded them to President **George Washington** (1732–1799; served 1789–97) to be sent to the states for ratification.

The original Constitution provides that amendments do not become effective unless ratified by at least three-fourths of the states. Two of the twelve amendments proposed by Congress in 1789 failed to be ratified, but the required number of states approved the other ten amendments by December 15, 1791.

The Bill of Rights

The Bill of Rights contains rights and freedoms that the government of the United States is not supposed to violate. The freedoms of religion, speech, the press, and assembly (the right to gather in a group) are set forth in the **First Amendment**. The **Second Amendment** protects the right to bear arms. The **Third Amendment** prevents the government from forcing a homeowner to house a soldier during peacetime against the owner's consent. The **Fourth Amendment** prohibits the government from conducting unreasonable searches and seizures of people and their property. The protection of life, liberty, and property also appears in the **Fifth Amendment**.

The right to fair treatment in legal cases against a citizen appears in the **Fifth Amendment**, **Sixth Amendment**, **Seventh Amendment**, and **Eighth Amendment**. The **Ninth Amendment** says the provision of specific rights in the Constitution does not imply the denial of other rights. Finally, the **Tenth Amendment** says governmental power not given to the federal government by the Constitution is retained by the states and the people.

The Bill of Rights is a popular and controversial part of the Constitution. Many citizens celebrate it as the bedrock of freedom in America. Other citizens believe federal power has grown stronger than the rights and freedoms that the Bill of Rights is supposed to protect. Important **Supreme Court** decisions often depend on the interpretation of the Bill of Rights. More than two centuries after its adoption, the Bill of Rights retains an important role in drawing the line between fair and unfair government actions and between the rights of citizens as individuals and as collective members of a society.

Birmingham Baptist Church Bombing

During the **civil rights movement** of the 1950s and 1960s, the Sixteenth Street Baptist Church in Birmingham, **Alabama**, served as an organizing center for rallies and marches for racial desegregation, the process of ending the enforced separation of blacks and whites in public places. Many renowned civil rights leaders, such as Fred L. Shuttlesworth (1922–), Dick Gregory (1932–), **Ralph Abernathy** (1926–1990), and **Martin Luther King Jr.** (1929–1968), used the church as their headquarters at one time or another.

Birmingham was a seat of white resistance to desegregation. The city's public safety commissioner, T. Eugene "Bull" Connor (1897–1973), was extremely hostile to the civil rights movement and scorned federal orders to integrate his city. Governor George Wallace (1919–1998) of Alabama was a strong segregationist as well and had vowed to disobey federal court orders to desegregate the schools. The **Ku Klux Klan**, a national white supremacy organization known for its use of violence, intimidation, and terrorism, was very strong in Birmingham.

Birmingham Sunday

On September 15, 1963, four hundred African Americans gathered to worship at the Sixteenth Street Baptist Church. Just a few days earlier, the courts had ordered the Birmingham schools to be desegregated, and tensions between white segregationists and blacks were high. (See

Desegregation of Public Schools.) Four girls—Cynthia Wesley, Carole Robertson, and Addie Mae Collins, each of them age fourteen, and Denise McNair, age eleven—were in the basement of the church when a bomb exploded, killing them instantly. Others in the church were seriously injured. That same day, two white Eagle Scouts shot at two black boys on a bicycle, killing the thirteen-year-old riding on the handlebars. Worried about black reprisals for the bombing, Governor Wallace ordered three hundred state troopers to patrol Birmingham. That evening, an officer shot and killed a fleeing black man.

King spoke at a joint funeral for three of the girls, urging African Americans to keep up their struggle for equality despite the murders. Eight thousand people gathered for the funeral, some of whom were white. No Birmingham city officials attended.

Slow justice

The **Federal Bureau of Investigation** (FBI) quickly began to examine four suspects in the bombing, Robert Chambliss (1904–1985), Bobby Frank Cherry (1930–2004), Thomas Blanton, and Herman Cash. All were white supremacists (people who believe that white people are superior to other races). Cherry was an expert with explosives and had been seen placing the bomb in the church. Chambliss was charged with murder and possessing dynamite without a permit. He was found not guilty of murder and received a six-month jail sentence for having the dynamite. The FBI did not bother to provide the prosecution with the ample evidence it had uncovered of the four men's connection to the bombing. FBI director **J. Edgar Hoover** (1895–1972), explained that he did not believe it was a worthwhile pursuit because a local jury would never convict these men of murder. The FBI dropped its own investigation.

The case was reopened in the 1970s. Using the evidence on hand, Chambliss, at the age of seventy-three, was tried and convicted of first-degree murder in the bombing. He went to prison in 1977 and died there in 1985. Another of the suspects, Cash, died in 1994. In 2000, thirty-seven years after the bombing, Blanton and Cherry were finally brought to trial for their part in the murders. Cherry had been bragging about it for years. Both men were convicted of murder and sentenced to life in prison. Cherry died in prison in 2004.

Birmingham Protests

In the early 1960s, Birmingham, **Alabama**, had a rocky history concerning race relations. The city had a population of 340,000 people, 40 percent of whom were African American, and it was reputed to be the most

The Birmingham protests were among the largest ever launched during the civil rights movement. AP IMAGES

segregated city in the United States. (Segregation is the enforced separation of blacks and whites in public places.) In 1961, the freedom riders, a group of activists bent on achieving desegregation on buses and in bus stations across the South, had been violently attacked there. (See **Freedom Rides**.) More than fifty unsolved bombings had earned the city the nickname of "Bombingham" among southern blacks. Despite the danger, in 1963 civil rights leaders decided to fight the city's racist policies.

One of the great leaders of the **civil rights movement** in Birmingham was the outspoken Baptist minister Fred L. Shuttlesworth (1922–). When the Alabama legislature outlawed the **National Association for the Advancement of Colored People** (NAACP) in the state in 1956, Shuttlesworth organized the Alabama Christian Movement for Human Rights (ACMHR). It had grown to be the largest civil rights organization in the state. Realizing that local activism was not strong enough to overcome Birmingham's racial problems, in late 1962 Shuttlesworth invited the renowned nonviolent civil rights leader **Martin Luther King Jr.** (1929–1968) to come to Birmingham to lead an all-out campaign to confront the city's segregation and economic discrimination.

King knew that segregation was unlikely to be defeated in the South without a greater degree of involvement by the federal government. He believed a well-publicized campaign in Birmingham could be the means to force President **John F. Kennedy** (1917–1963; served 1961–63) and his administration to take an active role in protecting the rights of African Americans. King and Shuttlesworth began planning.

"Bull" Connor

Politics in the city of Birmingham delayed the protest. Birmingham's commissioner of public safety, the staunchly segregationist T. Eugene "Bull" Connor (1897–1973), controlled Birmingham's fire and police departments and dominated the city government. He had embarrassed many prominent citizens of the city with his refusal to go along with court-ordered desegregation. Connor was running for mayor in March 1963, and many hoped he would lose. King decided to postpone the Birmingham protests until the elections were over, not wanting to provoke racial tensions that could strengthen Connor's campaign. Connor lost the election.

Rev. Ralph Abernathy, left, and Rev. Martin Luther King Jr. being arrested in Birmingham, Alabama, on April 12, 1963. AP IMAGES

Demonstrations begin

On April 3, King's **Southern Christian Leadership Council** (SCLC) and the ACMHR began a large-scale, nonviolent campaign of protest marked by a **sit-in movement** (demonstrations in which protestors would sit down and refuse to move), marches, and a well-organized economic boycott (refusal to do business) against downtown businesses. But even though he was voted out of office, Connor would not step down as public safety commissioner without a fight; as the protests began, he filed a lawsuit to remain in his job. Although the Alabama Supreme Court eventually ruled against Connor (on May 22, 1963), the short-term result was a confusing situation in which Connor was left in control of Birmingham's law enforcement.

The Birmingham protests were among the largest ever launched during the civil rights movement; they continued for sixty-five days and nights. One week after they began, Connor obtained an injunction, or order, from the state court against further demonstrations. King openly defied the injunction.

"Letter from a Birmingham Jail"

On April 12, police arrested King and a number of other demonstrators. While he was in jail, a newspaper published a letter from clergymen that questioned his timing for the protest and his defiance of the injunction. In response, King wrote his famous "Letter from a Birmingham Jail." Originally penciled in the margin of a newspaper, the letter became a classic expression of the moral injustice of segregation and the urgency of the civil rights movement.

King was released after eight days, but more demonstrators went to jail. In early May, running short of adult protesters, King encouraged children from the public schools to demonstrate. Up until this time, Connor had been fairly restrained in his handling of the protests. Infuriated by the continuation of the protests, he attempted to shut down the demonstrations by using greater force, including police dogs and fire hoses. At the peak of the demonstration on May 6 and 7, approximately two thousand protesters had been arrested, and the state fairgrounds had been pressed into service as a temporary jail.

Growing concern

By this time, Birmingham was the nation's leading news story. Photographs and films of protesters being attacked by dogs and blasted by fire hoses were being seen around the country and overseas. On May 7, some young blacks had vented their anger and frustration by battling with police and other whites in the downtown area. Many began to fear a major riot would erupt.

Birmingham's white and black leaders began serious talks. The Kennedy administration sent Assistant Attorney General Burke Marshall (1922–2003) to the city to pressure both sides to come to terms. During the final stages of negotiations, both the president and his brother, U.S. attorney general **Robert F. Kennedy** (1925–1968), kept in frequent contact with Marshall.

Finding agreement

On May 8, the demonstrations were suspended, and two days later a formal agreement was signed. Downtown merchants agreed to desegregate lunch counters, drinking fountains, and other facilities, and to hire at least some African Americans in clerical jobs. In addition, a permanent biracial committee (one with both black and white members) was to be established. Any demonstrators still in jail were to be released. The agreement occasioned a heated argument between King, who supported the terms, and Shuttlesworth, who thought the terms were too open to evasion. Segregationist extremists made a last-ditch attempt to disrupt the agreement by bombing the Gaston Motel, which had served as the protest's command center. Despite a night of rioting, the agreement held.

Impact

The "Battle of Birmingham" was one of the most dramatic confrontations of the civil rights movement. The newspaper and television pictures of nonviolent protesters—some of them no more than six years old—being bitten by police dogs or swept off their feet by high-pressure fire hoses provided the movement with some of its most powerful images. The violent images made thousands of Americans aware of the injustices African Americans faced in the Deep South. This made it easier for civil rights organizations to raise funds. The protests also inspired African Americans across the South; about two hundred communities organized similar campaigns in 1963.

Events in Birmingham also succeeded in achieving King's goal of promoting a greater federal role in eliminating segregation in the South. In an address in June 1963, President Kennedy called for a new civil rights bill. The landmark **Civil Rights Act of 1964** would not pass for another year, but much of its groundwork was laid by the events of 1963.

The agreement in Birmingham was a milestone, but within the city racial tension remained strong. Hostility to desegregation ended in tragedy on September 15, 1963, when a bomb was detonated by white supremacists at the Sixteenth Street Baptist Church, killing four African American girls (see **Birmingham Baptist Church Bombing**).

Black Codes

Black codes were laws passed immediately following the American **Civil War** (1861–65) by the former **Confederate States of America**. They were designed to prevent blacks from having the full rights of citizens and to restore, as much as possible, the labor and racial controls of **slavery**. The first black codes were passed in **South Carolina** and **Mississippi** in 1865, and they quickly appeared in other states throughout the South. Although they differed in form from each other, their aims were the same.

Before the Civil War, many states throughout the United States had laws that prevented blacks from enjoying the same rights as whites. By the end of the Civil War, much of that had changed in the North. This became increasingly true with America's adoption of the **Fourteenth Amendment** and **Fifteenth Amendments** of the **Constitution** in 1868 and 1870, which require equal protection under state laws and the right to vote, respectively.

The situation was quite different in the South. The emancipation of four million slaves dramatically affected southern white society. The system of slavery had empowered whites to keep blacks subordinate and had allowed the southern economy to thrive on the cheap labor of slavery. The system had been legalized by slave codes that defined the limited rights of blacks in the South.

With slavery abolished under the **Thirteenth Amendment** in 1865, the legal status of blacks became uncertain. Southern legislatures began to enact black codes based largely on the pre-existing slave codes. In many instances the black codes seemed to provide legal rights for newly freed slaves. They allowed blacks to marry, own property, negotiate contracts, and have limited participation in court proceedings against other blacks.

In reality, however, the black codes provided inferior rights and thereby ensured that southern blacks would remain subordinate to whites. The laws restricted where blacks could live and which trades they could practice. Many laws put limitations on labor contracts and property ownership, so blacks found themselves effectively slaves again to their employers or landlords. The punishments for breaking many of the laws were extremely harsh. Although many of the black codes attempted to mask racial intentions by avoiding the specific mention of race, they were obviously aimed at black southerners.

The black codes shocked many northerners and sparked concern about the effectiveness of reintegrating the southern states into the **Union**. The requirements for reintegration in the **Reconstruction** plan of President **Andrew Johnson** (1808–1875; served 1865–69) were easily met and demanded little change from the southern state governments. As a result, the enactment of black codes provoked conflict between the **executive branch** and **legislative branch** of the federal government for control of the process of Reconstruction.

The Republican Congress seized control of Reconstruction efforts and forced changes in policy. By requiring new constitutions and governments in the southern states, Congress managed to abolish some black codes. Congress passed legislation to protect the rights of freed slaves, including the **Civil Rights Act of 1866** and proposals for the Fourteenth and Fifteenth Amendments. Such legislation attempted to guarantee full citizenship and rights for blacks.

After Reconstruction, however, many of the racially discriminatory policies that shaped the black codes began to reappear. So-called **Jim Crow laws**, named for a character in a popular minstrel show, reintroduced similar inequality that resulted in black segregation and subordination until passage of the **Civil Rights Act of 1964**.

Black Friday

Black Friday is the nickname given to September 24, 1869. On that day, thousands of American investors lost their fortunes.

During the American **Civil War** (1861–65), the government attempted to keep the economy steady by issuing a large sum of money backed by nothing but credit. The American public understood that the plan after the war was to have the government buy back the "greenbacks," as they were called, with gold. The greenbacks that the government would buy back would be replaced with currency backed by gold.

Two men—stockbroker James Fisk (1834–1872) and financier **Jay Gould** (1836–1892)—did not want the government to rid itself of the gold. They hoped to buy up as much gold as possible and hold onto it while its value rose. When they could sell it at a profit, they would. The government's plan would ruin their scheme because it would put more gold on the market, which would force the value down.

Gould was smart enough to know he could not convince President **Ulysses S. Grant** (1822–1885; served 1869–77) to do what he wanted on his own, so he and Fisk befriended financier Abel Rathbone Corbin (1808–1881), Grant's brother-in-law. Together, the three men approached the president, who gave no clear response to their proposal. Gould and Fisk were encouraged that the president even took the time to speak with them, so they kept at their plan. Corbin knew the assistant treasurer of the United States, Daniel Butterfield (1831–1901), who agreed to let Fisk and Gould know when the government was ready to sell gold.

All seemed to be going according to plan, but Grant became suspicious of his brother-in-law's unusual interest in the gold market. He happened upon a letter written by his sister to his wife, and in the letter was an explanation of Gould's scheme. Grant, furious that he had been conned by family, contacted Corbin and ordered him to stop the plan. He then ordered the sale of $4 million in government gold.

Gould and Fisk began buying as much gold as they could on September 20, 1869. They watched gleefully as the value soared. On September 24, the price of an ounce of gold peaked at $162.50. But when the $4 million worth of government gold hit the market, people panicked at the prospect of their own gold losing value, and they attempted to sell their gold while the price remained high. Within fifteen minutes the price of gold dropped to $133 per ounce. Investors could not get rid of their gold fast enough, and many men lost their fortunes in what became known as Black Friday. Railway stocks lost nearly all their value, and businesses across the nation were left paralyzed.

Black Panther Party

The Black Panther Party, originally called the Black Panther Party for Self-Defense, was founded by Bobby Seale (1937–) and Huey P. Newton (1942–1989) in October 1966 in Oakland, **California**. Seale and Newton began working together as students at Merritt Community College, where they successfully fought for a black studies curriculum. Having carefully researched California gun laws, they established armed Black Panther patrols to curb police brutality.

On April 1, 1967, police killed an unarmed black man in a town near Oakland. The man's family came to the Black Panther Party for assistance. Organizing armed street rallies and confronting the local sheriff, the Panthers mobilized massive support. When a bill was introduced to the state legislature that would make it illegal for the Panthers to carry their arms in public, the group took its protest right into the capitol building in Sacramento. Images of members of the Black Panther Party at the capitol with their black berets, powder-blue shirts, black leather jackets, and large guns shocked Americans across the nation.

Stokely Carmichael, a Black Panther prime minister, gives a rousing speech to an attentive university campus crowd. AP IMAGES

Growing membership

The strategy of armed self-defense attracted many frustrated blacks to the party, particularly impoverished African Americans living in cities. Many were followers of **Malcolm X** (1925–1965), who had strongly questioned the nonviolent tactics of the **civil rights movement**. Malcolm X called for black nationalism, or the promotion of a distinct black identity, as opposed to integration into white society.

Eldridge Cleaver (1935–1998), the author of a widely read book of prison essays called *Soul on Ice* (1967), joined the group in its early days. He was soon followed by **Student Nonviolent Coordinating Committee** (SNCC) activist Kathleen Neal Cleaver (1945–), whom he married in 1967. When Newton was arrested in October 1967 following a confrontation in which a police officer was killed, the Cleavers stepped into leadership positions in the party, traveling coast to coast to gather support for the "Free Huey" campaign. (Newton was convicted of murder in 1968 but acquitted on a technicality in 1970.) Eldridge Cleaver, who had spent nine years in prison for attempted murder, had a gift for attracting media attention and was largely responsible for the growth of the party over the next several years. About forty chapter offices opened throughout the United States, and the Black Panther Party grew to more than five thousand full-time members.

Black Panther philosophy

The Black Panthers identified themselves as part of an international struggle to overthrow capitalism (free-market economic systems, such as those in the United States and most of Europe, in which individuals and companies compete for their own economic gain with little governmental interference). They were self-proclaimed Marxists, people who professed the ideas of nineteenth-century socialist philosopher Karl Marx (1818–1883), who believed that all of history was a struggle between the working classes and the wealthy.

An extremely powerful influence on the Panthers was the writing of black Caribbean revolutionary psychologist Frantz Fanon (1925–1961), who had played an important role in the struggle for Algerian independence from France. From Fanon, the Panthers derived their belief that black Americans' history and culture had been dominated, distorted, and nearly destroyed by whites. They believed the white "colonizers" imposed their own culture and system of values on blacks, a conquered people. The Panthers believed that the solution was to reeducate blacks to their true cultural identity—a process of empowerment best undertaken by separating from white society.

From the start, the Black Panther program emphasized social needs. The party provided free direct services to the poor and disabled, including breakfast for children, testing for disease, ambulance services, shoes, escorts for senior citizens, and legal aid. The Black Panthers' Intercommunal Youth Institute, a school, was honored by the governor of California for providing the highest level of elementary education in the state.

Because their revolutionary goals went beyond the interests of African Americans, the Panthers built coalitions with many nonblack organizations. They were the only major black organization to endorse gay and lesbian rights in the early 1970s. Further, they established official diplomatic relations with a number of revolutionary governments internationally, including Algeria, China, Cuba, and Vietnam.

SNCC merges with the Panthers

By 1967, many SNCC members were frustrated with the slow pace of the well-known group's nonviolent protest methods. In February 1968, the Black Panthers and SNCC announced that the two groups would merge. **Stokely Carmichael** (1941–1998), a leader of SNCC, was named Black Panther prime minister. The union was brief and controversial. Cleaver and Carmichael were soon arguing about the place of whites in the movement; Cleaver criticized Carmichael's "paranoid fear" of whites. In August, SNCC officially disassociated itself from the Black Panthers.

FBI targets the Panthers

The U.S. government saw the activities of the Black Panthers as a serious threat. **J. Edgar Hoover** (1895–1972), the director of the **Federal Bureau of Investigation** (FBI), ranked the Black Panther Party as the number-one threat to American security and made the group a target of COINTELPRO (the Counter Intelligence Program), an FBI program that investigated and, if possible, disrupted radical political organizations within the United States. FBI agents went undercover, joining the Panthers for the purpose of causing as much trouble as they could from within the group. Police also raided Panther offices. The FBI operation leveled against the Panthers resulted in divisions within the party, shootouts between Panthers and police, arrests, and killings of key Panther leaders.

Ultimately, internal division and constant police raids brought about the end of the Black Panther Party. The group had played a dramatic role in the struggle for racial equality and justice at a time when the tactics of nonviolent civil disobedience were faltering. By organizing poor and alienated blacks into a powerful political movement, the Black Panther Party transformed the face of urban politics.

Black Power Movement

The black power movement became a force among African Americans around 1965. It was so diverse and loosely coordinated, it is almost impossible to define. Although white Americans tended to interpret the "black power" slogan as a call to racial violence, blacks most often understood it as a call for racial pride and the achievement of political and economic power.

Frustrations in the mid-1960s

In the mid-1960s, the African American **civil rights movement** had seen many successes. Nonetheless, some activists were frustrated with the slow pace of change. They heard the call of the revered civil rights leader **Martin Luther King Jr.** (1929–1968) to remain nonviolent in the face of brutality, but they were not convinced that sit-ins (see **Sit-in Movement**), marches, and **Freedom Rides** were the answer.

The nonviolent civil rights movement of 1954–65 had produced expectations that were difficult to fulfill. Blacks could enter restaurants, but many lacked the money to pay for a meal. Blacks could vote, but they had not gained the power to improve their lives through the political system. Many civil rights activists began to respond to the words of African American leader **Malcolm X** (1925–1965), who believed that African Americans should remain separate from the white population because, in his view, American society was—and always would be—racist.

SNCC and black power

The **Student Nonviolent Coordinating Committee** (SNCC; pronounced "snick") was founded upon nonviolent principles in 1960 by student activists who were committed to confronting American racism and segregation. Operating in the most oppressive areas of the South and facing constant danger, dedicated SNCC workers were celebrated for their courage in the face of white intimidation in the early 1960s. By 1965, they were frustrated with the federal government's failure to protect their rights, and they faced continuing racism and economic and political inequality. That year, the SNCC gave up its nonviolent methods and its goals of organizing southern communities. It adopted instead the philosophy of black power promoted by SNCC leaders **Stokely**

Stokely Carmichael was an influential figure in the black power movement, which promoted racial pride as well as political and economic success within the black community. AP IMAGES

Carmichael (also known as Kwame Turé; 1941–1998) and H. Rap Brown (later known as Jamal Al-Amin; 1943–).

At that point, the SNCC voted to exclude whites from important positions. The organization increasingly pushed for withdrawing from the American mainstream and forming a separate black society. From its offices in Atlanta, the organization churned out "black power" bumper stickers depicting a lunging black panther and history pamphlets that stressed the teachings of Malcolm X. This turn toward militancy created tension between the SNCC and some of the veteran civil rights leaders.

The Black Panthers and beyond

The most aggressive wing of the black power movement was the **Black Panther Party** for Self-Defense, organized in 1966. The Panthers carried loaded firearms to public appearances and considered themselves at war with the white power structure. By the end of the decade, the militant party had considerable support, especially among young African Americans. For a short time, the Black Panthers and the SNCC merged.

The Panthers were only one among many activist groups. While some black power groups called for their own black nation in Africa, others wanted to establish a new homeland in the United States. The majority of black power groups tried to create black communities in which African Americans controlled their own economic and political destinies and took pride in their own history and culture.

What is "black power"?

Carmichael popularized the term "black power" in 1965. He defined black power many times, and not always in the same way, but the general idea was that African Americans had the right to define and organize themselves as they saw fit and to protect themselves from racial violence. The term was disconcerting to moderate African American leaders, who feared it would provoke hostility among whites and undo their progress in civil rights. The term did, in fact, terrify many mainstream whites, who interpreted the term to mean African American domination and possibly even race war rather than simply black empowerment.

"Black power" was a political slogan, but it also denoted a cultural movement. African Americans emphasized their enhanced sense of pride through art and literature. Playwright and poet LeRoi Jones (1934–), who changed his name to Amiri Baraka, became a leader of the black arts movement, which sought to create positive images for blacks. Popular black singers such as James Brown (1933–2006) and Aretha Franklin (1942–) expressed the spirit of "soul." Sports figures such as boxer Cassius Clay (1942–), who changed his name to Muhammad Ali, also identified with black power sentiments. At the 1968 Olympics, two African American athletes raised clenched fists in a "black power salute" on the victory stand after their event. At numerous colleges and universities, black students demanded black studies programs that would emphasize the contributions of African and African American people.

The influence of black power groups like the Black Panthers dwindled during the 1970s, but the commitment to black power within the African American community remained strong.

Black Tuesday

Tuesday, October 29, 1929, is remembered as Black Tuesday in the United States. That day, the value of stocks on the **New York Stock Exchange** (NYSE) plummeted, and many Americans lost their savings. Black Tuesday is commonly regarded as the beginning of the **Great Depression**, an economic recession in which much of the country struggled to keep food on the table and a roof overhead.

Economic prosperity

The United States had a great sense of prosperity during the 1920s. A strong economy and technological advancement brought luxury items like radios, vacuum cleaners, and automobiles into the lives of average Americans. Many such items could be bought on credit by paying in monthly installments. The growing sense of optimism and prosperity in the country led many people to acquire heavy loads of debt, or borrowed money that they had to repay.

The dream of making a fast fortune and the ability to buy stocks on credit prompted ordinary Americans to invest their small savings in the stock market. Stocks, or shares, represent part ownership in a company. An investor chooses to buy stocks in hopes that the value of the stock will go up, so they can sell the stocks for more than they paid. Stock prices can rise as more people become interested in the stock or if the company performs well. Likewise, the value will fall if few people buy the stock or if the company is not successful. When that happens, investors lose money. Stocks are bought and sold at stock exchanges, and in 1929 the NYSE was the primary exchange in the country.

Buying on credit

Buying stocks in the 1920s was made easy by brokerage firms. Investors were encouraged to buy stocks "on margin." This meant the investor paid a small percentage of the total cost of the stocks and borrowed the rest from the broker. If the value of the stock rose, then the investor still made money. If the value of the stock dropped, however, then the broker could demand more money to cover some of the loss, an act known as a "margin call." If the money was not paid, the broker could choose to sell the stock at current market prices. This meant that the investor would not only lose the investment but also often end up owing more money to the broker. As stock prices were rising steadily through the 1920s, many investors thought buying on margin was safe.

During the 1920s, there was little regulation of the stock market. Certain unregulated practices inflated the value of stocks. Often the value of stocks reflected investor interest in a company rather than the performance of the company. Some powerful investors took advantage of inside information to manipulate stock prices and make immense profits. With stocks performing so well, few people recognized the subtle signs that companies were actually struggling.

The crash

Stock prices reached a record high on September 3, 1929, then began a slow but steady decline. Although there were small rallies of increased value, the decline continued through September and October. By the end of October, fear and apprehension began to mount among all investors. As more and more brokers demanded their money with margin calls, values continued to drop.

Stock prices began to plummet on Thursday, October 24, when thousands of brokers placed margin calls to their investors. Bankers prevented a complete collapse of the market on that day, but only temporarily. By Tuesday, October 29, the continued loss of stock values created panic among investors. Selling occurred at such a rate that the market crashed. Many investors, large and small, not only lost their savings but also found themselves in great debt.

Stock market prices continued to decline for the next two and a half years. The stock market crash of Black Tuesday developed into a long-lasting depression that affected every aspect of American life for a decade.

Blacklisting
See **Hollywood Blacklisting**

Elizabeth Blackwell

The first woman in America to receive a medical degree, Elizabeth Blackwell crusaded for the admission of women to medical schools in the United States and Europe.

Elizabeth Blackwell was born in England on February 3, 1821, and when she was twelve her parents emigrated with their nine children to New York City. Her father became an ardent supporter of the **abolition movement** (someone who wants to eliminate **slavery**). In 1838, the Blackwells moved to Cincinnati, **Ohio**, but within a few months Blackwell's father died. The three oldest girls supported the family for several years by operating a boarding school for young women.

Medical school

In 1842, Blackwell accepted a teaching position in Henderson, **Kentucky**. Local racial attitudes offended her strong abolitionist convictions, and she resigned at the end of the year. On her return to Cincinnati, a friend urged her to study medicine. The following year, Blackwell moved to Asheville, **North Carolina**, and later to Charleston, **South Carolina**, where she taught school and studied medicine in her spare time.

When her attempts to enroll in the medical schools of Philadelphia, **Pennsylvania**, and New York City were rejected, she wrote to a number of small northern colleges. In 1847, she was admitted to the Geneva Medical College in **New York**. Because women had never gone to medical school, all eyes were upon her, and Blackwell proved to be an outstanding student. In 1849, at the top of her class, she became the first woman to graduate from medical school; the event was highly publicized in the United States and Europe. Because no hospitals in the United States would hire her, she went to Paris, France, to work at a women's and children's hospital for further study and practical experience. While working with the children, she contracted a severe eye infection that left her blind in one eye.

Practice in the United States

Handicapped by partial blindness, Blackwell gave up her ambition to become a surgeon and began practice at St. Bartholomew's Hospital in London. In 1851, she returned to New York, where she applied for several positions as a physician but was rejected because of her sex. She established a private practice in a rented room, where her sister Emily, who had also pursued a medical career, soon joined her. Their modest practice later became the New York Infirmary and College for Women, operated by and for women. The Women's Medical College opened in

November 1868, adjacent to the New York Infirmary, with Blackwell as professor of hygiene. It was the first school devoted entirely to the medical education of women.

During the **Civil War** (1861–65), she organized a unit of women nurses for field service. The army at this time had no hospital units. This association soon became the U.S. Sanitary Aid Commission, officially appointed by President **Abraham Lincoln** (1809–1865; served 1861–65).

In 1869, Blackwell set up practice in London and continued her efforts to open the medical profession to women. Her articles and her autobiography attracted widespread attention. From 1875 to 1907, she was a professor at the London School of Medicine for Women. She died at her home in Hastings in 1910.

Bleeding Kansas
See **Kansas-Nebraska Act**

Bluegrass Music
See **Country Music**

Bomb
See **Atomic Bomb;** *Enola Gay;* **Manhattan Project**

Daniel Boone

Daniel Boone's life spanned the final days of the original **thirteen colonies** and the birth of the United States as a nation-state. His adventures included wartime service as a soldier, exploration west of the Appalachian Mountains, and political service with Americans such as **Patrick Henry** (1736–1799) and **Thomas Jefferson** (1743–1826).

Early life

Boone was born on November 2, 1734, in a rural township near Reading, **Pennsylvania**. He was the sixth child of eleven born to Squire and Sarah Boone. The Boone family farmed their homestead and operated a blacksmith shop. Boone learned reading, writing, and math at home.

Boone received his first rifle at age twelve. He spent much time learning to hunt and explore in his wooded surroundings. His family left

Pennsylvania in 1747 when they were rejected from their **Quaker** church because Boone's older brother, Israel, married a woman who was not a Quaker. They settled in **Virginia** and then in western **North Carolina**.

War and love

From 1754 to 1763, the British colonies fought in the **French and Indian War** against France and its Native American allies. Boone served for the British as a teamster (wagon driver) and blacksmith in a campaign against Fort Duquesne led by General Edward Braddock (c. 1695–1755), who died in the attack. During the campaign, Boone met John Finley, with whom he would work as an explorer.

Boone was back in North Carolina when he wed Rebecca Bryan in August 1756. They had met in 1754 when Boone's sister Mary married William Bryan. Together, the Boones had ten children. Rebecca birthed another child whom she had with Daniel's brother, Edward, during Daniel's absence in another battle of the French and Indian War. Rebecca told Daniel that she thought he had died, and that Edward had comforted her through the difficult time.

Explorer, politician, and soldier Daniel Boone.

The pioneer

Frontier hostilities between Britain and France ceased around 1760. In November of that year, Boone and other explorers crossed the Blue Ridge Mountains to explore what became **Tennessee**. Boone made land claims in his travels, but had trouble throughout his life enforcing them.

In 1769, a judge hired Boone to lead an expedition into **Kentucky**. Along with Finley and others, Boone traveled through the Cumberland Gap into Kentucky. Boone helped cut a trail that would be used for decades by pioneers headed west.

In 1775, Boone became head of a colony in Kentucky called Boonesborough. He was captured in 1778 by Shawnee Indians and lived with them for four months. When he learned of their plan to attack

Boonesborough, he escaped to warn the colony. The colony survived the attack, but Boone, then a colonel in the American army's efforts to end British control of the colonies, was court-martialed for his time with the Shawnees, who were friends of the British. Boone won the trial and was promoted to the rank of major.

Politics, wanderlust, and final years

Boone was elected to the Virginia legislature twice in his life, in 1771 and 1781. He disliked politics, however, and moved his family a number of times in the ensuing years, including to **Ohio** and to what became **West Virginia**.

By 1799, Boone had lost most of his land holdings to lawsuits and creditors. At age sixty-five he moved his family to Alta Luisiana, or Upper **Louisiana**, which was still controlled by Spain. The Spanish gave Boone 850 acres of land plus more for family members to attract him to their colony. After the United States took control of the territory in the **Louisiana Purchase** of 1803, U.S. land commissioners ruled that Boone's land claims were invalid. Congress, however, later confirmed some of the grant.

Boone's wife Rebecca died in 1813. Boone spent his remaining years wandering and living with some of his many children. He died at his son Nathan's house in **Missouri** on September 26, 1820. In 1845, the Kentucky legislature arranged to have his remains moved to a burial site in Kentucky in honor of his pioneer work there. The Daughters of the **American Revolution** erected a memorial at the original gravesite in Missouri in 1915.

Boone's legendary status took root while he was alive. In 1784, John Filson published a biography called *The Adventures of Colonel Daniel Boone*. Three years after Boone's death, Lord Byron wrote the poem "Don Juan" with seven stanzas on Boone.

Boston Massacre

On the evening of March 5, 1770, tensions between English soldiers and the civilians of Boston, **Massachusetts**, erupted into a violent encounter now known as the Boston Massacre. An incident that began with the harassment of one English soldier ended with the deaths of five colonists and injuries to six others. The incident was an indication of colonial dissatisfaction with English rule. Later it would be depicted as a fight in the battle for colonial liberty.

Tensions rising

The roots of the Boston massacre lay in the deep colonial resentment of measures taken by the English Parliament. The **Townshend Acts** of 1767, in particular, had imposed taxes that affected businesses employing the working poor. As colonial resistance to the acts increased, England sent soldiers to America in 1768 to maintain order.

Tensions rose as the colonists began to suspect that the English soldiers were permanently stationed within the colonies. Soldiers began to bear the brunt of the citizens' anger and frustrations and were subjected to harassment and acts of violence. The culmination of this tension was the Boston Massacre.

The incident

On March 2, an English soldier approached a rope maker in hopes of finding extra work during his off-duty hours. The rope maker insulted the soldier. Eventually the argument turned into a fight that involved other citizens and soldiers and lasted into the next day.

On March 5, angry townspeople confronted another soldier who was on duty and began to harass him. Several other soldiers came to his defense. Captain Thomas Preston ordered them not to fire, but the crowd began pelting the soldiers with mud, ice, and snow. Although Preston attempted to maintain order, the soldiers fired. One soldier later claimed he had received an order to do so. Three colonists died immediately, two others died later, and six others were injured.

Preston and his soldiers were arrested and taken into custody. Most Bostonians believed that the soldiers deliberately fired into the crowd. A trial did not come until October 1770. **John Adams** (1735–1826), who later became the second president of the United States, served as the defense lawyer for the accused. Preston and six of his men were acquitted (found not guilty). Two soldiers were convicted of manslaughter, but they received the small punishment of branding on their thumbs before returning to their regiments. The Boston Massacre added to growing colonial resentment of England, which resulted in the start of the **American Revolution** in 1775.

Boston Tea Party

On the evening of December 16, 1773, a group of angry Boston citizens boarded three ships belonging to the East India Company docked in Boston Harbor. In protest of the British Parliament's **Tea Act** (1773), the group quietly dumped more than ninety thousand pounds of tea into the harbor. The incident has become known as the Boston Tea Party. It triggered a series of events that led directly to war and eventually to independence for America.

Parliamentary acts

The Boston Tea Party represents the difficult relationship between England and the **thirteen colonies** following the **French and Indian War** (1754–63). The French and Indian War was the last and most expensive of the colonial wars between France and England. The cost of defending the American colonists throughout the war had wiped out the British treasury.

Thinking that the colonies should help pay for past war debts and for the future cost of keeping English soldiers for their defense, Parliament passed a series of acts to raise money from the colonies. Among the measures passed by Parliament, the **Townshend Acts** (1767) were most unpopular. Instead of placing a direct tax on materials the colonists bought and sold, these acts imposed duties on items imported into the colonies. This made certain important items such as lead, glass, paint, paper, and tea more expensive.

Citizens protested by refusing to buy the taxed products and by signing nonimportation agreements throughout the colonies. Faced with such widespread opposition, the British government repealed the Townshend duties (taxes) in March 1770. To prove that Parliament had the right to tax the colonies, however, it preserved a three-penny duty on tea.

Corporate affairs

Between 1771 and 1773, the relationship between the colonies and England seemed fairly calm. However, Parliament's passage of the Tea Act in 1773 brought the period of peace to an abrupt end. The Tea Act was not passed with the intention of disciplining the American colonies. It was instead an attempt to revive the struggling East India Company.

The tension between the original thirteen colonies and England boiled over with the Boston Tea Party, when colonists snuck onboard English ships and dumped 342 chests of tea into the harbor. TIME & LIFE PICTURES/GETTY IMAGES

The legislation effectively cut wholesalers out of the tea trade by allowing the East India Company to sell tea directly to its own agents in America.

By avoiding the cost of using wholesalers, the East India Company was able to sell tea more cheaply than other tea companies could. This allowed the company to monopolize, or dominate, tea sales in the colonies. The monopoly angered colonists at all levels of society. Business for wholesalers and local merchants decreased. Tea smugglers were hurt by the competition of more affordable tea on the market.

In November of 1773, the first shipments of East India Company tea since the passage of the Tea Act began to arrive in ports throughout the colonies. They were met with hostile receptions. In New York and Philadelphia, angry crowds forced officials to send the tea ships back to England without unloading their cargoes. A tea ship was burned in Annapolis, **Maryland**, and arsonists in **New Jersey** burned a warehouse where unloaded tea was stored. The governor of Massachusetts, Thomas

Hutchinson (1711–1780), decided to face down the demonstrators in his colony.

Boston's tea

Three ships from the East India Company attempted to unload tea in Boston. A group of Boston citizens, led by revolutionary statesman Samuel Adams (1722–1803), refused to allow the tea to be taken off the ships. Governor Hutchinson called on the Royal Navy to blockade the harbor so the ships could not leave the port. Knowing that British law required ships to unload cargo after twenty days in port, the governor hoped to sidestep the demonstrators.

On December 16, the twenty-day period came to an end. Although Adams and others tried to convince Governor Hutchinson to allow the ships to return to England, he refused. Later that evening, a group of about seventy colonists disguised as American Indians silently boarded the ships. They broke open and dumped 342 chests of tea into the harbor.

In response to the Boston Tea Party, Parliament passed a series of measures, known as the Intolerable Acts, to punish the citizens of Massachusetts. The punitive laws, however, served to unite the colonists, who soon organized the First Continental Congress to plan a strategy for dealing with England. (See **Continental Congress, First**.) The conflicts between England and the colonies soon escalated into violence and the **American Revolution** (1775–83).

William Bradford

William Bradford was an Englishman who settled **Plymouth Colony** with the **Pilgrims** in 1620. The Pilgrims traveled to the New World to find a place where they could practice religion and community life without interference from the Church of England. As governor of the colony for most of his adult life, Bradford helped it survive hardships to become a permanent settlement.

Early life

Bradford was born in Austerfield, Yorkshire, England, in March 1590. His father, a farmer named William, died when Bradford was one. His mother, Alice, died six years later in 1597. Relatives cared for Bradford after that.

Bradford began attending a Puritan church when he was twelve. **Puritans** were Christians who wanted to reform the Church of England, which Puritans felt had too many fancy rituals. Around age sixteen, Bradford joined a church of Separatists in Scrooby, England, led by John Robinson (1575–1625) and William Brewster (c. 1566–1644). Separatists were Puritans who wanted to separate from the Church of England.

The Church of England considered Puritanism a threat to its power, so Puritans were often harassed in England. In 1608, the Scrooby congregation moved to Holland to practice religion freely. For twelve years, first in Amsterdam and then in Leyden, the Scrooby congregation experimented with living as an English community in a foreign land. Bradford worked in the textile industry during this time and married Dorothy May. He had a son with Dorothy and three children with Alice Carpenter Southworth, whom he married in 1623 after Dorothy's death years earlier.

The Pilgrims

The Scrooby congregation eventually decided to leave Holland. Living in Dutch country made it hard for the community to retain its English character and customs. The congregation did not wish, however, to return to persecution in England.

In London, the Scrooby congregation found investors from the Virginia Company who wanted to send settlers to the New World for harvesting its resources for a profit. In 1620, Bradford and about one hundred others sailed on the *Mayflower* with plans to settle in the area that would become **Virginia**. In November they arrived around present-day Cape Cod, **Massachusetts**, and by December they landed at Plymouth Bay and settled for the winter.

At Plymouth Bay, the Pilgrims were outside the area where the Virginia Company had power to establish colonies. (See **Colonization**.) This forced the Pilgrims to create their own government, which they did under a legal agreement called the Mayflower Compact.

Settling into colonial life

Half of the colonists at Plymouth died during the winter of 1620, including Governor John Carver (c. 1576–1621). The colonists elected

Bradford to be their new governor. Bradford organized the colonists to build a community, find food, and negotiate with Native Americans as necessary. He also had responsibility for overseeing justice and managing the colony's business affairs.

Bradford and the colonists met a Native American named Squanto, who had spent some time in England and spoke English. Squanto (1600?–1623) taught the colonists how to plant corn and preserve fish. Bradford negotiated with the chief of the local Wampanoag tribe for a peace treaty that lasted four decades.

Over the years under Bradford's guidance, Plymouth Colony survived early hardships and became a permanent settlement. The investors did not find it as profitable as other New World colonies. Still Plymouth Colony managed to pay off its initial debt by 1648.

Later years

In his later years, Bradford taught himself how to read the Bible in Hebrew, and he studied Greek, classical poetry, and philosophy.

From 1630 until 1650, Bradford wrote a book about the Pilgrims, called *Of Plymouth Plantation.* The book reflects Bradford's transition from viewing Native Americans as savages to respecting them. Toward the end of his life, Bradford thought that the colonists should purchase native lands that they wished to use, an idea that other colonists rejected.

Bradford died in Plymouth Colony in May 1657.

Broadway

Broadway is a street in New York City running the length of the borough of Manhattan. A few theaters were built along Broadway around the turn of the nineteenth century; more soon followed. In the twentieth century, the Broadway district became the center of mainstream American theater and the home of some of the best-known musical and dramatic productions in the English-speaking world. In 2007, thirty-nine professional theaters made up the Broadway theater district.

The early theaters

The earliest theater in the Broadway district, the elegant Park Theater, opened in 1798. By 1820, a few more were built in the area, notably the

Vaudeville shows were popular variety acts featuring comedians, jugglers, singers, and dancers. Vaudeville started out rowdy and crude, with audience participation sometimes spiraling out of control, but eventually evolved into a more cultured theater experience. © UNDERWOOD & UNDERWOOD/CORBIS

3,000-seat Bowery Theater and Chatham Gardens. The Park brought in English actors to perform classic drama such as the plays of William Shakespeare (1564–1616). The other theaters catered to more popular tastes. With the rise of industrialism and immigration in the mid-1800s, increasing numbers of the working class attended these urban theaters.

Melodrama, blackface minstrelsy, and vaudeville

The most popular form of play in the early nineteenth century was the melodrama, with its exaggerated moral conflicts, stock characters (types used over and over again), and predictable format. Some of the better melodramas drew a mix of sophisticated and uneducated audiences. One example was the six-act adaptation of Harriet Beecher Stowe's 1852 novel *Uncle Tom's Cabin* by George L. Aiken (1830–1876). The play had the basic elements of the melodrama, with its arch villain, suffering innocents, thrilling spectacles, comic relief, and poetic justice. It also dealt seriously with **slavery**, the most heated social issue of its time.

Blackface minstrelsy, another popular form of entertainment, was featured in Broadway theaters beginning in the late 1820s. It usually consisted of several white male performers imitating in an exaggerated style the songs, dances, and speech patterns of southern blacks. Performers blackened their faces with burnt cork, dressed in rags, and played banjos, fiddles, and tambourines.

Vaudeville shows were popular variety acts featuring comedians, jugglers, singers, and dancers. In its original form, vaudeville was rowdy and often crude, with audience participation sometimes spiraling out of control. By the end of the nineteenth century, theater owners began to produce "refined vaudeville" acts for family audiences. The 3,200-seat Niblo's Gardens was one of the first Broadway theaters for the new vaudeville.

In 1866, *The Black Crook: An Original Magical and Spectacular Drama in Four Acts* opened at Niblo's Garden. This is considered the first American "book musical"—that is, a musical with a plot and characters. The rather high-brow cultural event at a low-brow vaudeville house was the most commercially successful Broadway play up to that time.

The Syndicate

By 1900, theatrical touring troupes based in New York took their long-running Broadway shows on the road, performing them in theaters throughout the country. The system of booking plays nationwide was complicated, and six New York theater owners took advantage of the turmoil. Emulating the **robber barons** of the steel, railroad, and oil industries (business leaders whose unethical practices often involved driving competitors out of business), these theater owners formed the Theatrical Syndicate in 1896. They brought order to theater bookings, but took nearly complete control over American theater in the process.

By 1900, the Syndicate controlled more than five thousand U.S. theaters, including virtually every first-class stage. To maximize its profits, the Syndicate began to cut costs, undermining the quality of its shows. It soon faced competition from ambitious new rivals such as the Shubert brothers (Lee, Sam, and Jacob), who in 1905 began building their own chain of theaters. They managed to break the Syndicate's monopoly on the American theater in 1915, but like the Syndicate, the Shuberts exerted tight control over their extensive theatrical empire.

Because of the Syndicate's emphasis on profits in the early years of the century, Broadway theater became, and has remained, an extremely conservative commercial enterprise. It produces expensive shows designed to appeal to large audiences and make a large return on investors' money. Broadway is not known for experimenting with new art forms.

The boom period

Around the turn of the twentieth century, there were sixteen theaters on Broadway, with others nearby and many new theaters under construction. The theater district extended more than a mile, from Thirteenth Street to Times Square (formerly Longacre Square). Streetlights illuminated the thriving area, which became known as the Great White Way. Broadway theaters offered about seventy plays in the 1900–1901 season, and that number increased each year.

As the **Roaring Twenties** began, Broadway was in its heyday. In 1917, 126 plays were produced; that number soared to 264 in 1928. The Broadway district was home to seventy to eighty theaters. Melodrama and vaudeville gave way to many new forms, ranging from serious drama to musical comedy to light entertainment.

Development of musical theater

In 1900, vaudeville performer George M. Cohan (1878–1942) began to focus his ambitions as a playwright, songwriter, and performer on the Broadway theater. In 1904, Cohan created the patriotic musical comedy *Little Johnny Jones,* which featured the hit songs "Give My Regards to Broadway" and "Yankee Doodle Boy." Other Cohan musical comedies included such popular songs as "You're a Grand Old Flag" and the popular **World War I**–themed "Over There." Audiences craved his simple patriotic messages and upbeat songs. The title of one of Cohan's 1901 shows, *The Man Who Owns Broadway,* soon became his own nickname.

By the 1910s, musical forces such as **Irving Berlin** (1888–1989) and George (1898–1937) and Ira Gershwin (1896–1983) were putting their song-writing talents to work to create generally mediocre musical plays featuring outstanding songs. These artists first wrote the songs and then developed a thin plot to tie them together in a show. The Gershwin production *Lady Be Good* in 1924 introduced dancing star Fred Astaire (1899–1987). Singer Al Jolson (1886–1950) made his debut (first appearance as a performer) at the Winter Garden Theatre in 1911, winning the audience over with a brilliant performance.

In 1907, Florenz Ziegfeld (1867–1932) presented the *Follies* of 1907, the first of his famous series of revues featuring beautiful showgirls in lavish costumes. The *Ziegfeld Follies* became the longest-lived series of musical revues in show-business history. As the *Follies* progressed, the acts became more elaborate. Rope-twirling humorist Will Rogers (1879–1935) made his *Follies* debut in 1916, and singer-comedian Eddie Cantor (1892–1964) in 1917. Together with Fanny Brice (1891–1951) and W. C. Fields (1880–1946), these comics added a crucial dimension to the beautiful-girls show.

During the 1910s and 1920s, Ziegfeld mounted more than three dozen Broadway shows in addition to his *Follies,* most of them musical comedies. Perhaps his greatest triumph was the 1927 production of *Show Boat,* by Jerome Kern (1885–1945) and Oscar Hammerstein II (1895–1960). The musical featured acclaimed songs such as "Ol' Man River" and "Can't Help Lovin' Dat Man." *Show Boat* is considered the forerunner of the modern American musical drama.

The Depression and World War II

The Roaring Twenties were followed by the stock market crash of 1929 and the **Great Depression** (1929–41), a time of economic troubles around the world. Many Broadway theaters went out of business; others greatly reduced their productions. Many former theaters became movie houses, as movies took over a significant portion of theater audiences. Despite the obstacles, Broadway produced some of its greatest musicals in the 1930s. It was the prime era for the Gershwin brothers' work, and for musicals from new composers such as Cole Porter (1891–1964).

The turning point for the modern Broadway musical occurred during **World War II** (1939–45) with the Richard Rodgers (1902–1979) and Oscar Hammerstein musical play *Oklahoma!* Taking up where *Show Boat* had left off, **Rodgers and Hammerstein** wrote the play for this musical first and then made everything in it, including the songs, work to develop the plot, characters, and drama. *Oklahoma!* was an instant success, setting a record for its Broadway run and forever changing the nature of the American musical. The 1950s saw many more musical dramas, including *My Fair Lady* (1956), which set the record for the longest run of any theater production in history; *West Side Story* (1957); and Rodgers and Hammerstein's final musical, *The Sound of Music* (1959).

Attendance at musicals dropped during the late 1960s and 1970s. As tastes changed with the introduction of rock music, some musicals, such as *Hair* and *Grease,* attempted to adapt to the times. Broadway still had its share of traditional musicals, and some continued to be smash hits. But the decrease in productions and audiences continued into the 2000s.

Non-musical Broadway plays

The 1920s brought a boom in serious American drama as well as musical productions. In 1920, *Beyond the Horizon,* the first full-length play by Eugene O'Neill (1888–1953), debuted on Broadway and won that year's Pulitzer Prize. O'Neill probed the dark side of humanity and bucked the trend towards lighter fare. His plays were critical successes, and many cultural observers felt he raised the artistic standards on Broadway.

Continuing the development of realism were the two major playwrights of the 1940s and 1950s, Arthur Miller (1915–2005) and **Tennessee Williams** (1911–1983). Miller's first major triumph, *Death of a Salesman*, premiered on Broadway in 1949. It was America's first tragedy of a common man, Willy Loman. Williams's *The Glass Menagerie* premiered on Broadway in 1945, using Williams's own troubled family relations as subject matter. *A Streetcar Named Desire*, which opened on Broadway in 1947, was directed by Elia Kazan (1909–2003) and starred Marlon Brando (1924–2004).

Most Broadway plays of the 1950s were written and directed by white men, but in 1959 *A Raisin in the Sun,* a play by Lorraine Hansberry (1930–1965) about an African American family confronting racism, debuted to a standing ovation. It was the first play by a black woman to be produced on Broadway. Gradually, Broadway stages began to reflect the multicultural society. By the 1980s, many plays written by and about minorities and women were commercial and critical successes.

Non-musical Broadway plays were not universally serious. Neil Simon (1927–) became Broadway's most reliable and commercially successful playwright beginning in the 1960s by dedicating himself to light entertainment. Simon's well-made Broadway comedies include *The Odd Couple* (1965) and *The Sunshine Boys* (1972).

Off-Broadway and Off-Off-Broadway

In the 1950s, the enormous expense of producing theater on Broadway led to the development of smaller theaters outside Times Square, collectively referred to as Off-Broadway. Off-Broadway provided a challenge to Broadway, opening the door for alternative theater. The 1960s saw the rise of Off-Off-Broadway, alternative theatrical performances staged in small coffeehouses off Broadway's main theater row. These coffeehouses boomed, allowing experimentation in drama to flourish. By 1966, the number of Off-Off-Broadway productions was twice that of Broadway and Off-Broadway combined.

Broadway today

Broadway celebrates its own players every year with the Antoinette Perry Awards, better known as the Tony Awards, established in 1947. These awards are only for productions that open in the major Broadway theaters.

In 2007, Broadway had only about half the number of theaters it had in the 1920s. It has never been able to regain the popularity it enjoyed during the 1920s. Still, some of the best writers, directors, performers, costume and set designers, composers, and many other theater professionals continue to bring their talents to this center of U.S. theater. The thirty-nine official Broadway theaters remain a popular tourist attraction in New York City and continue to draw crowds. Total Broadway attendance in 2005 was just under twelve million.

Brown Berets

The Brown Berets were a militant Chicano (Mexican American) civil rights group, modeled in part on the African American **Black Panther Party**. Like the Black Panthers, the Brown Berets arose out of a desire to fight discrimination and especially to defend the Mexican American community from police brutality.

A youth group

The Brown Berets got their start at a Mexican American youth conference in East Los Angeles, **California**, in 1966, at which high school students gathered to discuss problems facing Mexican Americans. The students continued to work together over the next year, and their group took the name Young Chicanos for Community Action (YCCA).

In late 1967, the YCCA opened the Piranya Coffee House as a site from which to promote community consciousness and recruit members. The YCCA adopted a brown beret as a part of its uniform and thus became known as the Brown Berets. Emphasizing the right of self-determination and defense against aggression, the Brown Berets considered themselves nationalists—that is, they identified themselves first and foremost as Chicanos and rejected the idea that they should adjust their traditions and culture to assimilate (blend in) with the mainstream U.S. culture. They had a formal code of conduct and ethics.

In practice, the Brown Berets emphasized opposition to police brutality and discrimination in the schools. During the group's main period of activity—from 1967 through 1972—the Brown Berets developed more than twenty chapters and published the newspaper *La Causa*. In May 1969, the Brown Berets opened the East Los Angeles Free Clinic, offering a range of medical services.

The Brown Berets participated in the major events of the Chicano movement, including the East Los Angeles "Blow Outs," organized demonstrations in which more than ten thousand students walked out of Garfield, Roosevelt, Lincoln, and Belmont high schools to protest educational discrimination against Chicanos.

The Chicano Moratorium

In late 1969, the Brown Berets formed the Chicano Moratorium Committee, which organized annual marches to protest the large number of Chicano soldiers dying in the **Vietnam War** (1954–75). A year later, they called for a national Chicano Moratorium to protest not only the Vietnam War but also oppression by police. The Moratorium, held in Los Angeles in 1970, became one of the country's largest antiwar protests, with nearly twenty thousand people in attendance. Overreacting to a minor incident, the police attacked the peaceful demonstrators. In the ensuing violence, respected Chicano journalist Ruben Salazar (1928–1970) was killed.

In 1971, the Brown Berets conducted a March Through Aztlán, marching one thousand miles from Calexico, California, to the state's capital, Sacramento, to protest police brutality, racial discrimination, and the Vietnam War. In 1972, they occupied Santa Catalina Island off the

Southern California coast, arguing that the island had not been specifically named in the Treaty of Guadalupe Hidalgo of 1848, which ended the **Mexican-American War** (1846–48) and resulted in Mexico ceding California to the United States. Therefore, according to the Brown Berets, the island still belonged to Mexico. In late 1972, in response to repeated harassment by police, the Brown Berets disbanded. In the 1990s and 2000s, local Brown Beret groups formed for many of the same purposes and with the same basic principles as the original group.

Brown, John
See **Harpers Ferry Raid**

Brown v. Board of Education

The **Fourteenth Amendment** to the U.S. **Constitution**, adopted in 1868, gives all Americans, regardless of race, equal rights and equal protection under state and federal laws. Yet at the beginning of the 1950s, American society was still separated into black and white. Hotels, trains, parks, restaurants, apartment houses, and even state voting precincts were segregated by race through state statutes called **Jim Crow laws**. African Americans were criminally prosecuted and jailed for attempting to ride the same trains or eat in the same restaurants as whites.

Racial **segregation** (the separation of races) had been established by law in the United States in 1896 in the **Supreme Court** case called *Plessy v. Ferguson*. Homer Plessy was an African American man who attempted to ride in a whites-only railroad car in **Louisiana**. When he was charged with violating Louisiana's Jim Crow law, Plessy argued all the way to the Supreme Court that the law was unconstitutional. In a seven-to-one vote, the 1896 Court declared that the Fourteenth Amendment did not prohibit state laws from treating people differently according to the color of their skin as long as that treatment was "equal." The "separate but equal" doctrine created by the *Plessy* decision lasted for nearly sixty years, until the 1954 decision of *Brown v. Board of Education*.

Topeka, Kansas, 1950s

In 1950, Oliver Brown was told that his eight-year-old daughter could not attend the Topeka, **Kansas**, neighborhood elementary school four blocks from their home because Kansas law required African Americans

George Hayes (left), attorney
Thurgood Marshall (center),
and James M. Nabrit (right)
celebrate the landmark Brown
v. Board of Education *U.S.*
Supreme Court decision in
Washington, D.C., in 1954.
THE LIBRARY OF CONGRESS

to attend separate schools. Brown joined with other African American families to engage the **National Association for the Advancement of Colored People** (NAACP; a prominent civil rights organization) to file a lawsuit against the board of education of Topeka. They claimed that segregation violated their children's constitutional rights under the Fourteenth Amendment. For four years, the families lost their case but appealed it to progressively higher courts. In 1954, *Brown v. Board of*

The plaintiffs in the Brown v. Board of Education *case that attempted to obliterate the "separate but equal" doctrine.* CARL IWASAKI/TIME & LIFE PICTURES/GETTY IMAGES

Education reached the U.S. Supreme Court along with three similar cases.

The plaintiffs' attorney, **Thurgood Marshall** (1908–1993), later a Supreme Court justice, argued that racially segregated public schools were not equal and could not be made equal. He believed, therefore, that the laws were in violation of the Fourteenth Amendment. He claimed that the only way for the Court to uphold segregation in 1954 was "to find that for some reason Negroes are inferior to all other human beings." The Supreme Court agreed and unanimously rejected the "separate but equal" doctrine of *Plessy v. Ferguson,* stating that "in the field of public education the doctrine of 'separate but equal' has no place."

Reaction

The *Brown* decision hit the country like a bombshell. At the time of the ruling, 40 percent of public-school students lived in areas that required segregation by law. Mandatory-segregation laws were in effect in **Alabama**, **Arkansas**, **Delaware**, **Florida**, **Georgia**, **Kentucky**, Louisiana, **Maryland**, **Mississippi**, **Missouri**, **North Carolina**, **Oklahoma**, **South Carolina**, **Tennessee**, **Texas**, **Virginia**, **West Virginia**, and **Washington, D.C.**

Heated opposition to *Brown* came immediately. Several states defied the court decision. Louisiana and Georgia voters enacted bills to permit racially segregated education in November 1954. Georgia allowed public educational funds to be provided to individuals to establish private segregated schools. **Michigan** voters approved, almost two to one, a state constitutional amendment to permit the abolition of public schools if there was no other way to avoid racial desegregation of schoolchildren. Similar actions were taken in Alabama, Mississippi, North Carolina, and South Carolina.

"All deliberate speed"

Reversing segregation was not going to come easily, and the Court realized the tremendous resistance local politicians and school boards would have to its decision. Therefore, the *Brown* decision was argued again over the issue of how to bring about desegregation. In *Brown II* (1957), Chief Justice Earl Warren (1891–1974) and the Supreme Court required local federal district courts to assess local obstacles to integration and decide whether local school boards were making honest attempts at the **desegregation of public schools**. The nation's public schools were ordered to desegregate "with all deliberate speed."

Desegregation was extremely unpopular. Attempts by African American students to follow court-ordered integration resulted in riots in cities such as Milford, Delaware; Mansfield, Texas; Clinton, Tennessee; and New Orleans, Louisiana. President **Dwight D. Eisenhower** (1890–1969; served 1953–61) believed that the Supreme Court had attempted to force the nation to integrate too quickly and offered no help. Even many African American leaders and intellectuals, such as writer Zora Neale Hurston (1891–1960) and activist W. E. B. Du Bois (1868–1963), disliked the idea, doubting that African American children would be treated equally in desegregated schools.

White southerners continued to use tactics of obstruction and delay. Desegregation did not occur in the Deep South until the mid-1960s.

Nonetheless, *Brown* had an immediate effect on the hearts and minds of African Americans, and many historians consider it the start of the modern **civil rights movement**. Movement leaders stated that *Brown* influenced their activities, if only because it showed that the nation's highest court believed that the Constitution supported their civil rights.

James Buchanan

James Buchanan devoted his presidency to trying to maintain the **Democratic Party**'s North-South coalition (voting bloc), which he believed would keep the United States intact in the years prior to the **Civil War** (1861–65). He was unable to keep his party or the United States intact, and he is probably most often remembered for this failure.

Buchanan was born on April 23, 1791, and raised in a large, respected family in **Pennsylvania**. He received a good education in his hometown and graduated from Dickinson College in 1809. After college, Buchanan studied law, and he was admitted to the Pennsylvania bar in 1812. He quickly established a successful law practice. The two main ingredients of his success were his knowledge of the law and his talent for giving speeches and debating.

Enters politics

Buchanan's political career began with his election to the Pennsylvania House of Representatives in 1813. As a Federalist (a member of the **Federalist Party**, which sought a strong central government and an industrialized society), he opposed the **War of 1812** (1812–15), a conflict between England and the United States over trade issues. He feared that it would be harmful to northern industries. Once war was declared, though, he enlisted in the military.

Buchanan became a member of the U.S. House of Representatives in 1820. The U.S. victory in the War of 1812 had destroyed the Federalist Party, leaving the United States with only one political party, the **Democratic-Republican Party**. In the election of 1824, four Democratic-Republicans ran for president, splintering the party. Those who supported **Andrew Jackson** (1767–1845) would become the

Democratic Party, and those who supported **John Quincy Adams** (1767–1848) formed a new party, the **Whigs**. The majority of former Federalists joined the Whig party, but Buchanan supported Jackson.

A Jacksonian Democrat

Adams won the election of 1824, although Jackson had gotten the majority of popular votes. During the Adams administration, Buchanan actively opposed many of the president's efforts. It was during this time that he made his first public statement on **slavery**, calling it a moral and political evil, but one that would endure for years to come.

James Buchanan, the fifteenth president of the United States, was minister to Russia and Great Britain but is most remembered for his failure to prevent the secession of South Carolina. THE LIBRARY OF CONGRESS

After ten years in the House, Buchanan became the minister (diplomatic representative) to Russia. He returned in 1833 and was elected to the U.S. Senate. As a member of the Democratic Party, Buchanan realized he must support Jackson, who had followed Adams as president. When Jackson announced his ambition to crush the national bank (a commercial bank regulated by the federal government), Buchanan supported Jackson, even knowing that this action would hurt his home state of Pennsylvania, where the Second National Bank of the United States was located. The bank, located in Philadelphia, had held the nation's federal funds for nearly two decades. Buchanan chose to be a loyal Jacksonian Democrat in opposing the bank, motivated, at least in part, by his national (rather than state) political ambitions.

From 1845 to 1849, Buchanan served as secretary of state to President **James K. Polk** (1795–1849; served 1845–49), representing the government in foreign affairs, and then he became the minister to Great Britain. When he returned from England in 1856, Buchanan found the United States more deeply divided than ever by the 1854 **Kansas-Nebraska Act**. The act repealed the **Missouri Compromise** of 1820, which had permitted **Missouri** to be admitted as a slave state while banning slavery in the remaining northern portions of the **Louisiana Purchase**. The Democratic Party was bitterly divided between its members in slave-holding states and its members in free (non-slave-holding) states. Buchanan had avoided the conflict simply by being out of the country, and some believed he was the only candidate who could mend the Democratic Party's wounds and save the **Union**. Thus he became the party's candidate.

In the 1856 presidential election, Buchanan was not a favorite of either the North or the South, but those who opposed the Democratic Party were too divided to take the election. Buchanan did not get a majority of the popular votes, but he did win the presidency. He defeated the **Republican Party** candidate, **John C. Frémont** (1813–1890), and the **Know-Nothing Party** candidate, former president **Millard Fillmore** (1800–1874; served 1850–1853).

The presidency in 1856

Buchanan's administration was haunted by the question of slavery in the U.S. territories. He hoped that the **Supreme Court**'s verdict in the ***Dred Scott* case** in 1857 would settle the issue once and for all. Dred Scott (c. 1795–1858) was a slave who had sued for his freedom based on his residence in a free territory, where he and his slave owner had moved. The Supreme Court ruled against him, stating that he was still the property of his owner even though he had lived in a free state. To Buchanan and many others, the *Dred Scott* decision meant that only states—and not the federal government—had the authority to prohibit slavery within their boundaries.

Buchanan believed that the Democratic Party had held the Union together during the recent conflicts; as president, he felt it was his job to unite the party. He tried to keep Southerners from abandoning it by strongly upholding the right to own slaves in slave-holding states. In his zeal to please Southerners, he attacked abolitionists (people who sought to abolish slavery) and placed many prominent Southerners in high positions in Washington. But the South could not be appeased so easily. With most of the new states destined to be free of slavery, the North was sure to gain power at the South's expense. The old North-South coalition of the Democratic Party had been pushed to the breaking point. The territory of **Kansas** had reached a state resembling civil war over the issue of slavery. Buchanan's compromises were inadequate to stop the divide.

Buchanan chose not to run for president in 1860. The Democratic Party splintered into three sectional factions, whose candidates, Vice President John C. Breckinridge (1821–1875), U.S. senator Stephen A.

Douglas (1813–1861) of Illinois, and former U.S. representative John Bell (1797–1869) of Tennessee, lost to Republican candidate **Abraham Lincoln** (1809–1865; served 1861–65). Lincoln had spoken strongly of limiting the expansion of slavery. When Lincoln won the election, the South prepared to secede (withdraw from the Union). Buchanan had been warned, but he had not prepared for the secession. During his last days in office, his administration fell apart as the Civil War between the North and the South began.

Buchanan supported the Union throughout the Civil War. He died in 1868, remembered most for the last few months of his administration, when the country divided.

Buffalo Bill
See **William "Buffalo Bill" Cody**

Buffalo Soldiers

Approximately 20 percent of the U.S. Cavalry involved in the **Plains Indian Wars** (1866–90) were African American soldiers. These soldiers made up the Ninth and Tenth U.S. Cavalry Regiments.

The Cheyenne and Comanche tribes nicknamed these men Buffalo Soldiers because they were courageous and strong, qualities shared with the mighty buffalo. The hair of the Buffalo Soldiers reminded the tribal warriors of the tuft of hair between a buffalo's horns, as well. Given that the buffalo was important and necessary to the Native Americans' way of life, the nickname was an honor, and one the soldiers accepted with pride.

The Buffalo Soldiers fought in more than 177 conflicts against the Plains tribes, and at least seventeen Medals of Honor were awarded them throughout the Indian Wars.

Fighting was not all they did, however. The Buffalo Soldiers mapped miles of southwestern frontier territory (wilderness at the edge of a settled region) and strung hundreds of miles of telegraph lines. Without the protection of these famous soldiers, construction crews would not have survived long enough to build the railroads throughout the frontier.

The Buffalo Soldiers participated in many other wars, including the American **Civil War** (1861–65), the **Spanish-American War** (1898), and both **World War I** (1914–18) and **World War II** (1939–45).

Bulge, Battle of the
See **Battle of the Bulge**

Bull Run, Battles of
See **Battles of Bull Run**

Bunker Hill, Battle of
See **Battle of Bunker Hill**

Bureau of Indian Affairs

The Bureau of Indian Affairs (BIA) is the federal agency responsible for administering policies for Indian nations and communities.

Organization

The BIA was created in 1824 as a part of the U.S. War Department, a cabinet department that was the forerunner of the Department of Defense. Its task was to handle the growing problems caused by the **westward expansion** of the United States into territories mainly inhabited by the Indians. The early BIA had three levels of administration. Its leaders, including the commissioner, were stationed in **Washington, D.C.** BIA superintendents were posted throughout Indian-occupied lands, where they oversaw territorial-level agencies. Indian agents and subagents lived among the various tribes. The BIA remained within the War Department until 1849, when Congress transferred the Indian agency to the Department of the Interior.

The BIA was accused of abuse, mismanagement, and corruption from its early days and throughout the nineteenth century. Many of the agency's top administrators received their jobs as political favors; they were not qualified for the job or even interested in the plight of the American Indians. Many pocketed the money set aside for the Indians.

Taking the land

The BIA came into being around the same time that Congress passed the Indian Removal Act of 1830. The act authorized the federal government to transfer Indians living in the eastern part of the country to lands west of the Mississippi River. The BIA was responsible for the task of confin-

The Bureau of Indian Affairs, which manages policies for Indian nations and communities, has its own police force to monitor Indian affairs. AP IMAGES

ing them to designated **Indian reservations** in the West and training them to adapt to mainstream American ways. For several decades, the BIA concentrated on Indian removal and relocation, which involved dislodging, usually by force, entire Native American communities from lands throughout the ever-expanding United States.

By 1870, the federal government had secured most of the present-day United States from the Indians. It signed treaties with them that promised the Indians that they could remain on their reservation lands forever. In 1871, however, the government called for an end to treaties. The **Indian Appropriations Act** declared Indians to be wards (people under the protection and care) of the government and gave the BIA the authority to carry out the government's role as guardian on the reservations.

Allotment

On February 8, 1887, Congress passed the **Dawes Severalty Act** (General Allotment Act), designed to promote the concept of individual ownership of land by dividing the reservations into tracts and allotting one tract to each Indian. This was a tremendous change for most tribes, because Native American land was traditionally held in common by all members of the community and used for the good of everyone. Under the act, the individual tracts of land "given" to the Indians were to be held in trust (something held by one party for the benefit of another) for twenty-five years while the Indians received training in farming and other mainstream American customs.

The effect of the Dawes Act was to destroy the social and political systems of the tribes while transferring authority to powerful BIA Indian agents. The BIA staffed the tribal government, courts, and law enforcement agencies with hand-picked Indians who were willing to cooperate in pursuing the agency's goals. The BIA drafted a Code of Indian Offenses that prohibited many traditional cultural and religious practices. While the Indians were being trained to become farmers, the BIA rationed their food and necessities of life. The agency thus could starve into submission those Indians who refused to crop their hair short, who continued to paint their faces, or who persisted in engaging in traditional religious ceremonies. The bureau also assumed responsibility for the education of young Indians. Not surprisingly, its policy was to provide them with knowledge and skills necessary to fit into mainstream society. Students were not allowed to speak their native languages or practice many of their customs.

Indian New Deal

By the mid-1930s, it was clear that the Dawes Act had failed to benefit the Indians. The BIA-administered reservations were in disastrous shape, while those reservations owned and operated by the tribes as a group had fared much better. President **Franklin D. Roosevelt** (1882–1945; served 1933–45) promised reform. He appointed sociologist John Collier (1884–1968) commissioner of the BIA to help carry out the "Indian New Deal." Under Collier's direction, the BIA stopped trying to force Native Americans to adapt to the non-Indian ways. Management of reservations was turned over to the tribes. Reservation schools were free to teach traditional Indian culture and languages in the classroom.

The BIA was not always popular after the reforms of the 1930s. In 1972, the **American Indian Movement** (AIM) staged a demonstration in which the protesters took over BIA headquarters in Washington,

D.C., in protest of the federal government's Indian policies. In the 1990s, various groups accused the BIA of mismanagement of tribal funds. Nevertheless, in the early 2000s, the BIA continued to act as trustee over 55.7 million acres of land held in trust by the United States for the 561 federally recognized tribal governments. The agency is responsible for developing the forests, farms, and other resources of these lands and protecting water and land rights. The BIA also continues to provide education, health, and social services.

Aaron Burr

Aaron Burr was born on February 6, 1756, in Newark, **New Jersey**. His father, Aaron, was the pastor of the Newark Presbyterian Congregation. His mother, Esther, was the daughter of the well-known theologian Jonathan Edwards (1703–1758).

Before the younger Aaron was a year old, his father took a post as president of the College of New Jersey (later Princeton University), and the family moved to Princeton. His father died a few months later, in September 1757. The deaths of his mother and grandparents followed within the next year. Aaron and his older sister, Sarah, moved to the care of Timothy Edwards, a twenty-year-old uncle.

Burr prepared for college and graduated from Princeton at seventeen. He began to study theology to become a minister, but in 1774 he abandoned those studies. Instead he decided to become a lawyer. That plan, however, was delayed by the **American Revolution** (1775–83).

Military service

The Battle of Lexington, which opened the war, inspired Burr to join the Revolutionary cause. (See **Battle of Lexington and Concord**.) He and **Benedict Arnold** (1741–1801) fought in the expedition to take Quebec. Although the attack was unsuccessful, Burr served with distinction.

In the spring of 1776, Burr joined the staff of General **George Washington** (1732–1799) as a major. Their personalities conflicted, and Burr was transferred to the staff of General Israel Putnam (1718–1790). Burr served with distinction in the battle of Long Island and in the evacuation of **New York**.

In July 1777, Burr was appointed lieutenant-colonel in the Continental line. He earned a reputation for discipline and daring as the

Although a successful attorney, senator, and vice president, Burr's reputation declined at the end of his career and financial difficulties surrounded him until his death. THE LIBRARY OF CONGRESS

leader of a regiment stationed in Orange County, New York. The hardships of his stations, however, took a toll on Burr. His health began to suffer, and in March 1779 he submitted his resignation. After a long period of recovery, Burr returned to the study of law.

Law and politics

In 1780, Burr was well enough to begin his study of law with determination. He eventually relocated to Haverstraw, New York, and was admitted to the New York Bar as an attorney in early 1782. In July, he married Theodosia Bartow Provost, the widow of a British army officer. Over the course of their twelve years together, she gave birth to four children. Only one, a daughter, survived into adulthood, and she disappeared at sea in 1812. Theodosia died in 1794.

In the fall of 1783, the Burrs moved to New York City, where Burr established a law practice. He was a highly respected attorney. With the encouragement of a radical political group, Burr gained election to the New York State Assembly. He served from 1784 to 1785 but refrained from being nominated for another term.

Burr continued to be entangled in the work of the state's political factions. As a result, he earned an appointment as the state attorney general in 1789. In 1791, he began to serve in the U.S. Senate. It was during this time that Burr gained an enemy in **Alexander Hamilton** (1755–1804), who was secretary of the treasury under President Washington.

During his six years in the Senate, Burr became associated with the politics of **Thomas Jefferson** (1743–1826), President Washington's secretary of state. After **James Monroe** (1758–1831) left the Senate, Burr became the spokesman for the policies of the Jeffersonians. In 1796, both Burr and Jefferson ran for president, but Vice President **John Adams** defeated both of them. At that time, representatives from each state voted in the election; the first-place finisher was declared president, while the second-place finisher automatically became vice president. In

1796, that meant that Adams would be president and runner-up Jefferson would be vice president. Failing to gain reelection to the Senate the same year, Burr returned to New York in 1797. There, he was elected to the State Assembly again and served until 1799.

Vice presidency

During Adams's presidency, political parties became clearly defined in the young nation. Jefferson's supporters, including Burr, belonged to the **Democratic-Republican Party**. In the election of 1800, Jefferson and Burr received the same number of electoral votes, tying for the presidency. The **Constitution** required that the election be decided by the House of Representatives. In the tie-breaking vote there, Jefferson was elected president, and Burr became vice president, thanks in part to Hamilton's support for Jefferson. As vice president, Burr was not very popular with members of either the **Federalist Party** or the Democratic-Republican Party. By 1804, the Twelfth Amendment had been passed, which required electors to vote for president and vice president separately. New York governor George Clinton (1739–1812) wound up being elected as Jefferson's second-term vice president.

With Burr's days as vice president numbered, his political friends nominated him for the governorship of New York. Although he gathered some support, Burr's popularity had continued to decline. His political rivals, especially Hamilton, worked against him as well. He was defeated by a heavy majority.

Hamilton's scorn during the New York election infuriated Burr and prompted a duel between them. Burr fatally shot Hamilton on July 11, 1804, at Weehawken, New Jersey, while still serving as vice president.

Declining popularity

Burr's duel with Hamilton, while giving him political revenge, brought many difficulties as well. Although duels were still common, they were not legal in either New Jersey or New York. Hamilton was immensely popular and had many admirers who were angered by the event. Officials in both New York and New Jersey charged Burr with multiple crimes, including murder. He fled first to Philadelphia, **Pennsylvania**, and then to **South Carolina**. Although he eventually beat the charges and returned to complete his term as vice president, the end of his term in March 1805 effectively marked the end of his political career.

Another incident contributed to the decline of Burr's reputation. It appears that between 1805 and 1807 he was involved in plans either to separate the western states from the Union or to conquer the Spanish possessions of **Texas** and northern Mexico, or perhaps to accomplish both feats. The facts are so unclear that Burr's intentions remain clouded today. It is clear, however, that Burr was working toward some sort of uprising.

In preparation for his plans, Burr recruited volunteers, gathered supplies, and sought financial assistance. Among those plotting alongside Burr was the commanding general of the U.S. Army, James Wilkinson (1757–1825), who promised to supply Burr with troops. Wilkinson, however, changed his mind and decided to further his own career by revealing Burr's plans to authorities.

Burr was arrested and tried for treason. Fortunately for him, political sparring between President Jefferson and Chief Justice John Marshall (1755–1835) resulted in Burr's acquittal. Upon his release, Burr sought refuge in Europe.

Last years

Burr's reputation both socially and politically had plummeted. He was heavily in debt, and creditors were relentless. Burr retreated and set sail for England in June 1808. Ever hopeful of gathering support for his plans, Burr traveled from England to Sweden, Denmark, Germany, and France. He failed to gain support, however, and decided to return home to his daughter and grandson. Due to an unfortunate string of events, he did not return home until May 1812.

Burr returned to New York, where he had little difficulty reestablishing his legal practice. Within the year, both his grandson and daughter died. Financial difficulties continued to plague him. He suffered a minor stroke in 1830. In July 1833, Burr married a much younger and wealthier woman, Eliza Jumel. After only four months, they separated due to arguments concerning finances. Her request for divorce was granted after a dramatic trial. Burr died on September 14, 1836, the day the divorce was to become effective.

Bus Boycott

See **Montgomery Bus Boycott**

George H. W. Bush

A successful businessman, George Herbert Walker Bush emerged as a national political leader during the 1970s. After holding several important foreign policy and administrative assignments in **Republican Party** politics, he served two terms as vice president under **Ronald Reagan** (1911–2004; served 1981–89), and he went on to serve one term as president beginning in 1988.

George H. W. Bush was born on June 12, 1924, and led a privileged childhood as the son of a wealthy **Connecticut** senator. He graduated from a prestigious private school and was accepted at Yale University, but he changed his plans when the United States entered **World War II** (1939–45). Bush enlisted in the U.S. Naval Reserve, and by the end of 1943 he was the youngest fighter pilot in the navy. He was awarded the Distinguished Flying Cross for his actions on a September 2, 1944, mission in the South Pacific, during which his plane was shot down and he parachuted to safety. When he returned home, Bush married Barbara Pierce (1925–) and entered Yale. After graduating, he moved to **Texas**. By 1954, he was president of the Zapata Offshore Company. Drilling for oil in the Gulf of Mexico had already made him wealthy.

Enters the world of politics

Bush was active in the Republican Party in Texas, and in 1966 he was elected to the U.S. House of Representatives. In December 1970, he was appointed U.S. ambassador to the United Nations (UN). In 1973, Bush became the chairman of the Republican National Committee. The next year, he was appointed head of the U.S. Liaison Office in the People's Republic of China, and in 1975, President **Gerald R. Ford** (1913–2006; served 1974–77) called him home to head the **Central Intelligence Agency** (CIA; the government agency responsible for obtaining and analyzing information about foreign governments, corporations, and individuals). Bush served until 1976 and won high marks for improving agency morale.

George Herbert Walker Bush held several important foreign policy and administrative assignments before serving two terms as vice president and one term as the president of the United States. THE LIBRARY OF CONGRESS

Begins service under President Reagan

Bush sought the Republican presidential nomination in 1980. He was viewed as an attractive moderate alternative to the conservative Ronald Reagan, but he did not get the nomination. He accepted Reagan's offer of the vice presidential slot despite their differences of opinion on several key issues. During his two terms as Reagan's vice president, Bush loyally supported the Reagan agenda.

The presidency

In 1988, Bush was elected president. Immediately after taking office, he improved relations with Congress and the press. He preferred to negotiate differences between economic and political interests rather than take strong positions of his own. This was true in his foreign policy as well. During his first year in office, the Communist governments of the Soviet Union and Eastern Europe self-destructed, creating an entirely new balance of world powers. Bush supported the Russian reformist president Mikhail Gorbachev (1931–) and maintained a remote and formal relationship with all the countries of the former Soviet Union.

In the spring of 1989, Chinese students began massive demonstrations in support of democracy in Tiananmen Square, located in the heart of China's capital, Beijing. When the government crushed the demonstrations with military force, Bush at first spoke out against the actions of the Chinese leadership and imposed limited sanctions (punishments, such as stopping trade, to express disapproval), but he soon sent representatives to Beijing to ease the tension between the United States and China. Later he opposed congressional attempts to toughen the sanctions and restored China's most-favored-nations trade status.

Bush was initially halfhearted about U.S. initiatives to stop the drug-smuggling Panamanian dictator Manuel Noriega (c. 1935–). After an American soldier was killed by one of Noriega's soldiers in 1989, however, Bush authorized a full-scale military invasion of Panama. The majority of Noriega's forces surrendered after a few hours. Noriega was captured a few weeks later. In 1992, he was convicted in Florida on drug-dealing charges.

The Gulf War

Under the leadership of military dictator Saddam Hussein (1937–2006), Iraq invaded Kuwait in 1990 and proclaimed it a new Iraqi province. Bush launched Operation Desert Storm, mobilizing international forces that destroyed Hussein's air and land military capabilities in a six-week war that was televised virtually from start to finish. The action resulted in minimal U.S. casualties, and in the end President Bush's approval rating soared to a new high and established him as a powerful force in world affairs.

Despite the apparent total victory, the war failed to oust Hussein from power in Iraq. Bush ruled out further military action in Iraq but urged continued international economic sanctions against the Hussein regime.

Fails to win second term

After the Gulf War, many believed Bush would be unbeatable in the next presidential election. Yet by 1992, the nation's economy was in a downturn, the national deficit (the amount the federal government needs to borrow to make up the difference between what it spends and how much it collects in taxes) had soared, and crime was rising. In the general election, a popular independent candidate, Texas businessman Ross Perot (1930–), divided the Republican Party. (See also **Third Parties**.) The Republicans were further divided in the general election, with economic conservatives on one side and social and religious conservatives like Pat Buchanan (1938–)—who had challenged Bush in the Republican primaries—on the other. In the end, Perot took a whopping 19 percent of the popular vote, and the **Democratic Party** candidate, **Arkansas** governor **Bill Clinton** (1946–), won the election.

In retirement, Bush kept as low a profile as could be expected with two of his sons, President **George W. Bush** (1946–; served 2001–) and **Florida** governor Jeb Bush (1953–) prominently in the national spotlight.

George W. Bush

George Walker Bush was born on July 6, 1946, in New Haven, **Connecticut**, where his father, **George H. W. Bush** (1924–), was enrolled at Yale University. After his father graduated in 1948, the family moved to **Texas**, where the senior Bush worked as an executive in the oil industry. Like his father, George W. Bush attended Phillips Academy (a private school that prepares students for college) in Andover, **Massachusetts**, and went on to Yale University. He was an average student, president of his fraternity, and a member of an exclusive secret group, the Skull and Bones Society. While Bush was still at Yale in 1966, his father was elected to the U.S. House of Representatives. After serving in Congress, George H. W. Bush went on to hold positions in the presidential administrations of **Richard Nixon** (1913–1994; served 1969–74) and **Gerald R. Ford** (1913–2006; served 1974–77) before being elected vice president and president in the 1980s.

In 1975, George W. Bush earned a master's degree in business administration from Harvard. He served as a pilot for the Texas Air National Guard before beginning a career in the oil and gas business. He quickly gained a reputation for fast cars and occasionally heavy drinking. In later years, he admitted to being irresponsible in his youth. After working in the energy industry for several years, Bush met Laura Welch (1946–), an elementary school teacher and librarian. They married in 1977, and their twin daughters were born in 1981. Bush ran for a seat in Congress in 1978 but lost the election. He had some difficult times in the oil business, but eventually built a small, successful company.

Change of ways

In 1985, under the influence of Baptist evangelist minister **Billy Graham** (1918–), Bush experienced a religious conversion. A year later, he stopped drinking alcohol. To those who knew him, these events were seen as major turning points in his life. When his father won the Republican nomination for president in 1988, Bush helped manage his presidential campaign. He gained respect in **Washington, D.C.**, for rallying the campaign team through the ups and downs of the tight race.

Back in Texas after the election, Bush organized a group of wealthy investors to buy the Texas Rangers, a major league baseball team. Riding a wave of popularity, he decided to run as the Republican candidate for

Republican George W. Bush won the controversial 2000 election and became the forty-third president of the United States. AP IMAGES

governor of Texas in 1994. To the surprise of many, he won the election. After only a year in office, Bush was hailed as the most popular big-state governor in the country. He worked to improve public schools, cut taxes, and put welfare recipients to work, and he encouraged new business and job growth. Bush won reelection in 1998 with 68 percent of the vote.

By January 2000, Bush was the frontrunner of a large field of Republican presidential candidates and became the party's nominee that summer. Since some people questioned Bush's grasp of national issues and foreign affairs, he selected the experienced Dick Cheney (1941–) to be his running mate. Mixing a folksy approach with clear policy measures, Bush maintained a slight lead against the Democratic nominee, Vice President **Al Gore** (1948–), as the 2000 election approached.

A controversial election

Shortly after 8 PM on election day, Tuesday, November 7, 2000, news agencies began projecting that Gore had won the popular vote and seemed headed for an electoral college victory. (The electoral college is the group that directly elects the president and vice president. Each state is allotted a number of electors equal to the number of its representatives and senators in Congress, and each presidential candidate has a slate of electors assigned to that candidate. When a candidate wins the popular vote in a state, the electors assigned to that candidate vote for him or her in the electoral college.) Around 10 PM, news reporters began referring to **Florida**'s popular vote as too close to call. When daylight came on Wednesday morning, there was still no new president-elect.

The problem was in Florida. Vote tallies completed in Florida were extremely close, and serious voting problems had arisen in four Florida counties. Recounts began. Republican officials tried to have the recounts stopped since accepting the tallies as they were would have resulted in a victory, though a very narrow one, for Bush. Democrats took the matter before state judges. The Florida Supreme Court ruled unanimously (7–0) that manual recounts could continue. Bush's lawyers appealed the ruling to the U.S. Supreme Court. The nation waited to find out who would be the next president.

On December 12, a bitterly divided Supreme Court ruled 5–4 that the recounts were unconstitutional. It ordered a halt to all further recounts. Gore conceded the election to Bush.

The presidency

Bush took office ready to cut taxes, improve schools, build an antimissile defense system to intercept long-range missiles launched at the United States, create a White House department of faith-based (religious) initiatives, and reform immigration policy and Social Security. He drew criticism soon after taking office when he refused to sign the Kyoto Protocol, an amendment to the international treaty on climate change that required nations to reduce greenhouse gas emissions in their countries.

On September 11, 2001, terrorists hijacked commercial airliners and attacked the World Trade Center in New York and the Pentagon in Washington, D.C. (See **September 11, 2001, Terrorist Attacks**). With Congress uniting behind him, Bush announced a war on terrorism. In October, the United States led an invasion into Afghanistan (see **Afghanistan Conflict**), where **al-Qaeda**, the terrorist group responsible for the attack, was headquartered.

The Bush administration set up a new department, the **Homeland Security Department**, to consolidate the different government agencies that protect the nation from terrorist attacks and other disasters. Bush aides put together the **USA PATRIOT Act** of 2001, which gave law enforcement agents more power but caused controversy by treading upon civil rights.

Going on the offensive

Not long after invading Afghanistan, Bush announced that Iraq, North Korea, and Iran were "axes of evil," saying that they were illegally building up **weapons of mass destruction** (weapons capable of causing massive numbers of deaths, injuries, or destruction that fall into one of three categories: biological, chemical, and nuclear or radiological weapons) and that the United States would not allow them to do so. He stepped up his case against Iraq's president, Saddam Hussein (1937–2006), claiming that Iraq continued to build weapons of mass destruction even after the United Nations (UN) had concluded otherwise. The Bush administration also claimed that Iraq had links to al-Qaeda, and the administration asked the UN for a mandate to strike. The UN voted not to participate in an attack.

Proceeding without the United Nations, the Bush administration put together a coalition of forces dominated by American and British troops, with support from Australia, Denmark, and Poland, and drew up plans to invade Iraq. Worldwide opposition to an **Iraq invasion** was demonstrated on February 15, 2003, when protests drew between six and ten million people in hundreds of cities around the world. Nonetheless, the U.S. military assembled 125,000 troops in Kuwait; the United Kingdom assembled another 45,000. The coalition gave Hussein forty-eight hours to comply with requests for inspection and then attacked, starting the Iraq War. Investigations in Iraq after the war had started revealed no significant weapons of mass destruction; the link between Iraq and al-Qaeda was disproved. The initial attack overthrew Hussein, who was later hanged, but the war continued, fueled by Iraqi insurgents (rebels) who resented the American occupation of Iraq and by a growing civil war among Iraqi factions.

Although Bush tried to accomplish other things in his presidency, the ongoing Iraq War dominated his tenure in office nearly completely. During his first term in office, Bush was able to sustain popular support for his mission, and he was reelected to a second term. Soon after his reelection, however, his popularity began to plunge as the war dragged on. Then, on August 29, 2005, Hurricane Katrina, one of the most disastrous storms in U.S. history, struck the Gulf Coast, wreaking havoc in **Mississippi** and **Louisiana**. In New Orleans, the levees that protect the city from flooding broke down, causing 80 percent of the city to flood. For days, thousands of New Orleans citizens were stranded. Critics claimed that the Bush administration, and particularly the Federal Emergency Management Agency (FEMA), did not seem to grasp the severity of the situation in the city. Their delays in getting help to New Orleans caused chaos and suffering, which was meanwhile being viewed on nationwide television. For an administration that had prided itself on security and being ready for disaster, its handling of the rescue of New Orleans in the aftermath of Katrina was viewed as a black mark.

In the 2006 congressional elections, the Democrats won a majority in both the House and the Senate for the first time in more than a decade. The growing ranks of critics of the president accused him and his top aides of having manufactured evidence of weapons of mass destruction and al-Qaeda links to win support for the Iraq invasion. Critics also held that the administration had given too little thought to the political situation in Iraq and the Middle East and thus provided too few troops to handle the insurgency that followed the invasion. Even some Republicans broke rank, calling the administration's handling of the war incompetent. Bush's approval ratings in national polls slipped below 50 percent in January 2005 and continued to plunge, with a disapproval rating hanging in the mid-60s in 2007.

Busing for School Desegregation

In the 1954 landmark case *Brown v. Board of Education*, the **Supreme Court** ruled that segregated public schools (schools that separate black and white students) violated the constitutional right of equal protection for all citizens. A year after the *Brown* ruling, the Court convened again to determine how to desegregate, or end school **segregation.** (See also **Desegregation of Public Schools**.) The Court stated that desegregation should proceed with "all deliberate speed." Federal district judges were instructed to examine school systems on a city-by-city basis to create plans to correct illegal segregation. Since this guidance was vague, many school systems remained segregated for years.

In the 1960s, civil rights lawyers from the **National Association for the Advancement of Colored People** (NAACP) filed lawsuits on behalf of black parents and children requesting the courts to require desegregation plans for individual cities. In a 1969 decision, *Alexander v. Holmes County Board of Education,* the Supreme Court indicated that it would no longer tolerate delays in school desegregation. But exactly how to desegregate schools remained a question until the Supreme Court ruled on the *Swann v. Charlotte-Mecklenburg Board of Education* case in 1971.

Swann v. Charlotte-Mecklenburg

The Charlotte-Mecklenburg school district included the city of Charlotte, **North Carolina**, and rural Mecklenburg County. Twenty-nine percent of the district's school-age children were black, most of them concentrated in one area of Charlotte. Schools in the district were essentially either all-white or all-black, and the all-black schools were more poorly equipped than the all-white schools. In 1965, NAACP attorney Julius LeVonne Chambers (1936–) initiated a lawsuit to end racial segregation in the Charlotte public schools. The first ruling in *Swann v. Charlotte-Mecklenburg* made only vague requirements for change. Initially, the school district adopted a plan that supposedly permitted students to transfer between schools if there were open places available. After these changes, though, only 490 of the 20,000 black students in the district attended schools that contained any white students, and most of these students were in one school that had only seven white students. The few black students who attempted to attend all-white schools were often attacked by mobs of angry whites.

Chambers filed another legal action in 1969. Federal District Judge James B. McMillan (1916–1995) found that the Charlotte schools were still illegally segregated. With the assistance of education consultants, McMillan developed and imposed a desegregation plan in the public schools that involved transporting white children to previously all-black schools and black children to previously all-white schools to achieve desegregation. By mixing black children and white children in every school building, the school officials would no longer be able to provide adequate educational resources only for white students. Since blacks tended to live in one area of the city, this required transporting the children.

Many white residents did not want their children to attend schools with black children. Judge McMillan received threatening telephone calls and was ostracized (excluded from social events) by the community. Chambers was directly attacked. Firebombs and dynamite damaged his office, car, and home. The school board still wanted to avoid desegregation and appealed to the Supreme Court to overturn Judge McMillan's busing plan.

Many people expected at least some of the Supreme Court justices to rule against busing as a tool for desegregating schools. President **Richard Nixon** (1913–1994; served 1969–74) had campaigned against the forced busing of school children. Nixon's two appointees to the Supreme Court, Chief Justice Warren Burger (1907–1995) and Associate Justice Harry Blackmun (1908–1999), were presumed to agree with the president's view. Nonetheless, after much debate, on April 20, 1971, the Court ruled unanimously that judges could order school districts to use busing as a means to desegregate schools.

Busing plans nationwide

The use of busing spread as federal judges began to hear more lawsuits challenging discriminatory conditions in school systems. For once, desegregation plans were not limited to the South. In a 1973 case, the city of Denver, **Colorado**, was ordered to create a busing plan.

In 1974, a federal court ordered the schools in Boston, **Massachusetts**, to desegregate through an aggressive busing program. Boston's neighborhoods had long been divided by nationality and race. The court-ordered busing unleashed a storm of protest, frequent rioting, and even attacks on students. Residents of white neighborhoods threw rocks and bottles at buses and attacked black passersby. Violence between black and white students led to the presence of police on school grounds during much of the controversy. The violent conflict over busing in Boston lasted for years.

Eventually, most schools adjusted to busing, and desegregation became an accepted aspect of life in many public schools. In smaller cities, busing programs gave black students the opportunity to receive educational benefits that had previously been denied to them. Public opinion research indicated that, especially in southern states, the implementation of desegregation orders was accompanied by an increase in racial tolerance.

Milliken v. Bradley

In many large metropolitan (city) areas, however, schools failed to become racially mixed. Due to desegregation and busing requirements in the cities, many whites moved to the suburbs. As middle-class residents and businesses fled the cities, many cities were growing poor. Central city schools that often served poor minority students had significantly fewer resources than neighboring suburban schools for maintaining buildings and providing high-quality educational programs. To desegregate schools, the federal courts would have had to mix city school districts with neighboring suburban school districts.

After *Swann,* President Nixon had appointed four justices to the Supreme Court. In 1974, the Court issued a divided five-to-four decision in *Milliken v. Bradley* that prevented busing plans from crossing school district boundaries. Thus, in many large cities, segregation, and inferior education for black students, continued.

Where to Learn More

In addition to numerous U•X•L publications, the following sources were used to help compile the entries in this book.

Books

Altman, Linda Jacobs. *The American Civil Rights Movement: The African American Struggle for Equality.* Berkeley Heights, NJ: Enslow, 2004.

Ambrose, Stephen E. *Undaunted Courage: The Pioneering First Mission to Explore America's Wild Frontier.* New York: Pocket Books, 2003.

Anbinder, Tyler. *Nativism and Slavery: The Northern Know Nothings and the Politics of the 1850s.* New York: Oxford University Press, 1992.

Anderson, Terry H. *The Movement and the Sixties.* New York: Oxford University Press, 1996.

Anderson, Terry H. *The Pursuit of Fairness: A History of Affirmative Action.* New York: Oxford University Press, 2004.

Arsenault, Raymond. *Freedom Riders: 1961 and the Struggle for Racial Justice.* New York: Oxford University Press, 2006.

Bailey, Anne C. *African Voices of the Atlantic Slave Trade: Beyond the Silence and the Shame.* Boston: Beacon Press, 2006.

Baker, H. Robert. *The Rescue of Joshua Glover: A Fugitive Slave, the Constitution, and the Coming of the Civil War.* Athens: Ohio University Press, 2007.

Baker, Jean H. *James Buchanan.* New York: Times Books, 2004.

Barilleaux, Ryan J., and Mark J. Rozell. *Power and Prudence: The Presidency of George H. W. Bush.* College Station: Texas A&M University, 2004.

Barnes, Catherine A. *Journey from Jim Crow: the Desegregation of Southern Transit.* New York: Columbia University Press, 1983.

Bass, Patrik Henry. *Like a Mighty Stream: The March on Washington, August 28, 1963.* Philadelphia: Running Press, 2003.

Bates, Daisy. *The Long Shadow of Little Rock: A Memoir,* reprint ed. Fayetteville: University of Arkansas Press, 1987 (orig. pub. 1962).

Bauer, K. Jack. *Zachary Taylor: Soldier, Planter, Statesman of the Old Southwest.* Baton Rouge: Louisiana State University Press, 1985.

Beals, Melba Pattillo. *Warriors Don't Cry: Searing Memoir of Battle to Integrate Little Rock,* reprint ed. New York: Washington Square Press, 1995.

Beckwith, Francis J., and Todd E. Jones, eds. *Affirmative Action: Social Justice or Reverse Discrimination.* Amherst, NH: Prometheus Books, 1997.

Benn, Carl. *The War of 1812.* London: Routledge, 2003.

Berlin, Ira. *Many Thousands Gone: The First Two Centuries of Slavery in North America.* Cambridge, MA: Harvard University Press, 1998.

Bernstein, Peter L. *Wedding of the Waters: The Erie Canal and the Making of a Great Nation.* New York: W. W. Norton, 2005.

Bernstein, R. B. *Thomas Jefferson.* New York: Oxford University Press, 2003.

Bernstein, Richard. *Out of the Blue: A Narrative of September 11, 2001.* New York: Times Books, 2002.

Binder, Frederick Moore. *James Buchanan and the American Empire.* Selinsgrove, PA: Susquehanna University Press, 1994.

Blassingame, John W. *The Slave Community: Plantation Life in the Antebellum South.* New York: Oxford University Press, 1979.

Blue, Frederick J. *No Taint of Compromise: Crusaders in Antislavery Politics.* Baton Rouge: Louisiana State University Press, 2006.

Bonilla, Denise M. *School Violence.* New York: H. W. Wilson, 2000.

Bordewich, Fergus M. *Bound for Canaan, the Epic Story of the Underground Railroad: America's First Civil Rights Movement.* New York: Amistad, 2006.

Borneman, Walter R. *1812: The War That Forged a Nation.* New York: HarperCollins, 2004.

Bowen, Catherine Drinker. *Miracle at Philadelphia: The Story of the Constitutional Convention—May to September, 1787.* Boston: Little, Brown, 1966.

Bowen, William G., and Derek Bok. *The Shape of the River: Long Term Consequences of Considering Race in College and University Admissions.* Princeton, NJ: Princeton University Press, 1998.

Branch, Taylor. *At Canaan's Edge: America in the King Years, 1965–68.* New York: Simon & Schuster, 2006.

Branch, Taylor. *Pillar of Fire: America in the King Years, 1963–65.* New York: Simon & Schuster, 1998.

Brands, H. W. *The Age of Gold: The California Gold Rush and the New American Dream.* New York: Anchor, 2003.

Brands, H. W. *Andrew Jackson: His Life and Times.* New York: Anchor Books, 2006.

Brill, Marlene Targ. *James Buchanan: Fifteenth President of the United States.* Chicago: Childrens Press, 1988.

Buechler, Steven M. *Women's Movements in the United States: Woman Suffrage, Equal Rights, and Beyond.* New Brunswick, NJ: Rutgers University Press, 2007.

Burgan, Michael. *The Missouri Compromise.* Mankato, MN: Compass Point Books, 2006.

Burns, Stewart, ed. *Daybreak of Freedom: The Montgomery Bus Boycott.* Chapel Hill: University of North Carolina Press, 1997.

Bush, George. *All the Best, George Bush: My Life in Letters and Other Writings.* New York: Scribner, 1999.

Bush, George, and Brent Scowcraft. *A World Transformed.* New York: Knopf, 1998.

Cable, Mary. *Black Odyssey: The Case of the Slave Ship Amistad.* New York: Penguin Books, 1977.

Cagin, Seth, and Philip Dray. *We Are Not Afraid: The Story of Goodman, Schwerner, and Chaney and the Civil Rights Campaign for Mississippi.* New York: Bantam, 1991.

Carlisle, Rodney P., and John Stewart Bowman. *Perisan Gulf War.* New York: Facts on File, 2003.

Carnoy, Martin, et al. *The New Global Economy in the Information Age: Reflections on Our Changing World.* University Park: Pennsylvania State University Press, 1993.

Carson, Clayborn. *In Struggle: SNCC and the Black Awakening of the 1960s.* Cambridge, MA: Harvard University Press, 1995.

Carson, Clayborn, and Martin Luther King Jr. *Autobiography of Martin Luther King, Jr.* New York: Warner Books, 1998.

Chafe, William Henry, Raymond Gavins, and Robert Korstad, eds. *Remembering Jim Crow: African Americans Tell About Life in the Segregated South.* New York: New Press, 2003.

Clinton, Bill. *My Life.* New York: Knopf, 2004.

Colaiaco, James A. *Frederick Douglass and the Fourth of July.* New York: Palgrave Macmillan, 2007.

Colbert, Nancy A. *Great Society: The Story of Lyndon Baines Johnson.* Greensboro, NC: Morgan Reynolds, 2002.

Crapol, Edward P. *John Tyler, the Accidental President.* Chapel Hill: University of North Carolina Press, 2006.

Cunningham, Noble. *In Pursuit of Reason: The Life of Thomas Jefferson.* Baton Rouge: Louisiana State University Press, 1987.

Dallek, Robert. *Flawed Giant: Lyndon B. Johnson, 1960–1973.* Oxford: Oxford University Press, 1998.

Daniels, Roger. *Coming to America: A History of Immigration and Ethnicity in American Life.* New York: HarperCollins, 1990.

Darmer, M. Katherine B., Robert M. Baird, and Stuart E. Rosenbaum, eds. *Civil Liberties vs. National Security: In a Post 9/11 World.* Amherst, NY: Prometheus Books, 2004.

Davis, William C. *Lone Star Rising: The Revolutionary Birth of the Texas Republic.* College Station: Texas A&M University Press, 2006.

DiConsiglio, John. *Franklin Pierce: America's Fourteenth President.* Chicago: Childrens Press, 2004.

Dimond, Paul R. *Beyond Busing: Reflections on Urban Segregation, the Courts, and Equal Opportunity.* Ann Arbor: University of Michigan Press, 2005.

Douglas, Davison M. *Reading, Writing and Race: The Desegregation of the Charlotte Schools.* Chapel Hill: University of North Carolina, 1995.

Douglass, Frederick. *Narrative of the Life of Frederick Douglass.* Clayton, DE: Prestwick House, 2004.

Dyson, Michael Eric. *Making Malcolm: The Myth and Meaning of Malcolm X.* New York, Oxford University Press, 1995.

Egerton, Douglas R. *He Shall Go Out Free: The Lives of Denmark Vesey,* rev. ed. Lanham, MD: Rowman & Littlefield Publishers, 2004.

Ellis, Joseph J. *American Sphinx: The Character of Thomas Jefferson.* New York: Vintage, 1998.

Eskew, Glenn T. *But for Birmingham: The Local and National Movements in the Civil Rights Struggle.* Chapel Hill: University of North Carolina Press, 1997.

Etzioni, Amitai. *How Patriotic Is the Patriot Act? Freedom vs. Security in the Age of Terrorism.* Oxford, UK: Routledge, 2004.

Fairclough, Adam. *To Redeem the Soul of America: The Southern Christian Leadership Conference and Martin Luther King, Jr.* Athens: University of Georgia Press, 2001.

Farber, David R., and Beth L. Bailey. *The Columbia Guide to America in the 1960s.* New York: Columbia University Press, 2003.

Farmer, James. *Lay Bare the Heart: An Autobiography of the Civil Rights Movement.* New York: Penguin/Plume, 1986.

Fenton, William N. *The Great Law and the Longhouse: A Political History of the Iroquois Confederacy.* Tulsa: University of Oklahoma Press, 1998.

Finlayson, Reggie. *We Shall Overcome: The History of the American Civil Rights Movement.* Minneapolis, MN: Lerner, 2002.

Fitzgerald, Stephanie. *Little Rock Nine: Struggle for Integration.* Mankato, MN: Compass Point Books, 2006.

Flanagan, Alice K. *The Lowell Mill Girls.* Mankato, MN: Compass Point Books, 2005.

Fleming, Thomas. *The Louisiana Purchase.* Hoboken, NJ: Wiley, 2003.

Forbes, Robert Pierce. *The Missouri Compromise and Its Aftermath: Slavery and the Meaning of America.* Chapel Hill: University of North Carolina Press, 2007.

Franklin, John Hope, and Loren Schweninger. *Runaway Slaves: Rebels on the Plantation.* New York: Oxford University Press, 1999.

Frazier, Donald S., ed. *The United States and Mexico at War: Nineteenth-Century Expansionism and Conflict.* New York: Macmillan, 1998.

Freehling, William W. *Prelude to the Civil War: The Nullification Controversy.* New York: HarperCollins, 1968.

Gara, Larry. *The Presidency of Franklin Pierce.* Lawrence: University Press of Kansas, 1991.

Garrow, David G. *Bearing the Cross: Martin Luther King and the Southern Leadership Conference.* Norwalk, CT: Easton Press, 1986.

Gitlin, Todd. *Years of Hope, Days of Rage,* rev. ed. New York: Bantam, 1993.

Goldman, Roger, and David Gallen, eds. *Thurgood Marshall: Justice for All.* New York: Carroll & Graf, 1992.

Gonzalez, Juan. *Harvest of Empire: A History of Latinos in America.* New York: Viking, 2000.

Good, Timothy S. *Lincoln-Douglas Debates and the Making of a President.* Jefferson, NC: McFarland, 2007.

Greenblatt, Miriam. *John Quincy Adams: Sixth President of the United States.* Ada, OK: Garrett Educational Corp., 1990

Greenburg, Cheryl Lynn. *A Circle of Trust: Remembering the SNCC.* Rutgers University Press, 2005.

Grofman, Bernard, ed. *Legacies of the 1964 Civil Rights Act.* Charlottesville: University of Virginia, 2000.

Gumbel, Andrew. *Steal This Vote: Dirty Elections and the Rotten History of Democracy in America.* New York: Nation Books, 2005.

Gurko, Miriam. *The Ladies of Seneca Falls: The Birth of the Women's Rights Movement.* New York: Pantheon, 1987.

Hacker, Andrew. *Two Nations: Black and White, Separate, Hostile, Unequal.* New York: Ballantine Books, 1995.

Haley, Alex. *The Autobiography of Malcolm X.* New York, Grove Press, 1965.

Harms, Robert W. *The Diligent: A Voyage Through the Worlds of the Slave Trade.* New York: Basic Books, 2001.

Hasday, Judy L. *The Civil Rights Act of 1964: An End to Racial Segregation.* New York: Chelsea House, 2007.

Haugen, Brenda. *Frederick Douglass: Slave, Writer, Abolitionist.* Mankato, MN: Compass Point Books, 2005.

Haynes, Sam W. *James K. Polk and the Expansionist Impulse.* Edited by Oscar Handlin. New York: Longman, 1997.

Haynes, Sam W., and Christopher Morris, eds. *Manifest Destiny and Empire: American Antebellum Expansionism.* College Station: Texas A&M University Press, 1997.

Hendrick, George. *Why Not Every Man?: African Americans and Civil Disobedience in the Quest for the Dream.* Chicago: Ivan R. Dee, 2005.

Hickey, Donald R. *The War of 1812: A Forgotten Conflict.* Urbana: University of Illinois Press, 1989.

Higginson, Thomas Wentworth. *Black Rebellion: Five Slave Revolts.* Cambridge, MA: Da Capo Press, 2001.

Hindle, Brooke, and Steven Lubar. *Engines of Change: The American Industrial Revolution, 1790–1860.* Albany: State University of New York Press, 1981.

Hinks, Peter. *Encyclopedia of Antislavery and Abolition.* Westport, CT: Greenwood Press, 2006.

Howard-Pitney, David. *Martin Luther King, Jr., Malcolm X, and the Civil Rights Struggle of the 1950s and 1960s: A Brief History with Documents.* New York: Bedford/St. Martin's, 2004.

Hulnick, Arthur S. *Keeping Us Safe: Secret Intelligence and Homeland Security.* Westport, CT: Praeger, 2004.

Hunter, Tera W. *To 'Joy My Freedom: Southern Black Women's Lives and Labors After the Civil War,* reprint ed. Cambridge, MA: Harvard University Press, 1998.

Isenberg, Irwin, ed. *The City in Crisis.* New York: H. W. Wilson, 1968.

Jaffa, Harry V. *Crisis of the House Divided: An Interpretation of the Issues in the Lincoln-Douglas Debates.* Chicago: University of Chicago Press, 1982.

Johnson, Susan Lee. *Roaring Camp: The Social World of the California Gold Rush.* New York: W. W. Norton, 2001.

Jones, Howard. *Mutiny on the Amistad: The Saga of a Slave Revolt and Its Impact on American Abolition, Law, and Diplomacy.* New York: Oxford University Press, 1987.

Joseph, Peniel E. *Waiting 'Til the Midnight Hour: A Narrative History of Black Power in America.* Austin, TX: Holt, 2007.

Josephy, Alvin M., Jr. *Lewis and Clark Through Indian Eyes.* New York: Knopf, 2006.

Jurmain, Suzanne. *Freedom's Sons: The True Story of the Amistad Mutiny.* New York: HarperCollins, 1998.

Kagan, Elena, and Cass R. Sunstein. *Remembering "TM."* Chicago: University of Chicago Press, 1993.

Kaplan, Leonard V., and Beverly I. Moran, eds. *Aftermath: The Clinton Impeachment and the Presidency in the Age of Political Spectacle.* New York: New York University Press, 2001.

Kearns, Doris. *Lyndon Johnson and the American Dream.* New York: St. Martin's Griffin, 1991.

Kent, Zachary. *The Persian Gulf War: The "Mother of All Battles."* Berkeley Heights, NJ: Enslow, 2000.

King, Martin Luther, Jr. *Letter from the Birmingham Jail.* San Francisco: Harper, 1994.

Klausmeyer, David. *Oregon Trail Stories: True Accounts of Life in a Covered Wagon.* Emeryville, CA: Falcon, 2003.

Klees, Emerson. *The Iroquois Confederacy: Legends and History.* New York: Cameo Press, 2003.

Kornblith, Gary G. *The Industrial Revolution in America.* Boston: Houghton Mifflin, 1998.

Kukla, Jon. *A Wilderness So Immense: The Louisiana Purchase and the Destiny of America.* New York: Anchor, 2004.

Kupperman, Karen Ordahl. *Roanoke: The Abandoned Colony,* 2nd ed. Lanham, MD: Rowman & Littlefield, 2007.

Langford, R. Everett. *Introduction to Weapons of Mass Destruction: Radiological, Chemical, and Biological.* Hoboken, NJ: Wiley-Interscience, 2004.

Lavender, David Sievert. *Snowbound: The Tragic Story of the Donner Party.* New York: Holiday House, 1996.

Levin, John, and Jack Levin. *Domestic Terrorism.* New York: Chelsea House, 2006.

Levinson, Sanford, and Bartholomew Sparrow, eds. *The Louisiana Purchase and American Expansion, 1803–1898.* Lanham, MD: Rowman & Littlefield, 2005.

Levitas, Daniel. *The Terrorist Next Door: The Militia Movement and the Radical Right.* New York: St. Martin's Griffin, 2004.

Lewis, Meriwether, and William Clark. *The Journals of Lewis and Clark.* Edited by Bernard De Voto. Boston: Houghton Mifflin, 1953.

Lillegard, Dee. *James K. Polk: Eleventh President of the United States.* New York: Children's Press, 1988.

Linenthal, Edward T. *An Unfinished Bombing: Oklahoma City in American Memory.* New York: Oxford University Press, 2001.

Loevy, Robert D. *The Civil Rights Act of 1964: The Passage of the Law That Ended Racial Segregation.* Albany: State University of New York Press, 1997.

Lukas, J. Anthony. *Common Ground: A Turbulent Decade in the Lives of Three American Families.* New York: Vintage, 1986.

Madison, James. *Notes of Debates in the Federal Convention of 1787 Reported by James Madison.* New York: W. W. Norton, 1987.

Maxwell, Bruce. *Homeland Security: A Documentary History.* Washington, DC: CQ Press, 2004.

Mayer, Henry. *All on Fire: William Lloyd Garrison and the Abolition of Slavery.* New York: St. Martin's Griffin, 2000.

McAdam, Doug. *Freedom Summer.* New York: Oxford University Press, 1988.

McClymer, John F. *Mississippi Freedom Summer.* Detroit: Wadsworth, 2003.

McLynn, Frank. *Wagons West: The Epic Story of America's Overland Trails.* New York: Grove Press, 2002.

McPherson, Stephanie Sammartino. *"Lau v. Nichols": Bilingual Education in Public Schools.* Berkeley Heights, NJ: Enslow, 2000.

McWhorter, Diane. *Carry Me Home: Birmingham, Alabama: The Climactic Battle of the Civil Rights Revolution.* New York: Simon and Schuster, 2002.

Meed, Douglas V. *The Mexican War 1846–1848.* London, UK: Routledge, 2003.

Michael, George. *Confronting Right Wing Extremism and Terrorism in the USA.* New York: Routledge, 2003.

Miller, Douglas T. *Thomas Jefferson and the Creation of America.* New York: Facts on File, 1997.

Montejano, David. *Anglos and Mexicans in the Making of Texas, 1836–1986.* Austin: University of Texas Press, 1986.

Morganstein, Martin, Joan H. Cregg, and the Erie Canal Museum. *Erie Canal.* Mount Pleasant, SC: Arcadia, 2001.

Morris, Dick, and Eileen McGann. *Because He Could.* New York: HarperCollins, 2004.

Morrison, Toni. *Remember: The Journey to School Integration.* Boston: Houghton Mifflin, 2004.

Murphy, Jim. *Inside the Alamo.* New York: Delacorte Books, 2003.

Murphy, Virginia Reed. *Across the Plains in the Donner Party.* North Haven, CT: Linnet Books, 1996.

Myers, Walter Dean. *Amistad: A Long Road to Freedom,* reprint ed. New York: Puffin, 2001.

Myers, Walter Dean. *Malcolm X: By Any Means Necessary,* reprint ed. Bainbridge Island, WA: Polaris, 1999.

Nagel, Paul C. *John Quincy Adams: A Public Life, a Private Life.* New York: Knopf, 1997.

Newell, Clayton R. *The A to Z of the Persian Gulf War, 1990–91.* Lanham, MD: Scarecrow, 2007.

Nichols, Roy F. *Franklin Pierce: Young Hickory of the Granite Hills,* 2nd ed. Easton Press, 1988.

Niven, John. *John C. Calhoun and the Price of Union.* Baton Rouge: Louisiana State University Press, 1993.

Northrup, David, ed. *The Atlantic Slave Trade,* rev. ed. Boston: Houghton Mifflin, 2005.

Okin, J. R. *The Information Revolution: The Not-for-dummies Guide to the History, Technology, and Use of the World Wide Web.* Winter Harbor, ME: Ironbound Press, 2005.

Otfinoski, Steven. *William Henry Harrison: America's Ninth President.* Chicago: Children's Press, 2003.

Owsley, Frank Lawrence, Jr. *Struggle for the Gulf Borderlands: The Creek War and the Battle of New Orleans, 1812–1815.* Gainesville: University of Florida Press, 1981.

Packard, Jerrold M. *American Nightmare: The History of Jim Crow.* New York: St. Martin's Griffin, 2003.

Painter, Nell Irvin. *Sojourner Truth: A Life, A Symbol.* New York: W. W. Norton, 1997.

Pastan, Amy. *Martin Luther King, Jr.* New York: Dorling Kindersley, 2005.

Pauley, Garth E. *LBJ's American Promise: The 1965 Voting Rights Address.* College Station: Texas A&M University Press, 2007.

Peterson, Norma Lois. *The Presidencies of William Henry Harrison and John Tyler.* Lawrence: University Press of Kansas, 1989.

Postma, Johannes. *The Atlantic Slave Trade.* Gainesville: University Press of Florida, 2005.

Price, Richard. *Maroon Societies: Rebel Slave Communities in the Americas.* Baltimore, MD: Johns Hopkins University Press, 1996.

Ransom, Roger L. *Conflict and Compromise: The Political Economy of Slavery, Emancipation, and the American Civil War.* New York: Cambridge University Press, 2002.

Remini, Robert V. *John Quincy Adams.* New York: Times Books, 2002.

Riches, William T. Martin. *The Civil Rights Movement: Struggle and Resistance.* New York: St. Martin's, 1997.

Richter, Daniel K. *The Ordeal of the Longhouse: The Peoples of the Iroquois League in the Era of European Colonization.* Chapel Hill: University of North Carolina Press, 1992.

Ricks, Thomas E. *Fiasco: The American Military Adventure in Iraq.* New York: Penguin, 2007.

Rife, Douglas. *History Speaks: Seneca Falls Declaration of Sentiments and Resolutions.* Carthage, IL: Teaching and Learning Co., 2002.

Roberts, Jeremy. *Zachary Taylor.* Minneapolis, MN: Lerner Publications, 2005.

Romano, Renee Christine, and Leigh Raiford. *The Civil Rights Movement in American Memory.* Athens: University of Georgia Press, 2006.

Ross, Jim, and Paul Myers. *We Will Never Forget: Eyewitness Accounts of the Oklahoma City Federal Building Bombing.* Waco, TX: Eakin Press, 1996.

Russo, Peggy A., and Paul Finkelman. *Terrible Swift Sword: The Legacy of John Brown*. Athens: Ohio University Press, 2005.

Rutland, Robert A. *James Madison: The Founding Father*. New York: Macmillan, 1987.

San Miguel, Gaudalupe, Jr. *Contested Policy: The Rise and Fall of Federal Bilingual Education in the United States, 1960–2001*. University of North Texas Press, 2004.

Schwartz, Marie Jenkins. *Born in Bondage: Growing Up Enslaved in the Antebellum South*. Cambridge, MA: Harvard University Press, 2001.

Scott, Darrell, Beth Nimmo, and Steve Rabey. *Rachel's Tears: The Spiritual Journey of Columbine Martyr Rachel Scott*. Nashville, TN: Thomas Nelson, 2000.

Scott, John A., and Robert Alan Scott. *John Brown of Harpers Ferry*. New York: Facts on File, 1993.

Shapiro, Andrew L. *The Control Revolution: How the Internet Is Putting Individuals in Charge and Changing the World We Know*. New York: PublicAffairs, 2000.

Shaw, Ronald E. *Canals for a Nation: The Canal Era in the United States, 1790–1860*. Lexington: University Press of Kentucky, 1990.

Siebert, Wibur H. *The Underground Railroad from Slavery to Freedom: A Comprehensive History*. Mineola, NY: Dover Publications, 2006.

Siegenthaler, John. *James Polk: 1845–49*. New York: Times Books, 2003.

Sitkoff, Harvard. *The Struggle for Black Equality, 1954–1992*. New York: Hill and Wang, 1993.

Smith, Dennis. *Report from Ground Zero: The Story of the Rescue Efforts at the World Trade Center*. New York: Viking, 2002.

Smith, Elbert B. *The Presidencies of Zachary Taylor and Millard Fillmore*. Lawrence: University Press of Kansas, 1988.

Smith, Mark M. *Debating Slavery: Economy and Society in the Antebellum American South*. New York: Cambridge University Press, 2004.

Stefoff, Rebecca. *Andrew Jackson: Seventh President of the United States*. Ada, OK: Garrett Educational Corp., 1988.

Stegner, Page. *Winning the Wild West: The Epic Saga of the American Frontier, 1800–1899*. New York: Free Press, 2002.

Stevens, Carol B., ed. *William Henry Harrison*. Westport, CT: Greenwood Publishing Group, 1998.

Stewart, George R. *Ordeal by Hunger: The Story of the Donner Party*, rev. ed. New York: Adventure Library, 2002 (orig. pub. 1936).

Stick, David. *Roanoke Island: The Beginnings of English America*. Chapel Hill: University of North Carolina Press, 1983.

Stone, Geoffrey R. *Perilous Times: Free Speech in Wartime from the Sedition Act of 1798 to the War on Terrorism.* New York: W. W. Norton, 2004.

Street, Paul. *Segregated Schools: Educational Apartheid in Post–Civil Rights America.* London, UK: Routledge, 2005.

Stuart, Reginald C. *United States Expansionism and British North America, 1775–1871.* Chapel Hill: University of North Carolina Press, 1988.

Taylor, Eric Robert. *If We Must Die: Shipboard Insurrections in the Era of the Atlantic Slave Trade.* Baton Rouge: Louisiana State University Press, 2006.

Telgen, Diane. *Brown v. Board of Education.* Detroit: Omnigraphics, 2005.

Thompson, Frank T. *The Alamo.* Denton: University of North Texas Press, 2005.

Thompson, William, and Dorcas Thompson. *The Spanish Exploration of Florida: The Adventures of the Spanish Conquistadors.* Broomall, PA: Mason Crest, 2002.

Thoreau, Henry David. *Walden and "Civil Disobedience."* New York: Signet, 1960.

Time writers. *The Monsters Next Door: A Special Report on the Colorado School Massacre.* New York: Time Inc., 1999.

Truth, Sojourner. *Narrative of Sojourner Truth: A Bondswoman of Olden Time, with a History of Her Labors and Correspondence Drawn from Her "Book of Life."* New York: Oxford University Press, 1994.

Tushnet, Mark V. *Making Civil Rights Law: Thurgood Marshall and the Supreme Court, 1936–1961.* New York: Oxford University Press, 1994.

Tushnet, Mark V., ed. *Thurgood Marshall: His Speeches, Writings, Arguments, Opinions and Reminiscences.* Chicago: Lawrence Hill Books, 2001.

Vallelly, Richard M. *The Voting Rights Act: Securing the Ballot.* Washington, DC: CQ Press, 2005.

Walker, Dale L. *Eldorado: The California Gold Rush.* New York: Forge Books, 2003.

Walker, Jane C. *John Tyler: A President of Many Firsts.* Granville, OH: McDonald and Woodward, 2001.

Weatherman, Donald V. "James Buchanan," in *Great Lives from History.* Edited by Frank N. Magill. Vol. 1. Pasadena, CA: Salem Press, 1987.

Weisbrot, Robert. *Freedom Bound: A History of America's Civil Rights Movement.* New York: W. W. Norton, 1990.

White, Richard, and Kevin Collins. *The United States Department of Homeland Security: An Overview.* New York: Pearson, 2005.

Widick, B. J. *Detroit: City of Race and Class Violence.* Chicago: Quadrangle, 1972.

Wilentz, Sean. *Andrew Jackson.* Edited by Arthur M. Schlesinger Jr. New York: Times Books / Henry Holt, 2005.

Williams, Juan, and Julian Bond. *Eyes on the Prize: America's Civil Rights Years, 1954–1965.* New York: Penguin, 1988.

Wills, Garry. *James Madison.* New York: Times Books, 2002.

Winders, Richard Bruce. *Mr. Polk's Army: The American Military Experience in the Mexican War.* College Station: Texas A&M University Press, 1997.

Wood, Trish, and Bobby Muller. *What Was Asked of Us: An Oral History of the Iraq War by the Soldiers Who Fought It.* Boston: Little, Brown, 2006.

Wormser, Richard. *The Rise and Fall of Jim Crow.* New York: St. Martin's Griffin, 2004.

Wright, Lawrence. *The Looming Tower: Al-Qaeda and the Road to 9/11.* New York: Knopf, 2006.

Zarefsky, David. *Lincoln, Douglas, and Slavery: In the Crucible of Public Debate.* Chicago: University of Chicago Press, 1990.

Zinn, Howard. *SNCC: The New Abolitionists.* Cambridge, MA: South End Press, 2002.

Periodicals

Balleck, Barry. "When the Ends Justify the Means: Thomas Jefferson and the Louisiana Purchase." *Presidential Quarterly* Vol. XVII, no. 4 (fall 1992).

Beck, Melinda, and Stryker McGuire. "Get Me Out of Here!," *Newsweek* (May 1, 1995).

Dotson, J. "An American Tragedy," *Newsweek* 70 (August 7, 1967): 18–26.

Drummond, Tammerlin. "Battling the Columbine Copycats." *Time* (May 10, 1999).

Grecco, Michael. "The Gurus of YouTube." *Time* (December 16, 2006).

Mandel, Michael J. "The Internet Economy." *Business Week* (February 22, 1999).

Shattuck, Kathryn. "Kerouac's 'Road' Scroll Is Going to Auction." *New York Times* (March 22, 2001).

"A Young Mayor Seeks an Answer in the Ashes," *Life* 63 (August 11, 1967): 21–22.

Web Sites

"Adoption Laws in the U.S." *The Task Force.* http://www.thetaskforce.org/downloads/reports/issue_maps/adoption_laws_09_07_color.pdf (accessed on July 21, 2008).

Africans in America. http://www.pbs.org/wgbh/aia/home.html (accessed on July 21, 2008).

The Air Force Association. http://www.afa.org/ (accessed on July 21, 2008).

Almasy, Steve. "The Internet Transforms Modern Life." *CNN.com.* http://www.cnn.com/2005/TECH/internet/06/23/evolution.main/index. html (accessed on July 21, 2008).

"Amelia Earhart's Last Flight." *Virtual Exploration Society.* http://www .unmuseum.org/earhart.htm (accessed on July 21, 2008).

"American Masters: Aaron Copland." *PBS.org.* http://www.pbs.org/wnet/ americanmasters/database/copland_a.html (accessed on July 21, 2008).

"American Masters: McCarthyism." *PBS.org.* http://www.pbs.org/wnet/ americanmasters/database/mccarthyism.html (accessed on July 21, 2008).

"American Visionaries: Tuskegee Airmen." *National Park Service.* http://www.nps.gov/museum/exhibits/tuskegee/airoverview.htm (accessed on July 21, 2008).

"Amistad Trials, 1839–40." *Famous American Trials.* http://www.law.umkc.edu/ faculty/projects/ftrials/amistad/AMISTD.HTM (accessed on July 21, 2008).

"Andrew Carnegie." *PBS: American Experience.* http://www.pbs.org/wgbh/ amex/carnegie/sfeature/meet.html (accessed on July 21, 2008).

Army.mil: The Official Homepage of the United States Army. http://www.army.mil/ (accessed on July 21, 2008).

"The Atlantic Slave Trade." *PBS: The Story of Africa: Slavery.* http://www.bbc. co.uk/worldservice/africa/features/storyofafrica/9chapter4.shtml (accessed on July 21, 2008).

Aviation-History.com. http://www.aviation-history.com/ (accessed on July 21, 2008).

BarackObama.com. http://www.barackobama.com/index.php (accessed on July 21, 2008).

"Bill Clinton (1946–)." *Miller Center of Public Affairs, University of Virginia.* http://www.millercenter.virginia.edu/academic/americanpresident/clinton (accessed on July 21, 2008).

Brain, Marshall. "How Biological and Chemical Warfare Works." *How Stuff Works.* http://science.howstuffworks.com/biochem-war4.htm (accessed on July 21, 2008).

"A Brief History." *Levittown Historical Society.* http://www.levittownhistorical society.org/index2.htm (accessed on July 21, 2008).

"A Brief History of the American Red Cross." *RedCross.org.* http://www .redcross.org/museum/history/brief.asp (accessed on July 21, 2008).

"Brown v. Board of Education, 347 U.S. 483 (1954)." *The National Center for Public Policy Research.* http://www.nationalcenter.org/brown.html (accessed on July 21, 2008).

"The Call of the Wild." *SparkNotes.com.* http://www.sparknotes.com/lit/call/ (accessed on July 21, 2008).

"The Carter Family." *Southern Music Network.* http://www.southernmusic.net/ carterfamily.htm (accessed on July 21, 2008).

Carter, Jimmy, and Amy Goodman. "Palestine: Peace Not Apartheid ... Jimmy Carter in His Own Words." *Democracy Now!: The War and Peace Report.* http://www.democracynow.org/article.pl?sid=06/11/30/1452225 (accessed on July 21, 2008).

"Chasing the Sun: Aviation Timeline." *PBS.org.* http://www.pbs.org/kcet/ chasingthesun/timeline/1900.html (accessed on July 21, 2008).

"Chief Joseph." *PBS: New Perspectives on the West.* http://www.pbs.org/ weta/thewest/people/a_c/chiefjoseph.htm (accessed on July 21, 2008).

"Climate Change: Basic Information." *U.S. Environmental Protection Agency.* http://www.epa.gov/climatechange/basicinfo.html (accessed on July 22, 2008).

"Conflict of Abolition and Slavery." *The African American Mosaic: A Library of Congress Resource Guide for the Study of Black History and Culture.* http://www.loc.gov/exhibits/african/afam007.html (accessed on July 21, 2008).

"The Declaration of Sentiments, Seneca Falls Conference, 1848." *Modern History Sourcebook.* http://www.fordham.edu/halsall/mod/Senecafalls.html (acccessed on July 21, 2008).

"Despite Huge Katrina Relief, Red Cross Criticized." *MSNBC.com.* http://www.msnbc.msn.com/id/9518677/ (accessed on July 21, 2008).

"Directory of U.S. Political Parties." *Politics1.com.* http://politics1.com/ parties.htm (accessed on July 21, 2008).

"Disco." *Streetswing.com.* http://www.streetswing.com/histmain/z3disco1.htm (accessed on July 21, 2008).

Discovery: Space. http://dsc.discovery.com/space/index.html (accessed on July 21, 2008).

"Domestic Security: The Homefront and the War on Terrorism. The USA PATRIOT Act." *PBS: The Online NewsHour.* http://www.pbs.org/ newshour/indepth_coverage/terrorism/homeland/patriotact.html (accessed on July 21, 2008).

"The Doughboys of World War I." *OldMagazineArticles.com.* http://www .oldmagazinearticles.com/doughboys.php (accessed on July 21, 2008).

"Douglas MacArthur." *PBS: American Experience.* http://www.pbs.org/wgbh/ amex/macarthur/ (accessed on July 21, 2008).

Drye, Willie. "America's Lost Colony: Can New Dig Solve Mystery?" *National Geographic.* http://news.nationalgeographic.com/news/2004/03/0302_ 040302_lostcolony.html (accessed on July 22, 2008).

Edithwharton.org. http://www.edithwharton.org/edithwharton/ (accessed on July 21, 2008).

Elvis Presley: The Official Site of the King of Rock 'n' Roll. http://www.elvis.com/ (accessed on July 21, 2008).

Erbsen, Wayne. "Origins of Bluegrass in Western North Carolina." *Native Ground Music.* http://www.nativeground.com/originsofbluegrass.asp (accessed on July 21, 2008).

"Executive Order 11246: Equal Employment Opportunity." *PBS: American Experience: The Presidents.* http://www.pbs.org/wgbh/amex/presidents/36_l_johnson/psources/ps_execorder.html (accessed on July 21, 2008).

"Facts for Features: Oldest Baby Boomers Turn 60!" *U.S. Census Bureau.* http://www.census.gov/Press-Release/www/releases/archives/facts_for_features_special_editions/006105.html (accessed on July 21, 2008).

"Fahrenheit 451." *SparkNotes.com.* http://www.sparknotes.com/lit/451/context.html (accessed on July 21, 2008).

Federal Communications Commission. http://www.fcc.gov/ (accessed on July 21, 2008).

"Fifteen Years of the Web." *BBC News.* http://news.bbc.co.uk/1/hi/technology/5243862.stm (accessed on July 21, 2008).

"First Baby Boomer Files for Social Security Benefits." *FoxNews.com.* http://www.foxnews.com/story/0,2933,301997,00.html (accessed on July 21, 2008).

"Fog of War: The Gulf War." *Washington Post.* http://www.washingtonpost.com/wp-srv/inatl/longterm/fogofwar/fogofwar.htm (accessed on July 21, 2008).

"Fort Raleigh: National Historical Site." *National Park Service.* http://www.cr.nps.gov/history/online_books/hh/16/hh16toc.htm (accessed on July 21, 2008).

Giangreco, D. M. and Robert E. Griffin. "Marshall Plan." *TrumanLibrary.org.* http://www.trumanlibrary.org/whistlestop/BERLIN_A/MARSHALL.HTM (accessed on July 21, 2008).

"Global HIV Prevalence Has Leveled Off; AIDS Is among the Leading Causes of Death Globally and Remains the Primary Cause of Death in Africa." *UNAIDS.org.* http://data.unaids.org/pub/EPISlides/2007/071119_epi_pressrelease_en.pdf (accessed on July 21, 2008).

"Grand Ole Opry." *Southern Music Network.* http://www.southernmusic.net/grandoleopry.htm (accessed on July 21, 2008).

"The Grapes of Wrath." *SparkNotes.com.* http://www.sparknotes.com/lit/grapesofwrath/ (accessed on July 21, 2008).

"The Great War and the Shaping of the 20th Century (World War I)." *PBS.org.* http://www.pbs.org/greatwar/ (accessed on July 21, 2008).

Gross, Terry. "Get on the Bus: The Freedom Riders of 1961." *NPR.org.* http://www.npr.org/templates/story/story.php?storyId=5149667 (accessed on July 21, 2008).

"The Gulf War." *PBS: Frontline.* http://www.pbs.org/wgbh/pages/frontline/gulf/ (accessed on July 21, 2008).

"Hate Crime Legislative Update." *National Association of Social Workers.* http://www.socialworkblog.org/advocacy/index.php/2008/01/11/hate-crime-legislative-update/ (accessed on July 21, 2008).

"Henry Kissinger." *Nobelprize.org.* http://nobelprize.org/nobel_prizes/peace/laureates/1973/kissinger-bio.html (accessed on July 21, 2008).

"Hillary Clinton." *WiseTo.* http://socialissues.wiseto.com/Election2008/HillaryClinton/ (accessed on July 21, 2008).

Hillouse, R. J. "Who Runs the CIA? Outsiders for Hire." *Washington Post.* http://www.washingtonpost.com/wp-dyn/content/article/2007/07/06/AR2007070601993_pf.html (accessed on July 21, 2008).

"Historic Construction Company Project—Transcontinental Railroad." *ConstructionCompany.com.* http://www.constructioncompany.com/historic-construction-projects/transcontinental-railroad/ (accessed on July 21, 2008).

"A Historical Overview." *U.S. Coast Guard.* http://www.uscg.mil/history/articles/h_USCGhistory.asp (accessed on July 21, 2008).

"History of the American Flag." *AmericanRevolution.com.* http://www.americanrevolution.com/HistoryoftheAmericanFlag.htm (accessed on July 21, 2008).

"The History of AT&T." *AT&T.com.* http://www.corp.att.com/history/ (accessed on July 21, 2008).

"History of the Court." *The Supreme Court Historical Society.* http://www.supremecourthistory.org/02_history/subs_history/02_c.html (accessed on July 21, 2008).

"History of the FBI." *Federal Bureau of Investigation.* http://www.fbi.gov/libref/historic/history/text.htm (accessed on July 21, 2008).

"A History of Gay and Lesbian Rights." *Public Agenda for Citizens.* http://www.publicagenda.org/citizen/issueguides/gay-rights (accessed on July 21, 2008).

"HIV and AIDS." *KidsHealth.com.* http://www.kidshealth.org/parent/infections/std/hiv.html (accessed on July 21, 2008).

"Invisible Man." *SparkNotes.com.* http://www.sparknotes.com/lit/invisibleman/ (accessed on July 21, 2008).

"Iraq Coalition Casualty Count." *Icasualties.org.* http://icasualties.org/oif/Details.aspx (accessed on July 21, 2008).

"Iraq Poll 2007." *BBC News.* http://news.bbc.co.uk/2/shared/bsp/hi/pdfs/19_03_07_iraqpollnew.pdf (accessed on July 21, 2008).

"Irving Berlin: The Dean of American Songwriters." *Parlorsongs.com.* http://parlorsongs.com/bios/berlin/iberlin.php (accessed on July 21, 2008).

"Jacqueline Lee Bouvier Kennedy." *The White House.* http://www.whitehouse .gov/history/firstladies/jk35.html (accessed on July 21, 2008).

"Jimmy Carter." *The White House.* http://www.whitehouse.gov/history/ presidents/jc39.html (accessed on July 21, 2008).

"John Brown's Raid on Harpers Ferry." *Secession Era Editorials Project.* http://history.furman.edu/benson/docs/jbmenu.htm (accessed on July 22, 2008).

"John D. Rockefeller, 1839–1937." *The Rockefeller Archive Center.* http://archive.rockefeller.edu/bio/jdrsr.php (accessed on July 21, 2008).

"John McCain." *WiseTo.* http://socialissues.wiseto.com/Election2008/ JohnMcCain/ (accessed on July 21, 2008).

Johnson, Amy E. Boyle. "Ray Bradbury: Fahrenheit 451 Misinterpreted." *LAWeekly.com.* http://www.laweekly.com/news/news/ray-bradbury-fahrenheit-451-misinterpreted/16524/ (accessed on July 21, 2008).

"Karl Marx, 1818–1883." *The History Guide.* http://www.historyguide.org/ intellect/marx.html (accessed on July 21, 2008).

The King Center. http://www.thekingcenter.org/ (accessed on July 21, 2008).

"The Know Nothing and the *American Crusader.*" *The Historical Society of Pennsylvania.* http://www.hsp.org/default.aspx?id=446 (accessed on July 21, 2008).

"The Korean War." *The Harry S. Truman Library & Museum.* http://www .trumanlibrary.org/whistlestop/study_collections/korea/large/index.htm (accessed on July 21, 2008).

"The Liberty Bell." *U.S. History.* http://www.ushistory.org/libertybell/ (accessed on July 21, 2008).

"The Life of Henry Ford." *The Henry Ford.* http://www.thehenryford.org/ exhibits/hf/ (accessed on July 21, 2008).

Lincoln, Abraham. "'House Divided' Speech." *The History Place.* http://www.historyplace.com/lincoln/divided.htm (accessed on July 21, 2008).

"Lincoln Memorial." *National Park Service, National Register of Historic Places.* http://www.nps.gov/nr/travel/wash/dc71.htm (accessed on July 21, 2008).

"Lusitania." *PBS Online—Lost Liners.* http://www.pbs.org/lostliners/ lusitania.html (accessed on July 21, 2008).

"Lyndon B. Johnson." *The White House.* http://www.whitehouse.gov/history/ presidents/lj36.html (accessed on July 21, 2008).

"Making Mount Rushmore." *AmericanParkNetwork.com.* http://www.american parknetwork.com/parkinfo/content.asp?catid=92&contenttypeid=16 (accessed on July 21, 2008).

"Marine Corps History." *GlobalSecurity.org.* http://www.globalsecurity.org/ military/agency/usmc/history.htm (accessed on July 21, 2008).

"Marshall Plan." *Spartacus Schoolnet.* http://www.spartacus.schoolnet .co.uk/USAmarshallP.htm (accessed on July 21, 2008).

"The Marshall Plan (1947)." *America.gov.* http://www.america.gov/st/washfile-english/2005/April/200504291439291CJsamohT0.6520502.html (accessed on July 21, 2008).

Murphy, Gerald. "About the Iroquois Constitution." *Modern History Sourcebook.* http://www.fordham.edu/halsall/mod/iroquois.html (accessed on July 21, 2008).

"Narrow Use of Affirmative Action Preserved in College Admissions." *Law Center: CNN.com.* http://www.cnn.com/2003/LAW/06/23/scotus .affirmative.action/ (accessed on July 22, 2008).

NASA.com. http://www.nasa.gov/ (accessed on July 21, 2008).

Nichols, Bill. "8,000 Desert during Iraq War." *USA Today.* http://www .usatoday.com/news/washington/2006-03-07-deserters_x.htm (accessed on July 21, 2008).

"1986: Seven Dead in Space Shuttle Disaster." *BBC: On This Day.* http://news.bbc.co.uk/onthisday/hi/dates/stories/january/28/newsid_ 2506000/2506161.stm (accessed on July 21, 2008).

Oberg, James. "Seven Myths About the Challenger Shuttle Disaster." *MSNBC.com.* http://www.msnbc.msn.com/id/11031097/ (accessed on July 21, 2008).

"Oklahoma Bombing Report." *Washington Post.* http://www .washingtonpost.com/wp-srv/national/longterm/oklahoma/oklahoma.htm (accessed on July 21, 2008).

"Oklahoma City Tragedy." *CNN Interactive.* http://www.cnn.com/ US/OKC/bombing.html (accessed on July 21, 2008).

"Paris Peace Talks." *PBS: American Experience.* http://www.pbs.org/ wgbh/amex/honor/peopleevents/e_paris.html (accessed on July 21, 2008).

"The People's Vote: 100 Documents That Shaped America: The Truman Doctrine." *U.S. News & World Report.* http://www.usnews.com/ usnews/documents/docpages/document_page81.htm (accessed on July 21, 2008).

"Peter, Paul and Mary." *Classicbands.com.* http://www.classicbands.com/ ppm.html (accessed on July 21, 2008).

Peterson, Richard A. "Ten Things You Didn't Know about the Origins of Country Music." *University of Chicago Press.* http://www.press .uchicago.edu/Misc/Chicago/662845.html (accessed on July 21, 2008).

"Presidential Impeachment Proceedings: Bill Clinton, 42nd President." *The History Place.* http://www.historyplace.com/unitedstates/impeachments/ clinton.htm (accessed on July 21, 2008).

"Sandra Day O'Connor." *National Women's Hall of Fame.* http://www
.greatwomen.org/women.php?action=viewone&id=115 (accessed on July
21, 2008).

Scaruffi, Piero. "A Brief History of Country Music." *Scaruffi.com.*
http://www.scaruffi.com/history/country.html (accessed on July 21, 2008).

Selective Service System. http://www.sss.gov/ (accessed on July 21, 2008).

SNCC 1960–66: Six Years of the Student Nonviolent Coordinating Committee.
http://www.ibiblio.org/sncc/rides.html (accessed on July 22, 2008).

"Space Shuttle Columbia Disaster." *AerospaceGuide.net.* http://www
.aerospaceguide.net/spaceshuttle/columbia_disaster.html (accessed on July
21, 2008).

"Teaching with Documents: The *Amistad* Case." *The National Archives.*
http://www.archives.gov/education/lessons/amistad/ (accessed on July 22,
2008).

"They Changed the World: The Story of the Montgomery Bus Boycott,
1955–56." *Montgomery Advertiser.* http://www.montgomeryboycott
.com/frontpage.htm (accessed on July 22, 2008).

"This Week in History: October." *Peacebuttons.info.* http://www
.peacebuttons.info/E-News/peacehistoryoctober.htm (accessed on July 21,
2008).

"Thomas Jefferson Memorial." *National Park Service.* http://www.nps.gov/thje/
(accessed on July 21, 2008).

"Three Mile Island: The Inside Story." *Smithsonian National Museum of
American History.* http://americanhistory.si.edu/tmi/ (accessed on July 21,
2008).

"Three Mile Island: The Judge's Ruling." *PBS Frontline: Nuclear Reaction.*
http://www.pbs.org/wgbh/pages/frontline/shows/reaction/readings/tmi
.html (accessed on July 21, 2008).

"The Time 100: Billy Graham." *Time.com.* http://www.time.com/time/
time100/heroes/profile/graham01.html (accessed on July 21, 2008).

"The Time 100: Louis B. Mayer." *Time.com.* http://www.time.com/time/
time100/builder/profile/mayer.html (accessed on July 21, 2008).

"The Time 100: Mao Zedong." *Time.com.* http://www.time.com/time/
time100/leaders/profile/mao.html (accessed on July 21, 2008).

"The Time 100: Martin Luther King." *Time.com.* http://www.time.com/time/
time100/leaders/profile/king.html (accessed on July 21, 2008).

"The Time 100: Rosa Parks." *Time.com.* http://www.time.com/time/
time100/heroes/profile/parks01.html (accessed on July 22, 2008).

"The Time 100: William Levitt." *Time.com.* http://www.time.com/time/
time100/builder/profile/levitt.html (accessed on July 21, 2008).

Trinklein, Mike, and Steve Boettcher. "The Oregon Trail." *Idaho State University.* http://www.isu.edu/%7Etrinmich/Oregontrail.html (accessed on July 22, 2008).

"Twenty-third Amendment." *JusticeLearning.org.* http://www.justicelearning.org/justice_timeline/Amendments.aspx?id=22 (accessed on July 21, 2008).

"The Underground Railroad." *National Geographic Online.* http://www.nationalgeographic.com/railroad/ (accessed on July 22, 2008).

United States House of Representatives. http://www.house.gov/ (accessed on July 21, 2008).

"U.S. Constitutional Amendments." *FindLaw.com.* http://caselaw.lp.findlaw.com/data/constitution/amendments.html (accessed on July 21, 2008).

"U.S. Electoral College." *National Archives and Records Admininstration.* http://www.archives.gov/federal-register/electoral-college/faq.html#why electoralcollege (accessed on July 21, 2008).

"U.S.-Mexican War, 1846–1848." *PBS.org.* http://www.pbs.org/kera/usmexicanwar/index_flash.html (accessed on July 22, 2008).

"U.S. Military Deaths in Iraq War at 4,124." *MSNBC.com.* http://www.msnbc.msn.com/id/5972698/ (accessed on July 21, 2008).

The U.S. Navy. http://www.navy.mil/swf/index.asp (accessed on July 21, 2008).

"Vietnam Online." *PBS.org.* http://www.pbs.org/wgbh/amex/vietnam/ (accessed on July 21, 2008).

The Vietnam Veterans Memorial. http://thewall-usa.com/information.asp (accessed on July 21, 2008).

Wagner, Steven. "How Did the Taft-Hartley Act Come About?" *History News Network.* http://hnn.us/articles/1036.html (accessed on July 21, 2008).

"The Washington Monument." *National Park Service.* http://www.nps.gov/wamo/ (accessed on July 21, 2008).

"Weapons of Mass Destruction." *National Geographic.com.* http://magma.nationalgeographic.com/ngm/0211/feature1/ (accessed on July 22, 2008).

"Worldwide HIV & AIDS Statistics." *Avert.org.* http://www.avert.org/worldstats.htm (accessed on July 21, 2008).

Index

Italic type indicates volume number; **boldface** indicates main entries' page numbers; (ill.) indicates photos and illustrations.

A

AASS (American Anti-Slavery Society), *1:* 6–8; *3:* 665

Abenaki (Native American tribe), *6:* 1092, 1096

Abernathy, Ralph, *1:* **1–4,** 2 (ill.), 163 (ill.); *5:* 1024–26; *7:* 1451. *See also* Civil rights movement

Abington Township School District v. Schempp, 7: 1504

Abolition movement, *1:* 4 (ill.), **4–10,** 5 (ill.). *See also* Slavery

American Colonization Society, *1:* 6; 56–57

Amistad insurrection, *1:* 73–74

Atlantic slave trade, *1:* 111–12

Booth, Sherman, *3:* 613

Douglass, Frederick, *2:* 459–62

Free Soil Party, *1:* 8; *4:* 678; *5:* 846, 912; *6:* 1248

Grimké, Sarah and Angelina, *3:* 664–66; *7:* 1386

Harpers Ferry raid, *4:* 677–80; *8:* 1585

"House Divided" speech (Lincoln), *5:* 913

Liberty Bell as symbol, *5:* 904–5

literature of, *3:* 665–66

Mott, Lucretia, *5:* 1031–33

Philadelphia Female Anti-Slavery Society, *5:* 1031

Quakers, *5:* 1031; *7:* 1427–28

Truth, Sojourner, *8:* 1581 (ill.), 1581–83

Underground Railroad, *5:* 1033; *8:* 1583–85, 1602–4

World Anti-Slavery Convention, *8:* 1702

Abortion rights, *3:* 551–52; *7:* 1338–39, 1504, 1505

Abouhalima, Mahmud, *8:* 1709–10

Abraham Lincoln Brigade, *7:* 1456

Abstract expressionism, *1:* **10–11**

Abu Ghraib, *4:* 791

Abzug, Bella, *3:* 553

Acheson, Dean, *5:* 879, 982

ACLU. *See* American Civil Liberties Union (ACLU)

Acquired Immune Deficiency Syndrome. *See* AIDS

ACS. *See* American Colonization Society (ACS)

Adams, John, *1:* 11 (ill.), **11–17**

Alien and Sedition Acts, *1:* 15; 48–50

Jefferson, Thomas, *4:* 823

Marbury v. Madison, 5: 955–57

presidency, *1:* 14–16; *5:* 955–56

presidential election of 1796, *8:* 1588

presidential election of 1800, *8:* 1588

Treaty of Paris, *1:* 12 (ill.), 13

XYZ Affair, *1:* 48; *8:* 1735–37

Adams, John Quincy, *1:* **17–19,** 18 (ill.)

Amistad insurrection, *1:* 75

Jackson, Andrew, *1:* 18–19; *4:* 807

Manifest Destiny, *5:* 953

Van Buren, Martin, *8:* 1626

Adams, Samuel, *7:* 1312

Adams-Onis Treaty, *5:* 927

C

E

H

L

N

O

S

W

X

Y

Z

LAKE OSWEGO JR. HIGH SCHOOL
2500 SW COUNTRY CLUB RD
LAKE OSWEGO, OR 97034
503-534-2335